INDIAN ART AND AESTHETICS
Endeavours in Interpretation

INDIAN ART AND AESTHETICS
Endeavours in Interpretation

Editors
Maruti Nandan Tiwari
&
Kamal Giri

INDIAN ART HISTORY CONGRESS
GUWAHATI (ASSAM)
in association with
ARYAN BOOKS INTERNATIONAL
NEW DELHI

INDIAN ART AND AESTHETICS
Endeavours in Interpretation

ISBN-81-7305-263-8

First published in **2004** by
INDIAN ART HISTORY CONGRESS
Guwahati, Assam (India)
in association with
ARYAN BOOKS INTERNATIONAL
Pooja Apartments, 4B, Ansari Road, Darya Ganj, New Delhi-110 002 (India)
Tel. : 23287589, 23255799; Fax : 91-11-23270385
E-mail : aryanbooks@vsnl.com

Computer Typeset at Welcome Computers, New Delhi
Printed in India at Print Perfect, New Delhi

Cover Illustration :
Rāginī Toḍī, late 18th century, Jaipur, Collection: M.S. Man Singh II Museum

Preface

The study of Indian art has undergone several stages from art for art sake to the art as visual expression of religious concepts and philosophical ideas. Further in all its magnitude and forms, Indian art is taken to be the most vital, detailed and authentic record of the contemporary society, specially in respect of socio-cultural life. At present the study of Indian art is progressing with certain new dimensions and with the holistic and multi-disciplinary approach, particularly in reference to period and region.

No doubt a lot has been done but much is still to be done specially in the areas of folk and regional art forms which require extensive fieldwork and documentation to underline the living as well as past traditions of Indian art. For this undoubtedly energetic young scholars should come forward to take up this marathon task. In this connection the encouragement from senior scholars is also needed on several scores, including their career prospects.

The present volume comprises 18 articles. As usual the articles, contributed both by the senior and young scholars, pertain to the unpublished material and also to the analyses and fresh interpretations of different aspects of Indian art and aesthetics.

It is needless to write that the publication of this volume is possible only due to ungrudging help of the scholars who have been kind enough to contribute on different areas of Indian art. We are sure that their help will continue and the publication of these volumes will further be improved by the collective and collaborative efforts. The inspirations received from the Chairman, Dr. M.K. Nigam and the General Secretary, Dr. R.D. Choudhury have always encouraged us for which we express our gratefulness to them. Our thanks are due also to Dr. Shanti Swaroop Sinha and Dr. Anand Prakash Srivastava for their help in proof-reading and sundry matters. Lastly we also offer our thanks to M/s. Aryan Books International, New Delhi for publishing the volume nicely.

Vijayadashmi **Maruti Nandan Tiwari**

5.10.2003 **Kamal Giri**

Contents

Preface *v*
List of Plates *ix*
List of Contributors *xi*

1. A Rare *Yoginī* Sculpture with Bells 1
— *R.C. Agrawala*
2. Notes on the Origins of the Tibetan Iconography of Avalokiteśvara 5
— *Gian Giuseppe Filippe*
3. Fresh Light on the History of Indian Jade-Carving 13
— *M.L. Nigam*
4. Vision to Appreciate Art 19
— *R.C. Sharma*
5. The History and Art of Jaipur Painting: A Reappraisal 25
— *Chandramani Singh*
6. Representation of Rāmakathā in the Nīlkaṇṭheśvara Temple at Kekind 35
— *Neelima Vashishtha*
7. Objects of Beauty, Not Art Objects 39
— *Harsha V. Dehejia*
8. Decorated Bricks from Sarnath Museum 45
— *Niharika*
9. A Forgotten Jaina Centre: Bhālki 53
— *Hampa Nagarajaiah*
10. Apsaras Figures from Kaṅkālī Mound, Mathura 57
— *S.D. Trivedi*
11. Identification of Pitcher Carriers in Gaja-Lakṣmī Reliefs 67
— *A.L. Srivastava*
12. Some Aspects of Inscribed Jaina Images 75
— *Krishna Kumari Myneni*

13. Little Known Viśvarūpa Image from Himachal Pradesh 79
— *Subhashini Aryan*

14. Kapileśvara Temple of Charada 83
— *P.K. Nayak*

15. Symbols in Indian Art: An Overview 89
— *Savita Sharma*

16. A Study of Two Vaiṣṇava Manuscripts in the Western Indian Style : *Harilīlā-Ṣoḍaśa-Kalā* and *Prabodha - Candrodaya* 99
— *Rashmi Kala Agrawal*

17. Feminine Beauty in Divine Figures in Indian Art 103
— *Haripriya Rangarajan*

18. A Note on a Rare Viṣṇu Image from Varanasi 109
— *Kamal Giri & Pramod Giri*

List of Plates

Pl. 5.1 A folio from *Bhāgavata,* dated V.S. 1792, Jaipur, Collection: M.S. Man Singh II Museum

Pl. 5.2 *Rāginī Toḍī*, late 18th century, Jaipur, Collection: M.S. Man Singh II Museum

Pl. 6.1 Nīlakaṇṭheśvara Temple, Kekind (Rajasthan), *c.* 10th century AD

Pl. 6.2 Unconscious Lakṣmaṇa, pillar bracket, Kekind

Pl. 6.3 Rāma-Lakṣmaṇa-Hanumāna, pillar bracket, *maṇḍapa*, Kekind

Pl. 6.4 Hanumāna and monkeys, pillar bracket, Kekind

Pl. 6.5 Rāma with monkeys, pillar bracket, Kekind

Pl. 6.6 Rāvaṇa on chariot, pillar bracket, *maṇḍapa,* Kekind

Pl. 7.1 Ritual water container, 20th century

Pl. 7.2 Votive clay horse, 20th century

Pl. 7.3 Unguent container with mirror (brass), 20th century

Pl. 7.4 *Phaḍa* painting, Rajasthan, 20th century

Pl. 8.1 Brick with lotus pattern, Sarnath Museum

Pl. 8.2 Brick with human figure, Sarnath Museum

Pl. 8.3 Brick with step pattern, Sarnath Museum

Pl. 9.1 Jina with *śrīvatsa* mark, Bhālki (Karnataka)

Pl. 9.2 *Tīrthaṅkara*, Bhālki (Karnataka)

Pl. 9.3 Ambikā, Bhālki (Karnataka)

Pl. 10.1 Female figure in *śālabhanjīkā* motif, Kaṅkāli Ṭila, Mathura

Pl. 10.2 Bracket showing female beauty, Kaṅkālī Ṭīlā, Māthura

Pl. 12.1 Pārśvanātha, Gulbarga, Karnataka (Victoria & Albert Museum, London)

Pl. 12.2 Śāntinātha (Bronze), Victoria & Albert Museum, London

Pl. 13.1 Viśvarūpa, Bajaura, Himachal Pradesh

Pl. 14.1 Kapileśvara temple, Charada, Orissa

Pl. 14.2 Bāḍa, Kapileśvara temple, Charada, Orissa

Pl. 16.1 *Prabodha-Prakāśa*, late 15th century, Bharat Kala Bhavan

Pl. 16.2 *Harilīlā Ṣoḍaśa-Kalā,* AD 1529, Bharat Kala Bhavan

Pl. 17.1 Vārāhī

Pl. 17.2 Vasudhārā

Pl. 17.3 Vāgdevī
Pl. 17.4 Sarasvatī
Pl. 17.5 Tārā
Pl. 18.1 Viṣṇu, Varanasi, *c.* 11th cent. AD

List of Contributors

1. Dr. A.L. Srivastava
   1B/24/9, Bhilai - 490 009 (Chattisgarh)

2. Dr. Chandramani Singh
   C-76, Savarkar Marg, Tilak Nagar, Jaipur - 302 004 (Rajasthan)

3. Prof. Gian Guiseppe Filippi
   Dept. of Indological Studies, CA Foscari, University of Venice, Italy

4. Dr. Hampa Nagarajaiah
   Professor Emeritus, 1079, 18-A Main, 5th Block, Rajajinagar,
   Bangalore - 560 010 (Karnataka)

5. Prof. Harsha V. Dehejia
   256 New Street, Ottawa On, Canada

6. Dr. (Mrs.) Haripriya Rangarajan
   AB-13, Tilak Marg, New Delhi - 110 001

7. Prof. Kamal Giri
   Hony. Joint Director, Jñāna Pravāha, Samne Ghat, Varanasi - 221005 (Uttar Pradesh)

8. Prof. Krishna Kumari Myneni
   Dept. of History & Archaeology, Andhra University,
   Vishakhapatnam - 530 003 (Andhra Pradesh)

9. Dr. M.L. Nigam
   13-6-463/A/9, Ashok Vihar Colony, Kulsumpura,
   Hyderabad - 500 267 (Andhra Pradesh)

10. Dr. Neelima Vashishtha
    B-195C, University Marg, Bapunagar, Jaipur - 302 015 (Rajasthan)

11. Dr. (Mrs.) Niharika
    C/o. Shri. Ajay Srivastava
    Asstt. Archaeologist, Archaeological Museum, Sarnath, Varanasi - 221 007

12. Dr. P.K. Nayak
Reader, P.G. Dept. of History, Sambalpur University, Jyoti Vihar - 768 019, Sambalpur (Orissa)

13. Dr. Pramod Giri,
I.C.H.R. Post-Doctoral Fellow
Dept. of History of Art, Banaras Hindu University,
Varanasi - 221 005 (Uttar Pradesh)

14. Dr. Rashmi Kala Agrawal
Reader, Dept. of History of Art, Banaras Hindu University,
Varanasi - 221 005 (Uttar Pradesh)

15. Shri R.C. Agrawala
Ex. Director of Museums, 8/192, Malaviya Nagar, Jaipur - 302 017 (Rajasthan)

16. Prof. R.C. Sharma
Hony. Director, Jñāna Pravāha, Samne Ghat, Varanasi - 221 005 (Uttar Pradesh)

17. Dr. Savita Sharma
Curator, Bharat Kala Bhavan, Banaras Hindu University,
Varanasi-221 005 (Uttar Pradesh)

18. Dr. S.D. Trivedi
B-1/7, Sector G, Gyan Vihar, Aliganj, Lucknow - 226 024 (Uttar Pradesh)

19. Prof. Subhashini Aryan
2009, Sector 4, Urban Estate, Gurgaon - 122 001 (Haryana)

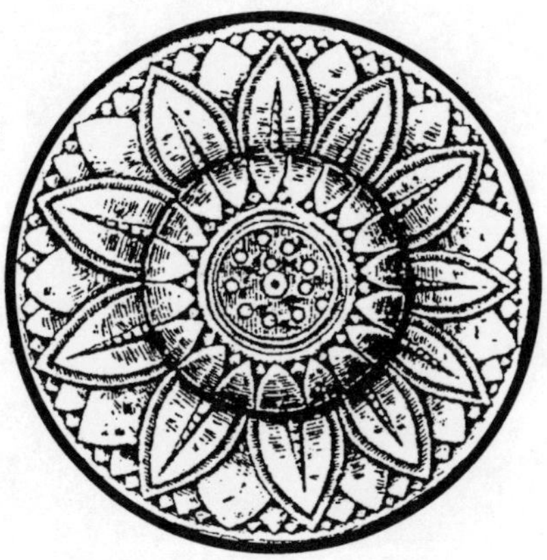

1

A Rare Yoginī Sculpture with Bells

R.C. Agrawala

It was more than ten years ago that Shri G.C. Singh, Excavation and Exploration Officer of the State Department of Archaeology, Govt. of U.P., Lucknow, gave me a blurred photograph of a goddess of great interest. The portion below the shoulder of the sculpture was missing and hence we had no idea of the *vāhana* of the goddess. Datable to the medieval period (10th to 12th century), it is an unusual icon of a *Yoginī* of the Śākta cult (Fig. 1). The figure shows only 14 hands while the remaining ones are completely missing. It appears that she was initially endowed with more than 20 hands. The provenance of the sculpture is also not known, it appears that it hailed from some part of Uttar Pradesh or Uttaranchal, probably Almora Hills or some place bordering Madhya Pradesh.

The upper-most vertically raised right and left hands of the goddess along with other hands on both sides carry bells, making the total number of bells ten. Other objects in her left hands are a manuscript and skull-crowned mace (*Khaṭvāṅga)* whereas one of the right hands carries trident in a damaged condition. The presence of a number of bells in her hands is quite unusual and amazing. However any other example of this kind is not available in any of the *Yoginī* centres of the country. Should we identify the present goddess as Ghaṇṭālī, an epithet which is found on pedestal inscription of 10th century *Yoginī* figure from Bheraghat, near Jabalpur in Madhya Pradesh? R.K. Sharma[1], an expert of *Yoginī* cult at Jabalpur too could not locate any such Ghaṇṭālī image endowed with numerous bells. A 15th century sculpture of Mahiṣamardinī in Govt. Museum at Jaisalmer[2] even furnishes the epithet *Ghaṇṭālī* for the Devī but that does not carry any weight in the study of the *Yoginī* figure under scrutiny. The importance of this unique Devī icon is further enhanced by the carving of ear-ornaments shown as bells, thus initiating us to identify the goddess as a composite form of Ghaṇṭālī and Ghaṇṭākarṇī. Further literary support will be eagerly awaited but this much is clear that the particular medieval sculptor has successfully delineated bells in hands and in the ear lobes with great charm, besides other important attributes, such as manuscript, *khaṭvāṅga, śakti,* etc.

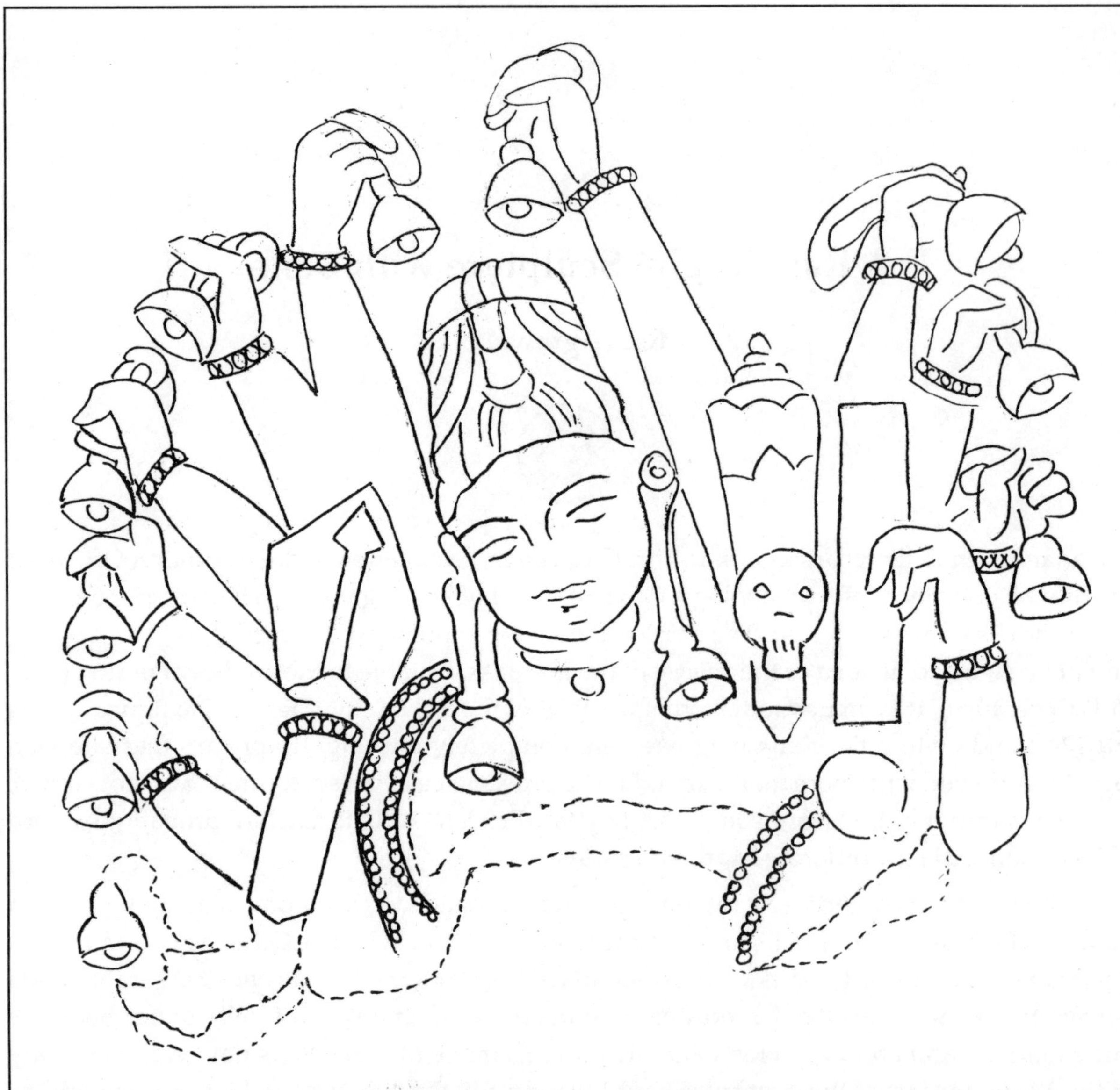

Fig. 1. *Yoginī* with bells, medieval period.

A passing reference may also be made to a modern temple of Goludeva at village Chitai, near Almora, which presents a rich feast of bells hanging on the exterior of this temple under worship. The devotees offer bells after their desires are fulfilled. We are of course not aware of the form of the deity under worship in this unusual shrine with hundreds of bells reported by Mamata Bharati.[3]

Presence of a single bell in one of the hands of Durgā and Mahiṣamardinī in Indian sculptures is well known. But the depiction of such a number of bells in the hands and even in the earlobes of the *Yoginī* requires further examination. A passing reference is essential to a Gandharan statue of Skanda examined by me in the reserve collection of Indian Art Museum at Berlin[4] in 1986 through the kindness of H. Hartel, Yaldiz and Lobo. The importance of this image is enhanced by the carving of a single bell in the right hand of the male Brahmanic deity who is invariably shown with Śakti, with victorious bells and banners; he has choice - bell; so he is called *Varaghaṇṭā.*

An unusual male *Yakṣa* type colossal statue from Tālā (Bastar area, Chhattisgarh) about 9 feet in height presents unusual details including carving of human heads on the body of the deity wearing the bells (Ghaṇṭā)[5] on earlobes. This is another enigmatic image of 6th century in Indian art. Another standing *Yakṣa* with curly hair from Mathura is pot bellied, nude and holds a club in the right hand and a vase in the left; a third eye is also shown on his forehead connecting him with Śiva. He wears big pendulous bells in the ears and is well identified as *Ghaṇṭā Karṇa Yakṣa.*[6] It is now preserved in the Govt. Museum at Mathura.

Acknowledgement

My thanks are due to Sri G.C. Singh for having favoured me with the photograph, which has helped me in having its line drawing sketch prepared with the kind assistance of my research student Mrs. Yojana S. Singh of the University of Rajasthan at Jaipur.

Notes and References

1. R.K. Sharma, *The Temple of Chausaṭha Yoginīs at Bherāghāt,* Delhi, 1978, p. 143, plate 88. All the hands of the *devī* here are missing but the bull is present below her seat. The actual details of this inscribed sculpture (*Śri Ghaṇṭālī*) are missing.
2. H. Goetz, *Art and Architecture of the Bikaner State,* Oxford, 1950, figure 20. It is from Pūgal (Bikaner) and was formerly preserved in Bikaner Museum.
3. Mamata Bharati, *Gaṇṭonwālā Goloudeva Mandira, Kādambinī* (Hindi), Delhi, November 2002, pp. 92-93. I wrote to her for further details but no response has been received so far. Further probe in the matter is essential.
4. R.C. Agrawala, Skanda with Cock and Peacock: A Rare Device in Gandharan Art, *Eastern Approaches: Essays on Asian Art and Archaeology,* ed. T.S. Maxwell, Delhi, 1992, pp. 130-132, plates 43-45. Consult P.K. Agrawala, *Skanda Kārttikeya: A Study in Origin and Development,* Varanasi, 1967, p. 20 for bell with Skanda.
5. *Riddle of Indian Iconography-Zetetic on Rare Icon from Tālā,* ed. L.S. Nigam, Delhi, 2000, p. 148, plates 33-38.
6. R.N. Misra, *Yaksha Cult and Iconography,* Delhi, 1981, p. 125, Fig. 67.

2

Notes on the Origins of the Tibetan Iconography of Avalokiteśvara

Gian Giuseppe Filippi

It has often been noted that the iconography representing the Dhyānī Bodhisattva Avalokiteśvara present various Śaiva features.[1] These features, however, have been viewed on the same plane of other symbolical components, which the Bodhisattva appears to share with other Brahmanical deities.[2] A more in-depth analysis has not yet been carried out, neither from a purely formal viewpoint, nor concerning various doctrinal and religious implications. The best procedure, in our opinion consists in the analysis of Avalokiteśvara's formal characteristics in the light of an iconography which is canonically fixed – such as that of the Guptas – and also by comparing it with the iconographic canon of *Vajrayāṇa.* Difficulties in gathering information may be obviated or corrected by approximation through the aid of data concerning other historical periods or through the help of the relevant literature. In any case, it is not our intention to reconstruct a hypothetical evolution or transition of Avalokiteśvara from Śaivism to Buddhism, which appears highly improbable from the point of view of its contents and actually impossible to demonstrate on historical grounds. We shall limit ourselves to highlight the intimate convergence of nature of these two mythical figures – Śiva and Avalokiteśvara – within Brahmanism and Buddhism, which can only be expressed through their symbolic identity.[3]

It is well known that Avalokiteśvara appears in India for the first time with the name of Padmapāṇi, who holds lotus in his hand. On a small pillar adorning the *vedikā* of the Great Stūpa of Sāñchī, is engraved as a bas-relief an impressive figure, his head adorned by a beautiful turban. He wears a *dhotī,* the edges of which fall from his shoulder; he also wears a heavy necklace and bracelets of precious stones. He leans to a tree and holds a lotus in his right, lifted hand. Coomaraswamy demonstrated that this is the oldest representation of the *yakṣa* Padmapāṇi.[4] Thus it is not the Bodhisattva as such that is represented here, but rather his corresponding *yakṣa,* as it happens in Buddhist and Jaina mythology in which this *yakṣa* flanks and protects both the *mānuṣībuddhas* and *Tīrthaṅkaras.* In the same work,

Coomaraswamy has identified the *yakṣa* Vajrapāṇi – which represents the Bodhisattva bearing the same name – with the *yakṣa* representing Maitreya. Along side these figures, another character is portrayed bearing a lance; this the Sinhalese scholar called *yakṣa* Śūlapāṇi. This name, however, does not appear in the traditional lists of the names of *yakṣas*. Moreover, his image is very similar to that of Śiva as it is sculptured on the *liṅgam* of Guḍimallam belonging to the same time period. A first connection could thus be established between these specimens belonging to the end of the second century BC, since both Padmapāṇi and Śiva appear to be represented under the guise of *yakṣas*.[5] We must also remember that Śiva is regarded as the head-chief of the multitudes of *yakṣas,* either directly or indirectly through his attendant and son Gaṇapati.[6] Throughout the centuries, Padmapāni's posture has remained practically the same in Vajrayāna iconography, with just one small variant: whereas the *yakṣa* Padmapāṇi holds a lotus in one hand and keeps the other resting on his side; the Bodhisattva Padmapāṇi however exhibits his empty hand in the *karuṇā-mudrā* pose.[7] He can also assume other postures, such as the *rājalīlāsana* and *padmāsana.* These icons are prior to the Mahāyāna period and do not yet show the symbolic characteristics, which appeared with the first manifestation of Buddhist Tantrism.[8] Only later on, i.e. in the Gupta period, the figure of the Bodhisattva Padmapāṇi bearing multiple heads and arms[9] appear: in turn, these representations gave rise to a rich symbolic iconography, which found its fullest elaboration in Tibet.[10]

It we now turn to Tibetan iconography, the first and most general characteristic to be noted about Avalokiteśvara is that he is usually represented as having a white or light grey skin, just like Śiva, since the deity has his body besmeared with ashes. Quite often, however, the god – in his angry aspect as Rūdra – is represented in red colour. Indeed, even Avalokiteśvara is often depicted in red, to demonstrate that he was manifested by the red Dhyānī Buddha Amitābha, an image of whom he often bears in the diadem he wears on his forehead. The rare and terrific images of Avalokiteśvara – just as the manifestation of Śiva known as Mahākāla – are represented in black.

Another common feature of Avalokiteśvara and Śiva is that both have been manifested from a light, which was projected out of the forehead of that divine principle which produced them, represented by Amitābha and Brahmā respectively. Alice Getty, who adds an observation of great value, which she perhaps didn't realize in all its import, has rightly evidenced this mythical detail:

> Rūdra is born from the wrinkle in the forehead of Brahmā, separates into male and female, and multiplies into eleven persons, *some of which are white and gentle and others black and furious.* These are evidently the eleven Rūdras quoted above, and correspond with the painted forms of Arya-Pāla.[11]

The assimilation of the eleven-headed Avalokiteśvara, known as Arya-Pāla, with the eleven Rūdras is of great relevance, especially if we consider the fact that in the oldest Brahmamical source these latter ones are interpreted as the eleven *prāṇas,* a person's vital energies.[12] In this way, the Bodhisattva identifies himself with the *sambhogakāya* of the perfect human being.

Almost all the various representations of Avalokiteśvara show him with a skin of a black antelope (*mṛga*) tied around his waist, worn as a Brahmanical cord. This appears to be linked to one of the most celebrated Śaiva myths, when the god Śiva decided to destroy Dakṣa's sacrifice. Śiva's irruption on the scene put to flight the gods who were assembled there; the sacrifice, personified in the form of a black antelope, tried to escape to the shies, but Śiva knocked him down with his arrow.[13] Consequently the bow and the arrow became the most recurrent symbols of the god. With the skin of the sacrifice, Śiva made his Brahmanical cord. For this reason, the skin of the black antelope has always been utilized as a garment by *Brahmacārins* and as meditation carpet by *Vedic vānaprasthins,* who do not perform sacrifices or any other kind of exterior rituals.[14] Thus, Avalokiteśvara wears the skin of the black antelope as an ascetic who refrains from all sorts of violent sacrifices.

Avalokiteśvara has his hair dishevelled and mixed with clay; the hair is knotted so as to form a high crest, identical to that of Śiva, which is known as *jāṭāmukuṭa,* i.e. a crown of matted braids. Part of these *jāṭas* even fall untidily upon his shoulders. This kind of hairstyle, still in use among the Śaiva *sādhus* of today, is also common among various schools of monks. No doubt, it is intended to represent the savage environment in which these renouncers retreat, though at the same time it calls to mind the image of Rūdra as bowman and wild hunter of antelopes, *mṛgavyādha.* In more recent times, even Avalokiteśvara – as the other Dhyānī Buddhas and Bodhisattvas – is represented with the typical *uṣṇīṣa* and the pointed tiara, with his unruly *jāṭas* hanging on the shoulders.

In some of his forms such as, for instance in the cases of Brahmadaṇḍa Lokeśvara[15] and Hālāhala Lokeśvara[16], the Bodhisattva is represented in the *ardhaparyaṅka* posture, along with his *prājña* Gītā seated on his left knee. Apart from some negligible variants, this posture is identical to that of Śiva and Pārvatī in their icon known as Umā-Maheśvara mūrti, in which:

> the image of Śiva and Umā should be seated on a seat, embracing each other. Śiva should have the *jāṭāmukuṭa* on his head with the crescent moon stuck in it, he should have two arms, in the right of which there should be a *nīlotpala* flower [blue lotus] and the left one should be placed in embrace on the left shoulder of Umā... The *Rūpamaṇḍana* informs us that Śiva should have four arms and that in one of the right hands there should be the *triśūla* and the other a *mātuliṅga* fruit (a kind of citron), one of the left arms should be thrown on the shoulder of Umā and there should be a snake in the other left hand.[17]

What especially strikes us here is the presence of the crescent moon along with the skull stuck in his hair, which we frequently find in the representation of Hālāhala-Avalokiteśvara.[18]

The most interesting form of the Bodhisattva, at least from our viewpoint, is that of Siṁhanāda Lokeśvara, the 'Lord of the world with the voice of a lion'.[19] Avalokiteśvara is here seated in the 'play posture', *līlāsana,* a variant of the *ardhaparyaṅka* posture. Apart from all the Śaiva features already described so far – the *jāṭāmukuṭa,* the skin of black antelope worn across his back, the blue lotus, the *triśūla* to which a cobra clings, and other elements – he also wears the skin of a tiger[20] as a sort of *dhotī* and bears the so-called 'third eye' on his forehead. Alice Getty observes that Siṃhanāda Lokeśvara bears a lotus in his left hand from which a sword comes out, and she connects this emblem to the iconography of Mañjuśrī.[21]

In reality, in the Brahmanical-Buddhist iconographic symbolism, the sword represents knowledge, that is, it is an instrument through which the ties of ignorance can be cut off. This weapon is often held by the god Śiva, as in the case of Raūdrapaśupati mūrtī, which simultaneously holds the sword and the noose (*pāśa).* Even more significant is the Vīrabhadra form of Śiva, bearing both the sword and the book of knowledge, and which – as such – comes close to the canonical representation of Mañjuśrī. In some cases, Siṁhanāda Lokeśvara also holds the *ḍamaru* the drum, the rhythmic sound of which beats the passing of time. It is clear from the image that the two parts, which make up the *ḍamaru,* are two skulls, in line with the purest Śaiva tradition. In this form of Avalokiteśvara, it is really difficult to identify even a single detail, which is not traceable in Śiva's own mythology. The mount of Siṁhanāda Lokeśvara is a lion, as his very name indicates. Siṁhanāda Lokeśvara is though to give aid to the sick people: indeed, according to tradition the hearing of the lion's roar assures the recovery from the most serious illnesses and it is even thought to operate the resurrection from the dead.[22]

The icons, which we have here described, are characterized by the *ardhaparyaṅka* posture, even in its *līlāsana* version, and thus exhibit the Bodhisattva attitude of intervening on behalf of all beings.[23] When the Bodhisattva has his legs crossed, especially in the *padmāsana* posture, it is meant to describe an attitude of contemplation and world-detachment. The image of Siṁhanāda Lokeśvara, the Lord of the Six Syllables, is representative of this attitude. In this case, Avalokiteśvara has his eyes half-closed, with two hands, which he keeps on his chest, he bears the jewel – *maṇi* – whereas in the other two hands he holds a blue lotus and an *akṣamālā* (rosary). If the jewel is totally alien to *Śaiva* mythology, the lotus and the rosary are two primary attributes of Śiva. This peculiar form of the Bodhisattva, however must be considered as embodying its essential personality. The six syllables form which give the name to this peculiar form the famous *mantra: Oṃ maṇi padme hūm,* which constitute Avalokiteśvara's secret essence.[24]

Up to this point, the data we have gathered and presented, tend to demonstrate a close symbolical affinity between Bodhisattva and the Brahmanical deity. What follows is to add more information concerning aspects which have not yet been considered in this light and which should offer more complete picture concerning the two deities.

Some of the forms representing Avalokiteśvara bear a baffling characteristic. Dharmadhātu Lokeśvara, the Lord of the Essence of Reality, Kamaṇḍalu Lokeśvara, the Lord of the Vessel for ritual ablution, Amoghapāśa the Lord of the infallible Noose, are three divine forms which are in charge of the manifestation, purification and destruction of the worlds. As it happens in the case of mythical figures involved in special activities, they are all represented in a standing posture, bearing the typical attributes which have already been described in this article.[25] The baffling characteristic is represented by their dress, which is worn down to the ankel of the right leg and down to the knee of the left leg. The dress thus worn appears to be without any explanation and indeed Alica Getty, who minutely describes the symbolic features of Avalokiteśvara, doesn't dare to mention this detail.[26] Schumann a couple of times admits that "the meaning of a dress gathered upon the left leg is unknown" and that "the meaning of the bareness of the left leg has not yet been clarifed.[27] Nonetheless, this scholar comes close to the solution of the problem, when he notes that the Bodhisattva "has a graceful attitude; the head being slightly bent and the hip protruding..."[28]

We propose the following quotation in order to solve the issue: "Ardhanārīśvara is the form of Śiva in which the god is depicted with his consort Pārvatī in a single human body depicting the left half of a female and the right half of a male."[29] Under the supreme form of the Androgyne, Śiva and Śivā were manifested from Brahmā's forehead in order to create the world. "Śakti is the same Mahādeva and Mahādeva comprises the Śakti. The entire universe, made up of mobile and immovable beings, is but a fragment of their supreme geatness."[30] The canonical representation of the Androgyne is described in various texts. Our main interest, however, focuses upon the description of the dress: "On the right side the ornaments should cover the body below the loins only up to the knee, and the material of the garment is to be tiger's skin and silk...the female half should be draped...in multicoloured silken female cloth, covering the body down to the ankles."[31] This description fits perfectly well with Avalokiteśvara's iconography, and it not only explains different length of the dress along the right and left leg, but it also explains why the female hip is more protruding than the other. Indeed, the creative function of the *Śaiva* Androgyne is clearly specular to that of the Avalokiteśvara-Tārā couple, which in the Vajrayāna tradition is viewed as the very root of the world.

The *Guṇa Kāraṇḍavyūha* text is dedicated to a description of the manifestation of the fourth world, the present one. Thanks to Padmapāṇi's intervention, which is quite similar to the cosmogony of the *Puruṣa Sūkta*. The creative function of the Bodhisattva is presented as his own self-sacrifice, as the disruption of the primeval oneness through androgenic duality. This explains why the Bodhisattva is always represented with smooth and graceful traits, which have been described by some as 'effeminate.' Actually, they are not 'effeminate' traits but truly feminine, due to his non-dual and hermaphrodite nature. This also explains the female characteristics of the rare Tibetan images of Avalokiteśvara. He holds the *cakra* of the Law, which in Brahminism is an attribute of the Viṣṇu and not Śiva, and this would appear in contrast with the thesis we have maintained till now. The wheel, however, is held by female half of the Androgyne, i.e. by Pārvatī, who, in the Brahmanical myth, is Viṣṇu's sister: she can thus legitimately bear this *Vaiṣṇava* weapon.

Of course, the hermaphrodite nature of Avalokiteśvara might suggest an answer to the still open question of the female representation of the same Bodhisattva in the Far East, under the names of Kaun Yin and Kannon.

In conclusion, Avalokiteśvara's Androgyne representation depicts him with a bare shoulder, the other being covered by the antelope skin – and with the opposite leg bare up to the knee. It is interesting to note that, still nowadays, some esoteric organizations of both the East – as some Chinese secret society – and the West – as the Free Masonry – request their aspirants to present themselves for initiation with their bare shoulder and bare opposite leg.[32] Evidently, this is a ritual allusion to the firm resolution which must animate the candidate of initiation in order to attain the primordial androgynic nature.

Notes and References

1. Mallar Ghosh, *Development of Buddhist Iconography in Eastern India: A Study of Tārā, Prajñās of Five Tathāgatas and Bhṛkuṭi,* Munshiram Manoharlal, New Delhi, 1980, p. 21.
2. "Although his first representation in India resembled Brahmā, with the hands in *Brahmāñjali mudrā* (devotional attitude), his functions were those of Viṣṇu, i.e. Preserver and Defender. But he also has much in common with Śiva..." Alice Getty, *The Gods Northern Buddhism,* Munshiram Manoharlal, New Delhi, 1978, p. 59.
3. Quite rightly, Taddei linked the presence of Hindu deities in the Buddhist iconography of Gandhāra to the peculiar 'skill' which various Bodhisattvas exhibit in assuming the form of the gods of different religions, with the aim of converting their followers to the true doctrine. In this regard, Taddei specifically notes the function of Avalokiteśvara. See Maurizo Taddei, "Non-Buddhist Deities in Gandharan Art: Some New Evidence", in W. Lobo and M. Yaldiz (eds), *Investigating Indian Art,* Berlin, 1987, pp. 349-362. Our case study, however, concerns a different aspect, that is, that of the essential identity of functions of the Hindu deity and the Buddhist Bodhisattva.
4. A.K. Coomaraswamy, *Yakṣas,* Munshiram Manoharlal, New Delhi, 1980 (2nd ed) part I, pp. 29-32.
5. *Ibid.,* p. 41.
6. A.A. Macdonell, *Vedic Mythology,* Motilal Banarsidass, Delhi, 1981 (3rd ed.), p. 101; E. Washburn Hopkins, *Epic Mythology,* Motilal Banarsidass, Delhi, 1986 (3rd ed.), p. 148.
7. Representations of the same period of the *yakṣa* Padmapāṇi clearly show that the Sāñchī posture was already canonical during the Śuṅga dynasty, as it can be proved by the relief on the Amin pillar as well as by the relief kept at the Government Museum, Lucknow. Concerning the iconography of Śūtapā'i, we may add that figure bearing the spear has often a peacock feather attached to his turban. In this case, the peacock is allusive of Śiva Nīlakaṇṭha, and not of Kṛṣṇa as some have suggested. Indeed, the peacock has a blue neck, just like Śiva. In time, the spear and the peacock will become the attributes of Śiva's son Skanda.
8. The presence of Śaiva iconography in the Buddhist sanctuaries of Central Asia is quite an ancient motif. For a detailed analysis of this important presence, see Ciro Lo Muzio, *L'iconografia di Śiva in Asia Centrale,* Univerdsita di Genova, 1994 (unpublished Ph.D. Thesis).
9. In Hindu iconography, Śiva is the deity that can be represented with the greater number of arms. Though he does not reach the amazing, countless arms of Avalokiteśvara as in the Vajrayāna tradition, nonetheless Śiva can exhibit a maximum of fifty arms , see R.S. Gupte, *Iconography of the Hindus, Buddhists and Jainas,* D.B. Tareporevala Sons & Co. Private Ltd., Bombay, 1972, p. 69.
10. "It is by now a documented fact that the fundamental elements of the Gupta style – together with the influences deriving from the semi-classic Gandhara school, which flourished between the 1st and 5th centuries – constitued the first form of the future evolution of this style of art, both in Ladakh and Central Asia. The entire group of mural paintings discovered in Miran, along the southern silk route, are clearly the products of this school of art. With the expansion of Buddhism along the silk route towards the East, various iconographic motifs as well as numerous works of art such as the archaic mural paintings of Tun-huang derived their inspiration from this source: the relation between the first paintings of Central

Asia and the Gupta style – together with its posterior of art – extended to the entire sequence of works-of-art, from the north-western region of Gandhara-known as Ysufzai (through the route passing across the Swat Valley) – to the southern tract of the silk route leading to China. These forms of art had a very important function especially around the middle of the 7th century, which was a time of frequent contacts among Nepal, Tibet and China..."; see Madanjeet Singh, *Arte himalyana,* Silvana Editoriale d' Arte, Milano, 1968, p. 52.

11. Alice Getty, *op. cit.,* p. 68.

12. *Śatapatha Brāhmaṇa,* XI. 6.3.7.

13. Stella Kramrisch, *The Presence of Śiva,* Motilal Banarsidass, Delhi, 1988, pp. 336-340.

14. "The consecrating magic of the black antelope skin was vested in the black antelope, Rudra's victim. 'Once upon a time the sacrifice escaped the gods, and having become a black antelope roamed about. The gods having there upon found it, stripped it of its skin' (*ŚB* 1.1.4.1). The black antelope was homologized with the sacrifice"; *ibid.,* p. 338.

15. "The Lord of the World, armed with a Brahmanic staff." The staff, which in India represents the power of the priestly caste, is in this case identified with Śiva's *triśūla; cfr.* Hans Wolfgang Schumann, *Buddhistische Bilderwelt,* Köln, 1986, 5.1.2. The Stutleys in their dictionary explain the compound *brahmadaṇḍa* as 'Brahmā's staff". The god Brahmā, however, does never bear a staff; he usually holds a sacrificial ladle. See James Stutely & Margaret Stutely, *A Dictionary of Hinduism,* London, 1977. It should also be noted that Lokeśvara and Lokanātha are both epithets of Śiva, quite commonly utilized in Tantric environments.

16. "The Lord of the World, Winner over the poison." This form of Avalokiteśvara has a variant called Nīlakaṇṭha, 'the One bearing a blue neck', which is a common epithet of Śiva celebrating his deed of drinking the *hālāhala* (poison), which emerged during the mythical churning of the Ocean of Milk.

17. T.A. Gopinath Rao, *Elements of Hindu Iconography,* Delhi, 1985 (2nd ed.), Vol. II, Pt. I, pp. 132-133.

18. Gupta, *op. cit.,* p. 129.

19. It corresponds in an astonishing way to the form of Śiva known as *siṁhakarṇa* meaning 'the One bearing the hearing of a lion;' *cfr.* T.A. Gopinatha Rao, *op. cit.,* Vol. II, Pt. I, pp. 129-130.

20. Various puranic myths narrate Śiva's adventure in the Dārukā forest, where the *ṛṣis* directed against him various extraordinary enemies; the demon elephant Gajāsura, the tiger demon Vyāghrāsura, the cobra demon, and the dwarf known as Apasmāra. Śiva killed the first two, making for himself a *dhotī* out of the tiger's skin, encircled his neck with the cobra, and crushed the dwarf with his foot; *cfr.* C. Sivaramamurti, *Natraja in Art, Thought, and Literature,* New Delhi, 1974, p. 154. As the winner against the elephant *asura,* Śiva bears in his hand the *aṅkuśa,* i.e. the special hook for elephants. In the not so common shape of Trailokyavaśankara Lokeśvara, the Bodhisattva is also endowed with the noose and the elephant hook.

21. Alice Getty, *op. cit.,* p. 69.

22. Hans Worlfgang Schumann, *op. cit.,* 5.1.1.

23. An exception to the rule can be found in an image published by Lokesh Chandra, which shows Simhanāda in the same position albeit with his legs fastened by a *yoga paṭṭa,* the sort of belt with which *yogis* tie both their legs in order to keep their bodies in the most difficult postures. This technique is said to favour meditation, although it is a clear hindrance to any

kind of movement; *cfr.* Lokesh Chandra, *Buddhist Iconography of Tibet,* Rinsen Book Co., Kyoto, 1986, Vol. I, p. 248.

24. Pratapaditya Pal, *Art of Tibet,* Los Angeles County Museum of Art/Mapin, Los Angeles, 1990, pp. 199-200.

25. With the exception of the *paśa* – not yet mentioned – i.e. the noose with which ordinary beings are put to death by suffocation. The same *paśa,* however, grants the initiation death to the *yogin. Cfr.* G.G. Filippi, *Dialogo di Naciketas con la Morte: Taittiriya Brāhmaṇa, III.11.8 - Kaṭha-upaniṣad,* Cafoscarina, Venezia, 2001, pp. 15-20; Lilia Arnoldo, "La Dea che uccide il Bufalo", A. Amadi (ed. by), *Il sangue nel Mito,* Venezia, AVIS ed., 2002, pp. 154-155. Since the time of the *Vedas,* the Lord of the noose in Brahmanism is of course Rūdra - Śiva; *cfr. AB,* 3.33; *ŚB,* 1.7.4.3.; *RV,* 10.92.9.

26. Pratapaditya Pal, commenting on two Tibetan bronzes representing Avalokiteśvara, describes their dress as a *dhotī,* without realizing that in both cases the dress is short on the left leg; see Pratapaditya Pal, *op. cit.,* pp. 193, 201.

27. Hans Wolfgang Schumann, *op. cit.,* 5.1.7; 5.1.8.

28. *Ibid.,* 5.1.5.

29. S.L. Nagar, *Śiva in Art, Literature and Thought,* Indus Publishing Co., New Delhi, 1994, p. 184.

30. *Śiva Purāṇa, Vās. S.,* II. 4.4.

31. S.L. Nagar, *op. cit.,* pp. 186-188.

32. (unknown author) *Rituale del Libero Muratore d'Inghilterra,* Roma, 'L'Acacia', 1948-49, pp. XI (primo grado), VI (secondo grado), VI (terzo grado); J.S.M. Ward, *The Hung Society,* or *The Society of Heaven and Earth,* The Baskerville Press, London, 1925, Vol. 1, pp. 108-109.

3

Fresh Light on the History of Indian Jade-Carving

M.L. Nigam

There has been a good deal of controversy about the origin and development of the art of jade-carving in India. The British scholars, who did the pioneering research work on this particular branch of knowledge, remained somewhat obsessed with the idea that the Indian artisans till the dawn of seventeenth century AD had no knowledge of jade and hence they were in no way competent to fashion jade specimens with such a superb and elegant workmanship which we notice in some of the jade vessels found inscribed with the name of the Mughal emperor, Jahangir and the dates given in the regnal era of the said emperor. In fact, some of the jade wine-cups of Jahangir also provide the place-names such as 'Mandu' and 'Fathpur' where they are recorded to have been produced. On this, the British scholars argue that such superbly finished jade wine-cups and jugs must have been carved in China which has a long history of the art of jade-carving and later they could have been brought to Mandu for engraving. This argument seems somewhat ridiculous because the tools and technique which are required for fashioning jade-objects and for inscribing legends over them are the same. So, if the Indian artisans possessed the technical knowledge and tools for engraving the legends on jade objects, then what prevented them from producing those very jade wine-cups which bear such legends ?

The British scholars are somehow not inclined to give the credit of fashioning some of the early jade specimens of Jahangir to Indian lapidars. According to S.H. Hansford, who wrote in 1968,

> But the design and execution of these superbly finished (jade) vessels is another matter. That Indian artists and craftsmen could possibly have equalled or surpassed the Chinese in this characteristically Chinese and highly specialised art and craft in the seventeenth century seems beyond the bounds of probability and, I venture to suggest, of possibility.[1]

Prof. Hansford also doubted whether Indian artisans possessed the hardstone technology and, if so, how ?

John Irwin, another British scholar, has opined,

It is possible that all these Jahangīrī Jades are of Persian workmanship, and with one exception (Plate 9) it is not possible to say with certainty that they were carved (as well as engraved) on Indian soil. However with absolute conviction we can say that by the end of Shah Jahān's reign a truly Mughal tradition of jade-carving had not only been firmly established but reached full maturity at the Mughal Court.[2]

Another noted scholar, Robert Skelton, who did most of the pioneering work on the history of Indian jade-carving, had acknowledged that India did possess the knowledge of working on hard stone technology right from the early historic periods. A number of beautiful crystal reliquaries have been found from the excavations of several Buddhist *stūpas* of Aśokan period which confirm Skelton's statement. Besides, the Indian technology using the bow lathe as against the Chinese craftsmen who worked on the treadle lathe would further prove that Indians did not adopt the Chinese technology and hence, the Indian jades belonging to Jahangir and Shahjahan's periods should not be considered as products of the Chinese artists.

Robert Skelton, however, has propounded a very far-fetched hypothesis that the earlier jade specimens of Jahangir's reign bear an unmistakable typological affinity with the Safavid metalware. The Safavid lapidars had borrowed the art of jade-carving from the Timurid art tradition. As the Indian Mughals had high regard for their Timurid ancestors, they borrowed the jade-carving tradition from Persia.[3] Thus, the early jade specimens inscribed with the name of Jahangir should be attributed to Persian jade-carvers. The Persian masters must have therefore trained the Indian craftsmen in the art of jade-carving.

The British scholars have taken it for granted that the technique of inlay workmanship came to India from Persia. The earliest jade object belonging to Jahangir is an archer's ring with the legend, "Shah Salim". As the inscription "Shah Salim" would suggest, the archer's ring was fashioned and inscribed at a time when Jahangir was still an heir-apparent. It has the traces of fine inlay workmanship in gold. It was also encrushed with precious stones which are now missing. It is because the gold-inlay is also found on the Perṣian metalware, and hence the above scholar attributes the workmanship of the said jade-archer's ring to Persian artisans. As we have mentioned it elsewhere, the inlay-technique was known to Indians in 9th century AD, if not earlier. The eyes of the metal images from Kashmir, datable to 9th century, exhibit the inlay technique.[4] Hence, it will be erronous to attribute all early Jahangir's jades to Persian artists. Robert Skelton further believed that the Indians did not have the knowledge of jade as raw material prior to the advent of Mughals in India. Thus, the art of jade-carving in India started right from the middle of Jahangir's reign. This hypothesis by Robert Skelton is not based on historical facts. Firstly, the similarity of forms of some of early jade-specimens belonging to Jahangir with the Persian metalware does not suggest that such jade objects, which are inscribed with the name of the Mughal emperor Jahangir and the dates given in his regnal years, should have been fashioned by the Persian artisans. There is no such evidence to support his hypothesis. The Persian art-forms, motifs and designs had already become familiar with Indian artists during the Tughlaq period. The gifted Indian artists, once they had already known these Persian forms and motifs atleast a century earlier to the advent of Mughals in India, had no difficulty whatever, to reproduce them as and when their new masters wanted them to do so. To assign all early jade vessels of Jahangir's reign to Persian craftsmen on typological basis alone is not correct. Secondly, the surmise that Indians did know jade as raw material prior to Akbar's period is also untrue. No doubt, the good variety of nephrite jade is not found in India. The mines of good quality jade are all located in Central Asia around Yarkand and Khotan regions, India had very close association with the said regions of Central Asia right from the beginning of the Christian era. The Buddhist missionaries from India had gone and settled in this area during 2nd-3rd centuries AD. There was a regular movement of Indians to these regions for the propagation of Buddhism. Thus, the plea that Indians remained unaware of jade as a commodity till seventeenth century is not very convincing.

In fact, Hiuen-Tśāng, the Chinese traveller who reached India via Central Asia during seventh century AD, clearly mentions jade as a commodity of regular transaction between India and Central Asian regions.[5] Hence, the argument of Robert Skelton, that Indians did not know of jade till Akbar's period is mere presumption and not based on historical facts.

Yet another factor which goes against the hypothesis of Skelton, which he himself admits, that the Safavid rulers did not much patronise the art of jade-carving. There are hardly a few jade specimens which can be ascribed to Persian workmanship on definite grounds. The Persian artisans of the Safavid court are known to have imbibed the art-forms of the Tumurid court tradition. Thus, there is no positive evidence to prove that the art of jade-carving came to India from Persia. In fact, the Persian artisans themselves did not evince much interest in the art of jade-carving.

There is no doubt that some of the jade-vessels belonging to Timurid rulers, viz. Ulugh Beg and Ala-al-daula were in the possession of the Mughal emperor Jahangir. The Mughal emperors of India were very proud of their Turkish lineage. Hence, they had a fancy for collecting the precious objects belonging to the royal treasury of the Timurid kings after the fall of their empire. In this regard, a reference in *Tuzuk-i-Jahangīrī* is noteworthy wherein Jahangir informs us that such rare treasures, "belonged to the jewel chamber of M. Ulugh Beg, the successor of M. Shah Rukh" and "in course of time, and by the revolutions of fate, had come into the hands of Safavid family".[6] The relations between Jahangir and the Safavid ruler, Shah Abbas were very cordial and friendly. They also used to send precious gifts to each other as a mark of goodwill. According to *Tuzuk-i-Jahangīrī*, the Persian monarch Shah Abbas had sent a special ruby, which was engraved with the name of Ulugh Beg, to Jahangir as a loving present. Thus, it is likely that some of the Timurid jade-vessels reached Jahangir through the Persian monarch. The Persian king, Shah Abbas got his name engraved on it and so also the name of Jahangir, son of Akbar, was inscribed on the same at a later date.

The Timurid court in Samarkand seems to have extended patronage to the art of jade-carving during the reign of Ulugh Beg in 15th century. A dragon handled jug with an inscription in Arabic characters bearing the name of Ulugh Beg, son of Shah Rukh and grandson of Timur, around its neck, must have been fashioned in Samarkand. Later it came in the possession of Jahangir and his son, Shahjahan whose names are also found engraved on the jug. Similarly, a wine cup with a bird handle in dark green nephrite and inlaid with silver wire is presently housed in the collection of Bharat Kala Bhavan, Varanasi. It is also inscribed with the names of Ulugh Beg and Jahangir. A small , jade - pot owned by Ulugh Beg's nephew, Ala-al- daula and later by the Mughal emperor Jahangir is now housed in the Avery Brunlage Collection, San Francisco. In addition to these, there are other Timurid jades found scattered in various museums and other private collectors of the world, which would suggest the flourishing of the jade-craft under the Timurid patronage in Central Asia.

As many inscribed jade-vessels of the Timurid royal house had come under the possession of Jahangir and Shahjahan and they are datable to 15th century, one would be tempted to surmise that the art of jade-carving had possibly reached India from Central Asia as a result of close contacts of the Indian Mughals with that region. All the so far known inscribed jade specimens in India, barring one example which we shall discuss later, are datable to 17th century. It led Western scholars to believe that the Central Asian craftsmen might have been imported by the Mughals to introduce this special art in the Indian sub-continent. However, there is no proof to subscribe to such a conjecture.

Meanwhile, our recent researches on the subject have thrown very valuable light on the history of Islamic jade-carving which further disapproves of such a possibility. A Persian manuscript, *Khawasul Jawahar* , presently housed in the Salar Jung Museum library, Hyderabad, contains very positive evidence regarding the history of jade-carving in Central Asian region. It is a rare manuscript dealing with the medicinal qualities of precious and semi-precious stones. The scribe of the manuscript, Mirza Lutf Ali Baig informs us that it was copied from an earlier treatise on the subject which was originally written by Mohammad Haji under the instructions of the Central Asian Monarch, Shah Rukh who was a great patron of learning and art. Mirza Lutf Ali copied it in the year 1270 Hijri. The period of Shah Rukh can be assigned to 15th century AD.

Our manuscript mentions that jade as a semi-precious stone was held in high esteem by the nobles of Khata. It was found in seven colours around the regions of Kashghar and Khata. According to this manuscript, it was the Kafirs living there who had the mastery over this craft. Their workmanship, both in engraving (Naqs-i-Khatai) and in carving out perfect figures, forms and motifs (*Sūratgirī*) was of such a high standard that the people got puzzled after witnessing the same. They also produced sword hilts out of jade. They were prized very high, so much so that a jade sword hilt (or belt) was sold in Khata for 5000 gold mohurs.[7] The Kafir's themselves, both men and women, took pride in possessing jade objects according to their social status. Even the tradesmen, who went to Khata, gained importance by acquiring beautiful jade objects.

The author of the manuscript further informs us that the Turks of Mawaraunhar and Khorasan initially did not evince much interest in this particular art. It was, however, from the reign of Shah Rukh, who himself collected jades, that the Turks got interested in this art and later on they not only learnt it but also became experts and produced a good number of craftsmen in the art of jade-carving. Gauharshad Begum, the wife of Shah Rukh, got prepared a "Pusht" (back of the throne) for her son, Baisanqar Mirza, by spending a large sum of money.[8]

The foregoing information based on an earlier treatise written for Shah Rukh, the ruler of Samarkand, is of special interest to us for knowing the history of jade-carving in Central Asia. Firstly, the art of jade-carving in Central Asian region was initially practised by the Kafirs living at Khata. Secondly, the first Central Asian monarch who took interest in the art of jade-carving was Shah Rukh. Thirdly, the Turks of Central Asia learnt this art from the Kafirs sometime during AD 1400 and later gained mastery over it. Fortunately for us, the information contained in the Persian treatise, "Khawasul Jawahar" is also confirmed by archaeological evidence. The first Central Asian jade specimen, which has come to light so far, is a dragon handled cup inscribed with the name of Ulugh Beg, son of Shah Rukh, presently housed in the British Museum, London. The story of Ulugh Beg's capture of two large blocks of jade during his Mughalistan campaign in 1425 is already known to us and one of these jade blocks is now placed on the tomb of Timur, the grandfather of Ulugh Beg. No jade specimen which can be ascribed to a date earlier than that of Shah Rukh has come to light so far from Central Asian region.

The next problem is that of the identity of the "Kafirs" who had introduced the art of jade-carving in Central Asia and who transmitted this knowledge to the Turks of Mawaraunhar and Khorasan. In the Islamic context, people other than those who believe in Allah, were called "Kafirs". The historical records further confirm that the area around north-eastern Afghanistan was known by the name of 'Kafiristan'. According to Hiuen-Tsang, it was a thriving seat of Buddhism. It is obvious that the so-called "Kafirs", found mentioned in the aforesaid manuscript, refer to the Buddhists inhabiting this region. The travel accounts of the Chinese travelers, viz, Fa-Hien and Hiuen-Tsang would testify that the entire Tarim basin had Buddhism as its flourishing religion during 6th and 7th centuries AD. Regarding the inhabitants it is mentioned,

> Their appearance is full of urbanity, their customs are well regulated '(They have chronicles). Their written characters (as well as their laws and literature) resemble the Indian model, the forms have been somewhat modified; the differences, however, are slight. The spoken language differs from that of other territories. The Law of Buddha is held in great esteem.[9]

Besides, the manuscripts found at Dandan-Uiliq and other sites, whether of Sanskrit or indigenous texts, further demonstrate the correctness of what the Chinese pilgrim Hieun-Tsang says about the writing of Khotan and the Indian base of its literature. Thus, there is no doubt that the Indian Buddhists were living in large numbers in Tarim basin during seventh century AD. The Chinese, who first controlled the entire Tarim basin, did not interfere with them. Yet, the conquest of Khotan by the Turkish rulers of Kashgar and its conversion to Islam took place sometime during AD 1000 . This political event must have proved a great setback to Buddhism and its followers. Some of the Buddhist missionaries, however, continued to live there and followed their arts and crafts to meet the requirements of the local population. As the Buddhist missionaries possessed the technique of jade-carving, they continued to practise the same in the region during the rule of Shah Rukh also. They were, however, called 'Kafirs' because they had not accepted Islam as their faith. It is thus, evident that the 'Kafirs', as found mentioned in *Khawasul Jawahar*, are none other than the Buddhist missionaries who had gone from India and settled in Tarim basin. Hence, it will not be inappropriate to suggest that the technique of jade-carving in Central Asia was initially taken from India by the Buddhists during the early centuries of the Christian era. Later, the art was learnt by the Turks who practised it with great skill and dexterity. The Indian Mughals, who had come to India from Central Asia, received the art of jade-carving in a modified form to suit the Islamic taste. The Mughals not only introduced and incorporated Central Asian and Persian motifs and forms but also provided greater incentive and vigour to the art of jade-carving.

It was Pinder Wilson who first wrote in 1963 that some of the jade wine-cups owned by the Mughal emperor Jahangir were produced in Samarkand for the Timurid ruler, Ulugh Beg.[10] The presence of some of the Timurid jade vessels in the court of Jahangir, however, does not mean that the art of jade-carving was introduced in India from Central Asia. They had descended from Central Asia. The Mughal emperors of India did acquire fancy art-objects from different countries as gifts or purchase to embellish their court which was famous for its royal grandeur all over the world. However, India had its own old art-traditions and techniques which continued during the Mughal era.

The recent discovery of the Persian manuscript, *Khawasul Jawahar* in the collection of Salar Jung Museum library has thus solved the long-awaited mystery of the origin and development of the art of Indian jade-carving. In fact, it was the other way round. The Indian Buddhist missionaries had taken along with them the technique of hardstone-carving to Central Asia and introduced the same among the Turks of that region. The Turks of Mawaraunhar and Khotan not only learnt this technique but they also produced beautiful jade-vessels, sword-handles and other objects of exquisite beauty to decorate the Timurid court of Samarkand. It was during the Mughal rule in India that the art of jade-carving came back to India from Central Asia in a modified form which suited the taste of Indian Mughals.

Notes and References

1. S.H. Hansford, *Chinese Carved Jades,* London, 1968, p. 97.
2. John Irwin, Mughal Jades, *The Times of India Annual,* 1998, p. 70.
3. Robert Skelton, The Relations Between the Chinese and Indian Jade Carving Traditions, *Colloquies on Art and Archaeology in Asia,* No. 3, University of London, 1972, p. 102.
4. M.L. Nigam, Jewellery-Inlay Work and Studding of Gems, *History of Technology in India*, Vol. I, A.K. Bag, (ed.) New Delhi, 1997, pp. 619-20.
5. S.Siyu-Ki Beal, *Buddhist Records of the Western World* , Vol. 1, p. 89.
6. *Tuzuk-i-Jahangiri*, trans. by Alexander Rogers, New Series, Vol. XIX, p. 379.
7. Mirza Lutf Ali Baig, *Khawasul Jawahar*, Folio 23 B.
8. *Ibid*., Folio, 24A.
9. Sir Aurel Stein, *Ancient Khotan*, p. 174.
10. R.H. Pinder Wilson, An Inscribed Jade Cup from Samarkand, *British Museum Quarterly,* Vol. XXIII, No. 1, London, 1960.

4

Vision to Appreciate Art

R.C. Sharma

By nature, man loves beauty, whether it is natural or created by himself. The works of art belong to the realm of beauty or aesthetics. These are to be seen or viewed in such a way that the mission of their creation is fulfilled. People do notice, appreciate, analyse or criticize as per their level of understanding, feelings and emotions. But only a few are able to discover the real beauty and message behind the object on view. There may be different approaches and layers of our vision from the mundane to the supermundane horizons.

In the Indian context, *kalā* (art) is derived from *kal,* meaning *ānanda* (joy or pleasure). Without this end being achieved, the role of art creation becomes insignificant. Those who advocate in favour of the theory of art for art sake dwell on the surface level only and are deprived of enjoying the bliss of art. The joy *(ānanda)* again has different layers of experience and one has to unfold Supreme Joy *(paramānanda),* which is beyond the scope of senses.[1] This is certainly a difficult target, but not impossible through constant endeavour.[2] For this, one has to develop his/her faculties and train the senses.

The domain of art is not mortal and if it is considered to be so, it is bound to be debased and fails to lead to the real joy. If an art piece is able to vibrate our emotions and elate us to higher consciousness, its mission is accomplished. Understanding of art is a two-way process, i.e. the spirit behind its creation and the training *(dīkṣā)* of the onlooker.

Art has been explained as the expression of thoughts in visual form. But the expression itself must be the result of the happy blend of beauty and spirit. The Indian aesthetics does not confine itself to the outer form, but the inward vision is equally or more significant. At this point, we reach somewhere near divinity *(divyatā)* as the opening of the inward vision does not merely depend on one's own effort, but the grace of divine is also a desideratum. When Arjuna longed to see the cosmic-form, the necessity of divine eye *(divyacakṣu)* was felt and was granted too.[3] When the entire universe is the manifestation of Supreme, the best art forms are also the reflection of the same.[4]

Even if one does not believe in the existence of Soul or Supreme, he has to realize that the man is not able to create, and also fails to understand and grasp the real significance of a number of best forms of nature, like sun, moon, galaxy, thunder, high peaks of mountains, ocean, etc. The efforts so far made in this direction touch only the periphery, but of course, made us conscious of our own dwarfishness. Though modern medical science, being based on the matter, soul cannot be grasped by an instrument, however, advanced it may be, as the instrument itself is made of matter. The sharp sword cannot slay, kill or cut the water, which will remain in its original shape, although struck a hundred times.

To realize the Soul or to listen to its message, we have to place ourselves on the pedestal of higher consciousness or a supermundane plane. This effort on our part has been called as *samādhi,* or a state of yoga *(yogastha).* If this is not done, we shall remain confined to the outer surface of beauty and shall miss the ocean of nectar in visualizing an art form.

Sri Aurobindo observes that the divine aspect always remains the integral part of an art form, although it may vary in degrees:

Its (Indian Art's) highest business is to disclose something of the Self through its expressions, the Infinite through its living finite symbols, the divine through his powers. Or the Godheads are to be revealed, luminously interpreted or in some way suggested to the soul's understanding... when this hieratic art comes down from these altitudes to the intermediate worlds behind ours, to the lesser godheads or genii, it still carries into them some power or some hint from above. And when it comes quite down to the material world and the life of man and the things of external Nature, it does not altogether get rid of the greater vision... there is always something more in which the seeing presentation of life floats in an immaterial atmosphere.[5]

About the spiritual contents, he thinks '...Indian art in fact is identical in its spiritual aim and principle with the rest of Indian culture'.[6]

Whatever has been said about the Indian art, the same is true for Indian architecture also. Percy Brown, while writing his introductory remarks on Indian architecture, seems very specific on this issue:

In each of the major historical developments of architecture, there is one basic principle underlying its conception, and one which is supremely distinctive. With Greeks this was refined perfection; Roman buildings are remarkable for their scientific construction, French Gothic reveals a condition of passionate energy, while Italian Renaissance reflects the scholarship of its time. In the same way, the outstanding quality of the architecture of India is its spiritual content. It is evident that the fundamental purpose of the building art was to represent in concrete form the prevailing religious consciousness of the people. It is mind materialized in terms of rock, brick or stone.[7]

This may be pointed out here that the art of a country cannot be studied in isolation; it is interwoven with architecture. In art, we view a single object, but in architecture, we examine piece by piece. The moods, modes and movements of the society are reflected in the mirror of art as well as of architecture. Some of the best art forms are seen on the exterior of *stūpas,* temples, *caityas,* memorials, palaces, etc. All these buildings are not just constructions, but these are the celestial specimens of art too. These are richly engraved or decorated with sculptures, motifs and flora and fauna, providing an aesthetic feast to the onlooker. At the same time, these are the messages of deep thought and divine message.

V.S. Agrawala, elaborately dealing with this aspect, opines that although the art is human creation *(mānuṣī-śilpa),* yet it remains very close to the Divine creation *(daivī-śilpa)* for the fact that it is through the divine inspiration that the artist creates a piece of art, and it is adorned with the divine beauty in its form *(rūpa)* and meaning (*artha*).[8] Manifestation of and dedication to divine has been the main function of Indian art and architecture. In early days, the Indian masses and even kings, did not bother to put up a monumental building for their residential purpose; hence their remains are extremely rare. On the other hand, we do have a large number of religious edifices to give them more strength and life. Non-perishable medium was used replacing forestry or timber. Same is the case with the engravers, carvers, artisans, painters and craftsmen, whose names generally remain obscure, anonymous and only a few are met with. They created a piece of art or architecture not as an art object, but an offering *(naivedya)* to the divine, and in the background of such faith, sentiments or emotions, the personal name was insignificant.

Being selfless has been the fundamental principle of Indian culture from the very beginning. The Vedic seer, after pouring each oblation into the fire, ended the hymn by uttering *'idaṁ na mama',* it is not for me. Perfect devotion and a sense of self-sacrifice has been the foundation of religious and spiritual attainment. Name *(nāma)* and figure *(rūpa)* of one's own self were not considered to be meritorious. When the concept of God and Soul remained subdued as a result of Buddhist, Jaina and other similar thoughts, the supermundane element and devotion continued and the homage was directed to the Buddha / Bodhisattva, *Tīrthaṅkara* and folk deities. This finds support from the canonical literature and archaeological evidence.

The merit earned in the installation of an image, which the art historians accept now as an object of art, did not go to the donor, but to the *ācāryas,* monks and parents. Sometimes, the welfare of people has also been aimed at the pedestal inscription, like that of a Buddha image by Yaśā, daughter of Grahadina, records that its purpose was the welfare of all beings.[9] Similarly, a Jaina *āyāgapaṭa* (tablet of homage) was set up in honour of the *Tīrthaṅkara* by a courtesan Vasu, the daughter of courtesan Loṇasobhikā.[10] Subsequently, the image was termed as *deyadharma* (pious gift) to a religious place and it aimed at achieving the Supreme knowledge *(lokottara-jñāna)* by all.[11] Thus, even if God and Soul are not recorded, the religious merit and the supermundane bliss, i.e. the divine aspect remained intact.

There are four basic elements behind the formation of an art object, viz., *rasa* (aggregate form of human emotions or sentiments), *artha* (meaning), *chanda* (rhythm) and *rūpa* (form). These are common to literature and to great extent to music also. The form *(rūpa)* represents *śabda* in case of literature. *Rasa* is the most vital of these and quite often it is expected to be the ultimate goal of art and literature. Divine has often been called as *rasa (raso-vai-saḥ).* These emotions are adequately tested in sculptures and paintings. If a piece of art is not able to generate at least one of the nine emotions,[12] the whole exercise in its creation is futile.

The second important element is *artha,* i.e. meaning or the message of an art product. It is through the message that the viewer is filled with a particular emotion. Without meaning, the production of any art piece is meaningless. In literature, the speech and meaning are inseparable, as both are essential in composition of a literature. These have been visualized as *Ardhanādrīśvara,* the composite aspect of male and female energy, being complementary to each other.[13] The message of icon or painting is conveyed through postures *(mudrās),* attributes *(āyudhas),* colours *(varṇas),* expression *(bhāva),* etc.

The third aspect is *chanda* (rhythm), which is an outcome of proper composition, symmetry and harmony of the figure. The fourth and last aspect is the *rūpa* or form, which imparts the visual shape to the vision and action of an artist through a medium, like clay, stone, metal, ivory, wood, cloth, paper, etc. The medium is transformed into an image, architecture, painting or a decorative motif.[14] The last aspect, i.e. *rūpa* dominates in the modern art production and the other three aspects, although more important than form, are often ignored. As such, one views only the one-fourth form of an art piece, although to the naked eye it appears full or complete as it does amuse in one way or the other. But this amusement is only superfluous and short-lived.

Coomaraswamy rightly observes, 'The life of pleasure only, one of which the end is pleasure, is subhuman, every animal knows what it likes and seeks for....'[15] He further explains, 'The Indian actor prepares for his performance by prayer. The Indian architect is often spoken of as visiting heaven and there making notes of prevailing focus of architecture, which he imitates below....'[16] Thus, the oriental, and particularly the Indian art or architecture, has much more to offer, to make the art as an offering to divine and in doing so, the artist or architect feels that he is an instrument *(nimitta)* and not the creator. This attitude changes the entire concept and elevates us from the lower strata to the higher level of divine consciousness.

The success of artist depends on the depth of his vision and the best form is the result of deep concentration what we call *samādhi* and *mahābhūtasamādhi,*[17] and the mortal initiation is ultimately transformed into immortal or *divya.* This was the expression for Dilīpa, and almost same sentiments are noticed from Śakuntalā,[18] that such outstanding beauty is the result of best contemplation and thought even by Brahmā, the Creator. To appreciate the significance, one has to develop his capacity of viewing. This again has multiple stages depending on the depth of the insight of the viewer or his keenness of observance. The first stage is that the onlooker should have the same wavelength as the artist. At this point, the art object is not a simple specimen, but it carries inner meanings, which have to be unfolded through deep and absorbing thought. The debased thinking should not persist and this is the first step or condition.[19]

To our good luck, such layers have been nicely exposed by the seers and poets, and particularly, the great exponent of Indian culture Kālidāsa. He presents different levels of viewing the beautiful things. The first stage of appreciation is *paśya,* simply to see and no effort seems necessary,

अमुं पुरः पश्यसि देव दारुं पुत्री कृतोऽसौ वृषभध्वजेन

रघु. 2.36

Or

पश्यानवद्यांगि विभाति गङ्गा भिन्न प्रवाहा यमुना तरगैः

रघु. 13.57

The second stage is when one sees with some curiosity and for this word *dadarśa* is selected:

स पाटलायां गवि तस्तिवांसं धनुर्धरः केसरिणं ददर्श

रघु. 2.29

The third stage is when one sees with effort and longing, and for this the word *prahitekṣaṇa* is used:

सा दुष्प्रधर्षा मनसापि हिंस्रैरित्यद्रि शोभा प्रहितेक्षणेन

रघु. 2.27

The next stage reflects the aspiration, i.e. keen desire to see and that is *didṛkṣā*:

सर्वोपमा द्रव्य समुच्चयेन यथा प्रदर्शं विनिवेशितेन।

सा निर्मिता विश्वसृजा प्रयत्नादेकस्थ सौन्दर्य दिदृक्षयेव।।

कु. 1.49

Brahmā aspired to see the beauty of the entire world at one place, and to fulfil this aim Pārvatī was created.

Another stage of viewing the best forms is when one totally forgets about himself and just concentrates on the figure. This happened when Indumatī appeared in the *svayamvara*:

तस्मिन् विधानातिशये विधातुः कन्यामये नेत्र शतैक लक्ष्ये।

नियेतुरन्तः करणैर्नरेन्द्राः देहैःस्थिता केवल मासनेषु।।

One more stage of looking at the beautiful objects has been expressed by the word *piva,* i.e drink through eyes:

पपौ निमेषाल सपक्ष्म पंक्तिरुपोषिताभ्यामिव लोचनाभ्याम्

रघु. 19

नेत्रैःपपुस्तृप्तिमनाप्नुवद्भिर्नवोदयं नाथमिवोषधीनाम्।

रघु. 2.73

निवात पद्मस्मितेन चक्षुषा नृपस्य कान्तं पिबतः सुताननम्।

महोदधेःपूर इवेन्दु दर्शनाद्गुरु : प्रहर्षः प्रबभूव नात्मनि।।

रघु. 3.17

Perhaps, the last stage of appreciating the beauty is to consider it as the greatest merit or the goal of the life:

अखण्डं पुण्यानां फुलमिव च तद्रूपघम्

अभि. शा. 2.10

Or sometimes, it is expressed as the best goal of the eye and nothing more is to be seen:

त्रिलोक सौन्दर्यमिवोदितं वपुः

अहो लब्धं नेत्र निर्वाणम्

कुमार. 5.41

These sentiments, expressions and emotions cannot be generated if the object is viewed at the surface or mundane level. One has to cultivate the habit of deeper perception and unfold the mysteries of art one after the other. This is the essence of Indian aesthetics. Matter *(sthūla)* or body-part *(śarīra)* is, of course, important and cannot be ignored, as it is the basis *(ādhāra)* of those thoughts, which are beyond the scope of matter and its analytical study. But our search must not confine to matter or surface only. We must go beyond and above in the realm of art or aesthetics, and appreciate the art objects from this angle. Only then, one can become a true connoisseur of art and enjoy its bliss, i.e. *rasa.*

Notes and References

1. सुखमात्यन्तिकं यत्तद्बुद्धिग्राह्यमतीन्द्रियम् । *Gītā.* 6.21
2. अभ्यासेन तु कौन्तेय वैराग्येण च गृह्यते । *Gītā.* 6.35
3. *Ibid.,* 11.8.
4. *Ibid.,* 10.41.
5. Sri Aurobindo, *India and Her Future,* 1971, p. 17.
6. Sri Aurobindo, *The Foundation of Indian Culture,* p. 208.
7. Percy Brown, *Indian Architecture* (Buddhist and Hindu Periods), 1956, p. 1.
8. V.S. Agrawala, *Indian Art,* 1965, pp. 4-5.
9. Mathurā Museum, No. 78.34.
10. R.C. Sharma, *The Splendour of Mathurā Art and Museum,* 1994, pp. 80-81 .
11. *Ibid.,* p. 139.
12. The number of the *rasas* is not certain. The *Nāṭyaśāstra* (11 .15-17) records eight *rasas: śṛṅgāra* (amorous), *hāsya* (comic), *karuṇā* (pathetic), *raudra* (furious), *vīra* (heroic), *bhayānaka* (terrible), *vībhatsa* (odious) and *adbhuta* (marvellous). Later, *śānta* (quiescent) was also added. The Vaiṣṇavas are keen to add two more, i.e. *mādhurya* (sweet) and *vātsalya* (fondness). *Dāsya* (service) is also sometimes treated as *rasa,* and Goswāmī Tulasīdāsa suggests one more, i.e. *sarala* (simple) – *Rāmacaritamānasa,* Ayodhyākāṇḍa 175.4.
13. वागर्थाविव सम्पृक्तौ वागर्थ प्रतिपत्तये ।

    जगत: पितरौवन्दे पार्वती परमेश्वरौ ।। Raghuvaṁśa 1.1.
14. V.S. Agrawala, *op. cit.,* p. 4.
15. A.K. Coomaraswamy, *Christian and Oriental Philosophy of Art,* 1941, p. 26.
16. *Ibid.*, p. 32.
17. तं वेधा विदधे नूनं महाभूत समाधिना। Raghuvaṁśa.
18. चित्ते निवेश्य परिकल्पित सत्त्वयोगा रूपोच्चयेन मनसा विधिना कृतानु ।

    स्त्रीरत्न सृष्टिरपरा प्रतिभाति सा मे धातुर्विभुत्वमनुचिन्त्यवपुश्च तस्या ।। Abhijñāna Śākuntalam 11.9
19. यदुच्यते पार्वति पापवृत्तये न रूपमित्यव्यभिचारि तद्वच: । Kumārasambhava V.36

5

The History and Art of Jaipur Painting: A Reappraisal

Chandramani Singh

In the beginning of the 20th century when A.K. Coomaraswamy, the pioneer among art historians, wrote about the painting produced for royal courts, temples and business houses of Rajasthan and Himalayan region which included Tehri Garhwal, at present a part of Uttranchal, he called it Rajput painting. Interestingly the cover of his book of the same name had a drawing showing two singing girls drawn in Jaipur style. Coomarawamy was the first to publish a portrait of master artist Sahibram and his work *Mahārāsa* (Coll. Man Singh II Museum).

One of Coomaraswamy's major works, *Rajput Painting,* was published in 1916 (2 vols.) and since then many of Indian and European/western art historians wrote on it; and in all these works Jaipur paintings were included. Independent works – books and monograph have also been written in subsequent years.[1]

Here we are going to discuss Jaipur style of painting, its major contribution to the art world along with certain questions related with it, but before we do so, we should look into the history of Kachawahas and their land briefly and then the style, which developed under their generous patronage.

Dulahrai, popularly known as Dhola, a prince from Narwar (Gwalior) family of the Kachawahas established a small kingdom in the north-eastern part of Rajasthan, then known as Dhūndhar, in the beginning of the 11th century. His son Kakildeva extended his territory and made Āmber his capital. Since then his family ruled in this region until the merger of the state into the Indian Union, with only the one change of capital from Āmber to Jaipur (which was founded by Sawai Jai Singh, 1699-1743 in 1727). The *rājās* of this dynasty took active part in Indian politics, especially during the Mughal rule, because of their cordial relations with the latter. During this long time period, the family patronized various arts and crafts. An atelier was maintained in the palace complex, works were executed by employees of *kārkhānā*/atelier and these were accumulated and finally developed into a large collection. Besides this, *jāgīrdārs* and *mahājans* also contributed in this activity and their collections are preserved in their families, temple and public institutions.

A well preserved and documented collection with written record in *toji bahīs* (coll. Rajasthan State Archives, Bikaner), provides valuable material for studying Jaipur style of painting. Our emphasis, in this articles will be on painting executed on paper although the tradition of wall painting is earlier than the former. Both these mediums are closely related and at times one feels that wall paintings are transferred on paper. Hence, literary references (late 16th and early 17th cent.) alongwith examples are being cited here.

Poet Amrit Rāi at the court of Mān Singh I, has mentioned painted walls of Āmber Palaces (1585). This is the earliest account of painting at Āmber. He writes.

सुचित्रित चित्र बनाई विचित्र, सुचाहि चरच्चिव चारू चरित्र।

लिखे जिय जंत अनंत बनाई, कहउब कहाँ लगि देउ गनाई।।[2]

There are beautiful paintings painted (on palace walls) illustrating different types of birds and animals, difficult to count them, says the poet.

Interestingly it corresponds with the subjects painted there.[3] There are birds and animals painted in squares, stylistically they are close to *Rāgamālā* series, preserved in the collection of M.S. Man Singh II Museum. Palette of this archaic looking style is dominated by chocolate, yellow and dirty blue.

Another text *Mān Carit Rāso* by Narottam *kavi* also refers to wall paintings at Āmber. The date of composition of this text is not known but the copy available to us (in the collection of City Palace, Jaipur) as prepared by Manohar Mahatma at Āmber on the 10th day of bright half of *Asoj* in V.S. 1697 (AD 1640). The related part reads.

लिषि रागरुप रागह जिमाल

लिषि भावसत्त अमरुरसाल।।

लिषि अष्ट नाइकनि भेदरंग,

नाइक्क चारि सुभसुभै संग।।

लिषि हंस परेवा अरू चकोर,

लिषि सुवा सारहिं बिंचह मोर।।

कटि बेलि बेलि बिच बिचै आंन,

लिषि कोक-कामिनी कितेउ थान।।[3]

These lines inform us the subjects of paintings painted on the walls of Āmber palace – *Rāgamālā*, paintings based on *Amrūśatak,* eight types of *nāyikā* and four types of *nāyaka,* among birds were swan, *cakor*, patridge, parrot, crane and peacock and in the middle of floral compositions were illustrations based on *kāmaśāstra.* These were all popular subjects in the 17th century painting.

Besides Mān Singh's palace at Āmber, there are paintings at Mughal gate at Bairath, in Maqdum Shāh's tomb, Āmber, in a *chatarī* at Bhaopura, near Jaipur and in the ruined palaces at Mozamabad (Jaipur).

I also feel that in order to understand the style of painting, one must look at the late 16th century Āmber, when the style was in formative stage. Its situation was slightly different than its counterparts in Rajasthan. Chiefs of Āmber were in close contact with Mughal emperors of Delhi which enabled them to see different parts of the country where they came in close contact with artists. Rājā Mān Singh invited five enameller families from Lahore to settle at Āmber and practise their craft, their descendants still live in Jaipur.[4]

He also encouraged paper industry at Sialkot, where paper makers prepared a special brand *Man Singh Sāhī Kāgaj,* named after their patron.[5]

Mān Singh had been travelling all over, busy in fighting but he did patronize art of miniature painting at Agra. Though we do not have any dated or signed example of the commissioned work of late 16th or early 17th century, but it may be assumed that the so called popular Mughal style was patronized by the Rajput princes of Jaipur and Bikaner, wealthy merchants and visiting dignitaries like Rev. Laud. Authors of Khajānchī collection catalogue were first to suggest that, 'there grew up outside the Imperial atelier a class of painting in which the patrons were Mughal noblemen of varying ranks who employed artists of their own or commissioned artists who were not in the pay of the Emperor.' They further added,

> But in fact not only noblemen but even the merchant classes were interested in this category, as is evidenced by the circumstance that the Jain Sangha of Agra commissioned the artist Sālivāhana in the year 1610 AD at Agra to paint the *Vijñapatipatra* (letter of invitation) which this Jaina Sangha sent to its religious preceptor Vijayasena Sūri then resident at Devakapaton in Saurashtra.[6]

We still do not have any dated support but a *Rāgamālā* series in the collection of Mahārājā of Jaipur painted in popular Mughal style strengthens our theory. These paintings came in the *Sūratkhānā* and artists must have had seen and inspired by them, thus this group played an important role in formation of the style.[7]

At this point, may be mentioned a number of Jain texts painted for the *mahājans* of Āmber, *Yaśodhar Carita* seems a popular text and many copies of this text were prepared for the Jain patrons. Raja Mān Singh had Jain *śresṭhis* in his service who accompanied him to Bengal and other parts of the country.[8] One such example – a copy of *Yaśodhar Carita* was copied at Akbarpur (Bengal) in 1604 for a Jain family of Āmber serving under Rājā Mān Singh.[9]

Due to liberal attitude of Āmber rulers towards other religions, Jainism flourished there and many illustrated texts were prepared. The earliest is *Yaśodhar Carita* dated *jeṭha sudī* 3 V.S. 1647 (AD 1591). Another work is also a copy of *Yaśodhar Carita,* dated *Bhādawa Sudī* 10, V.S. 1648 (AD 1592). It is in the collection of Pandit Lunakarna Digambar Jain temple, Jaipur. It seems that *Yaśodhar Carita* was a popular text in those days, especially for gifting to Ācāryas and religious personages. Late R.V. Somani also referred to one illustrated copy of this texts commissioned by Shah Shantu for presenting to Ācarya, Kshem Chandra. A folio from this work was published by S.Cary Welch.[10]

A style practised around Āmber was related with the style of *Caurapancāśikā* in the collection of Sansakar Kendra, Ahmedabad.[11] A discussion about its date and provenance continued for a long time among art historians and finally they agreed on *c.* 1550. It is further supported by a dated drawing in the collection of R.C. Sharma *Vyakul*, Jaipur[12] though I always felt that love lyrics of *Caurapancāśkā* ascribed to Vilhaṇa the Kashmiri poet, had some kind of association with Gwalior, but I could not assert at this point as it did not have any proof. Fortunately now I have two points in my favour on the basis of R.C. Sharma's *Vyakul*. The text of the manuscript was written at Gopācal durga which is Gwalior and a Hindi translation of *Caurapancaśikā* was also prepared there. This unpublished manuscripts is in the personal collection of Shri G.N. Bahura at Jaipur. Coming back to Āmber, two examples in the above mentioned style may be cited here-

(a) A line drawing with a date corresponding AD 1598 at Nagar in Tonk district of Rajasthan shows Gaṇeśa with two female attendants as suggested by late R.V. Somani. I am inclined to think that they are Riddhi and Siddhi. These female figures are close to the mid 16th century *Caurapancāśikā* type.

(b) Other landmark of this style is *Ādipurāṇa,* a Jain text in the collection of Terapanthi Jain temple, Jaipur. It was painted at Mozambad in V.S. 1663 (AD 1606). First published by Kastur Chand Kasliwal without illustrations[13], its paintings were studied by Sarayu Doshi later on. It is profusely illustrated and prove art activities in and around Āmber.

Summarising painters and their works in the region in the second half of the 16th and two decades of the 17th centuries which broadly corresponds to the time of Mān Singh I, it may be stated that artists were working at least in four different styles. (a)Archaic style which is close to the wall painting at Āmber and Bhaonagar. (b) Style which was used for Jain religious texts which developed into Mozambad *Ādipuraṇa* and *Caurapañāśikā* style which was in practice all over northern India; a *Bhāgavata* set, popularly known as Israda *Bhāgavata* had been painted in this style. Isarda, a small town near Jaipur was *thikāna* of former Jaipur state. Folios have come out from there hence named so. A number of illustrations from this *Bhāgavata* set are in Jaipur collection also. (c) The style used by the painters of sophisticated *Rāgamālā* paintings. They have strong Mughal flavour and I am inclined to think that painters were living at Agra and their patrons were Rajput princess,[14] and visiting dignitaries, i.e. Rev. Laud.[15]

Rājā Mān Singh passed away in 1614 and for seven years until the arrival of his great grandson Jai Singh, popularly known as Mirzā Rājā, in 1621, Āmber did not have good time. But after seven years of unrest Mirzā Rājā's arrival brought all peace and prosperity in the state. Mirzā Rājā was well versed in Turkish, Persian and Sanskrit and at the same time he was a great stateman and arch patron of art and letters. Diwān-i-ām, Sukh Mandir, Jas Mandir and gardens at Āmber executed during his time are of very high quality and even today they speak of his refined taste. But the quality of manuscript painting is archaic, two manuscripts illustrated for one of his *rānīes* Candrāwatijī, are folkish in nature. These are *Veli Kṛṣṇa Rukmiṇī rī* of Prithvīrāj of Bikaner and *Rasik Priyā* of Keshavdas.[16]

Both these texts remained highly popular among the patrons of medieval Rajasthan and Madhya Pradesh. A manuscript of *Veli Kṛṣṇa Rukmiṇī rī* containing four illustrations was painted at Āmber in 1640 for Vithaldas Bhai. The scribe and painter was Nanji, son of Kedar. At present it is in the Anup Sanskrit Library, Bikaner.[17] Late R.V. Somani once mentioned about a couple of folios of *Yaśodhara Carita* dated AD 1633 painted at Āmber but we did not get a chance to see it.

Bihari, a Brajabhaṣa poet, who lived at the court of Mirzā Rājā Jai Singh, composed *Satsaī* in the first half of the 17th century and soon it became a favourite of painters at Āmber, Mewar and in the 18th century in the Punjab Himalayan states. An illustrated manuscript of Bihari's *Satsaī* is reported to be in the collection of Thakur Mandhata Singh of Bikaner. It is dated V.S. 1703-04 and was painted at Āmber. H. Goetz had studied this series and observed that this set is purely Rajput composition. The shadowing colouring, sky effects are purely Mughal, yet there is no organic fusion between the two.[17a]

Here I would like to mention a half burnt page illustrating story of Rājā Gopī Chand.[18] It is a folio from a book now not available. Face of Rājā Gopī Chand shows strong resemblance with Mirzā Rājā. Following the medieval trend the facial features resemble with the ruler one can safely presume that it was painted during the time of Mirzā Rājā.

We come across a number of portraits of Mirzā Rājā Jai Singh, his son Rām Singh and grandson Krishna Singh, which are close to Mughal portraits, but in treatment of subject painting, Āmber artists or artists of Rajasthan in general do not have Mughal sophistication.

At this point I should mention that Āmber princes were posted in different parts of the country where they had their own establishments, which included artists also. When Kunwar Krishna Singh was at Aurangabad, artist Nūr Khān was working for him. He illustrated a text *Rasapradīpilkā*[19], a commentary on Sāraṅgadeva's *Sangīta Ratnākar,* written for the prince. All four illustrations in this manuscript are in characteristic of Golconda style. It is neither in Jaipur style, nor painted at Amber, but it became part of the Jaipur collection. Artists of *Sūratkhānā* must have seen it hence its or similar other texts indirect impact on the Jaipur style could not be overlooked.

Coming back of Āmber, in the closing years of the 17th century a very interesting work was commissioned by Mahārājā Vishnu Singh which was a treatise on massage related with Āyurveda.[20] Then came Sawai Jai Singh, when Āmber was under Mughals for a very short period, but soon it regained its past glory and emerged as one of the most important states of Hindustan. Emperor Muhammad Shāh depended on him for all political or to some extent personal matters. Eighteenth century brought peace and prosperity in the state, rulers spent most of their time in their homeland and under their tasteful and generous patronage Jaipur style flourished.

Seventeenth century was a period of experimentation. Artists were working in several groups, they had to change their medium from wall to paper which had its own limitation in space and technique, there was a change in subject also. On the other hand patrons, ruler of Āmber were posted in distant lands from where they brought new inspiration. Technique was imported from Mughal court, subject like *Kṛṣṇalīlā* in background of Mathura and Vrindavan, love lyrics *Heer-Rānjhā; Sohanī Mahīvāla* from Punjab and so on. Sanskrit and

Hindi texts were main source of inspiration, which were their own, Jaipur style combines all these and emerges in its full form in the 18th century.

The first decade of the 18th is represented by a series of *Rāgamālā*, dated AD 1709,[21] painted at Āmber. It shows Shahjahan period arches and columns at Āmber and Jaigarh, lower part of walls especially in the front portion of rooms have flowering plants painted in a highly delicate manner and doors have either brocade curtains of *chik* (curtain of straw). Two more series based on *Bārahamāsā* and *Rasikapriyā* had been also painted in the same style, though they do not bear date. In these manuscripts Āmber - Jaipur style characterized by enamel like colours, suave faces, decorative landscape and prominent architectural setting. Living at Agra Jai Singh commissioned a book on poetics, *Saras Rasa Grantha,* with 39 miniatures in which palette is dominated by yellows and vermilions.[22]

An important dated (1713) work of Jai Singh's period is a copy of *Yaśodhar Carita,* printed for a Jain Patani family at Sāngāner; at present preserved in the Jain temple at Sawai Madhopur.[23] It is a commendable work containing thirty-six paintings; but retouched at places. The paintings illustrate king's court; army marching, the king in *zenānā,* Jain monks and nuns, royal procession, ruler paying respect to mother goddess and elephant fight. The figure of king resembles to Sawai Jai Singh. Architecture, flora and fauna and treatment of animals are close to *Kānkrolī Rāgamālā* of 1709. The charm of these paintings lie in brilliant colour scheme and beautiful figures. Another Jain text worth mentioning is an illustrated *Kalpasūtra,* painted at Malpura in 1730 at present in L.D. Institute, Ahmedabad.

Sawai Jai Singh's son Iswari Singh (1743-50) seemed to have a fancy for animal fight and he commissioned many paintings based on this subject, they are on large canvas but some are in miniature also. *Lal Citerā* specialized in this branch and many of his works, preserved in the city palace collection, speak about his skill.

Ishwari Singh's younger brother Madho Singh I (1750-67) was fond of portraiture. Earlier formal portraits were made – Rājā standing with a sword with a hawk on his hand or with a flower but in the second half of the 18th century taste changed. Madho Singh got his likenesses painted in many different ways and moods engaged in day-to-day activities, playing chess, walking and worshipping in his room, perhaps this was the taste of the time all over Muhammad Shāh at Mughal court, Mahārāṇa Sangraṁ Singh in Mewar, Sansār Chand in Kangra, Balwant Deva at Jasrotā all got such portraits made.

Madho Singh spent his childhood at Udaipur, where Mahārāṇā took keen interest in portraiture, this also influenced him. He was interested not only in his likeness painted but also of his courtiers, his kinsmen and contemporary rulers. We are fortunate to have *tojī bahīs* (daily record) of his time, preserved in the Rajasthan State Archives, Bikaner, which gives a detailed account of the paintings prepared, artists and albums of paintings. Here is an account of *Saravan Sudi* V.S. 1814 (1757) when thirty-one portraits of the Mahārājā were prepared by his court painters, whose names also appear. In 1763, forty-three paintings were presented to the Mahārāja by the court painters – Sahib Ram 10, Khusal 8, Ramji 8, Heera 5, Nawala 5, Uda 3 and Pohkar 4. In the same year portraits of Mahārāṇa Amar Singh, Sangrām

Singh, Jagat Singh and his son Pratāp Singh were also painted. The records also show that paintings narrating details of battles, animal fights and royal procession were also executed.

The records inform that *citerā* (painter) Sāhib Rām was allowed to have three assistants and to send Rs. 30 and 8 annas per month. He also received an increment of Rs. 5 and 2 annas in addition to his salary Rs. 18 per month in 1762.

Besides portraits, a charming *Rāgamālā* series was painted during his period. Among other paintings are illustrations of *Mahābhārata, Kāmaśāstra* and *Bārahamāsā*.

During the time of Mahārājā Prithvī Singh (1767-1778), artists at *Sūratkhānā* were working and produced a number of portraits. His ultimately death took place in 1778 and his younger brother Pratāp Singh (1778-1803) became the next ruler.

S. Pratāp Singh, a devotee of Govind Devajī was a poet of repute and composed poems in Brajabhāṣā. His pen name was 'Brajnidhi'. It was natural that Kṛṣṇa became the centre of artistic activities in Jaipur. *Bhāgavata*[24] (1792) (Pl. 5.1), *Durgāpāṭha* (1779) and *Rāgamālā*[25] (Pl. 5.2) series were executed during his time. Tall, slender figures, prominent architectural background with one or two trees indicating landscape are characteristics of this period.

There are two series of *Rāgamālā* painted during the reign of Pratāp Singh. A series in the collection of Central Museum, Jaipur has 43 miniatures, 5 *rāgās*, 3 *rāginīs* and 8 *rāgaputras*. Their *swarūpa* or iconography closely follow the description given in *Rādhā Govind Sangīta Sāra*, a text composed at Jaipur during the reign of Pratāp Singh. Painters Mangal and Jiwan painted this series.[26]

Painters Sāhibrām, Uda, Ghasi, Gopāl, and Rāmjīdās[26] were still active and contributing to *Sūratkhānā*. There works show maturity. An area of Jaipur painting of Pratāp Singh time which is not discussed by art historian is portraits of courtiers professionals, artists, pet birds and animals which included horses and elephants in the royal stable also. Many of these have artists names. It was golden period of Jaipur style.

Among the texts illustrated in the last quarter of the 15th century, following texts deserves special attention:-

Bhāgavat dásam skandha (tenth chapter) deals with life of Kṛṣṇa. It has 366 folios, out of which 127 bear painters names, they are as follows, Chimana, Raju, Rām Sewak, Jīwan, Ghasī, Gopāl, Ghasī son of Sītārām, Sāligrām, Ghasī I, Jīwan, son of Rājārām, Ghāsi, son of Dayārām, Udai, Hukma and Hīrā. This work was completed in 1790, the colophon reads, *Śrī Bhāgavata Purāṇe Daśam Skanhe....Samvat* 1849 *Māgha māse śukla pakṣe* 5 *Budha vāsare likhitam mide pustakam Tek* Chand Brahmana - *Bhāgavata* tenth chapter was completed on Wednesday, 5th day of bright half of *Māgha* (month) in 1749 (AD 1792).

Durgāpātha was completed in 1799, has 102 folios, painted by Gopal, Uda, Hukma, Lakṣmana, Saligram, Ghasi, Jiwan, Radha Kishan and Ram Kishan,

An unusual size tinted drawing measuring 8 × 2½ in the collection of city palace museum illustrates battle fought between Kām Bakhsh and Bahādur Shāh for the throne of Delhi. Somehow, this incident took fancy of Pratāp Singh and ordered poet Chunnilal Bhatta to compose a text on this important event in history, after the text was composed, artists of *Sūratkhānā,* Hira, Hukma, Gopal, Saligram, Jiwan, Ghasi, Uda and Ram Sewak were asked to prepare a picture.

Besides the royal atelier, *Bhaktamāra Stotra* (1764) and *Yaśodhara Carita* all in the collection of Baḍā Mandir, Jaipur were illustrated for Jain patrons. Here we may refer to a voluminous work – *Mahābhārata* dated 1792 in the collection of Rajasthan Oriental Research Institute, Jodhpur, which was painted for an art lover.

Painted in Jaipur style a *vijñapti patra* was sent to Jinchandra on *Bhadawa Sudī* 11. VS 1853 (September 1796). There are many scenes of Jaipur city in this *patra.*

First quarter of the 19th century is represented by traditional miniature painting, illustrated, copies of *Gītā Govinda* of Jaideva, *Viṣṇu Sahaśranāma* (1807) and *Jagdeva Panwar rī bāta* (1812) were prepared by the artists of *Sūratkhānā.* Portraiture continued to be a popular subject, likenesses of rulers and his countries were executed.

Jaipur signed treaty with Britishers in 1803, which was again ratified in 1818 and soon after Jaipur felt British impact. British watercolour and European oil colour techniques were introduced. A portrait of Capt. Faiz Mohammad is published by Rita Pratap. Mid 19th century also witnessed introduction of photography and the traditional painters working in *Sūratkhānā* had to share it with photographers. Mahārājā Rām Singh II himself was a good photographer. It was a new technique hence was more in demand. The Mahārājā organized an exhibition of photography in 1883 where in he honoured eminent photographer Rājā Dindayal alongwith painters Fakira, Ramjilal, Ganga, Bishan, Murali, Chaju, Madhu, Mohanlal, Nandrama and Ganesh. Chaju painted illustrations for the census of Jaipur state (1901).

Time had been changing very fast, though *Sūratkhānā* was there, artists were doing only routine job for example painting Laksmi for *Deepāvalī pūjan*, Sravaṇ Kumār for *Sarāvaṇī Pūrṇimā* and Nīlkantha for *Duśehra.* On the other hand international style was introduced in the country through oil paintings of Raja Ravi Verma and artists trained in Sir J.J. School of Art. Wash technique came through Ram Gopal Vijay Vargiya who worked in this technique. Kripāl Singh who was trained at Shantiniketan experimented with traditional watercolour tempera and Jaipur drawing. He came out with a style of his own.

Though names of painters are mentioned at places in this article but I feel that it will remain incomplete without a word about them. Mohandas' name appears on a painting entitled *Princess and a Saint*, an early 17th century work acc. no. AG 1025, coll. Man Singh II Museum. Sahib Ram, the illustrious portrait painter painted formal portraits of Jaipur rulers from Jai Singh (1699-1743) to Jagat Singh (1803-1817). His portraits are available in many collections and was published by A.K. Coomaraswamy. Artists Fazil Mohammad and Sadiq Mohammad were invited by Jai Singh to his newly built capital. Their names appear in *Tojī* records – daily account book, where their monthly salary is mentioned Rs. 15 per month Pohkar, a popular name in Rajasthan, worked in the 18th century. He mastered in animal painting and one of his masterpieces show tiger fight, his name also appears in *Sūratkhānā* records, Lal *Citerā* was also an animal painter. Many of his works, mostly animal fights are in the collection of Mān Singh II Museum. Rāmjī Dās was a portrait painter, while Sahib Rām painted large sized portraits of the royal personages, Rāmjī Dās did mostly small sized likeness of king, courtiers, professionals engaged in the royal household, dancers and musicians. Besides these eminent ones there were a large number of painter engaged in *Sūratkhānā*.

Jaipur artists worked outside their home town also, they were commissioned by Jain traders and industralists. One Gaṇeśa *musavrir*, a resident of *Tahavildaron kā Rāstā,* Jaipur executed large panels in a Jain temple at Calcutta in 1868-69 for Shrimali Phophaliya Shikhar Chand. He also painted at Kesariyājī and Rāṇakpur (Rajasthan) and Pāvāpurī and Champāpuri (in Bihar). A *Vijñapti patra,* in the collection of Pratāp Singh Durgar, Calcutta, was also painted by him at Azeemganj, Agra. This *patra* was sent to Ratna Vijayji at Gwalior, it shows scenes of Jaipur. One group of Jaipur painters settled at Bikaner did mostly wall painting.[27] They still paint with same proficiency. Recently, I saw them working at Junagarh, the old fort at Bikaner, where restoration work was being done.

Today, we do not have *Sūratkhānā* but it survives in thousands of traditional painters, who are painting for open market. Traditional subjects illustrated in traditional manner are in demand both in national and international market.

Notes and References

1. Karl. J. Khandalavala, *Wall Paintings from Amber,* Lalit Kala Akademi, New Delhi, 1974. Rita Pratap, *The Panorama of Jaipur Paintings,* D.K. Printworld, New Delhi.
2. Gopal Narayan Bahura, *Mān Charitāvalī,* M.S. Man Singh II Museum, Jaipur 1990, p. 24/152.
3. *Ibid,* p. 148.
4. Ancestral house of Jaida family is located in Jadion ka Rastā, a branch of Chaurā Rastā, Jaipur. Late Sardar Kudrat Singh of this family was honoured with Padmashri by the Govt. of India.
5. G.N. Bahura, *Literary Heritage of the Rulers of Amber and Jaipur,* M.S. Man Singh II Museum, Jaipur 1976, p. 34.
6. Karl J. Khandalvala, M. Chandra and P. Chandra, *Miniature Painting: Catalogue of Sri Moti Chand Khajanchi Collection*, Lalit Kala Akademi, New Delhi 1960, Frontispiece and Fig. 22, pp. 14-15.
7. Based on discussion with Late Karl J. Khandalavala.
8. Source: Late R.V. Somani.
9. *Ibid.*
10. S. Cary Weleh, *A Flower from Every Meadow: Indian Painting from American Collections*, New York, 1973.
11. Karl Khandalavala and Moti Chandra, *New Documents of Indian Painting: A Reappraisal.* The Prince of Wales Museum of Western India, Bombay, 1969, Pl. 20.
12. Ram Charan Sharma 'Vyakul', *Paradisic Heritage,* SRC Museum of Indology, Jaipur, 1998, pp. XIV-XV.

13. Kastur Chandjī Kasaliwal, *Vir Vānī,* Vol. V.
14. Pramod Chandra, 'Ustad Salivahana and the Development of Popular Mughal Art', *Lalit Kala,* No. 8, 1960, pp. 25-46.
15. H.J. Stook and Karl J. Khandalavala, *The Laud Ragamala Miniatures,* Oxford, 1953.
16. G.N. Bahura, *Literary Heritage,* Pl. XXII (a & b).
17. Hermann Goetz, *Art and Architecture of Bikaner State,* London, 1935.
18. A.K. Das, 'Homage to Jaipur: Miniatures', *Marg,* Vol. XXX, No. 4, pp. 76-94.
19. *Ibid.*
20. *Ibid.*
21. Shridhar Andhare, 'A dated Amber Ragamala and the problem of provenance of the 18th cent. Jaipuri Painting', *Lalit Kala,* No. 15, 972, pp. 47-51 and related plates.
22. G.N. Bahura, *Literary Heritage,* Pls. IX, XII & XIII.
23. Kamla Garg, *Yashodhar Charit, Sachitra Pandulipiyan,* (Hindi), Bharatiya Jyanpith, New Delhi, 1991.
24. Anon. *Treasures of Dhoondhar Collection,* Series one, City Palace, Jaipur, Pl. V.
25. *Ibid.,* Pl. III.
26. A.K. Das, 'Ramjidas Chatera: An eighteenth century portrait painter from Jaipur, *Cultural Contours of India* (ed. V.S. Srivastava), Abhinav Publications, New Delhi 1981, pp. 317-323.
27. For Jain sources I am indebted to late Dr. Kastur Chand Kasliwal and late R.V. Somani. I have been working on Jaipur painting for many years and discussed my queries with them time to time. One of the aspect which I intended to highlight was peoples support to the art of painting, in which they were extremely helpful.

6

Representation of Rāmakathā in the Nīlakaṇṭheśvara Temple at Kekind

Neelima Vashishtha

Kekind, a derivative of Kiṣkindhā, is presently known as Jasnagar, and forms a part of the District of Nagaur in Rajasthan. It constituted a part of the erstwhile princely State of Jodhpur.

The Śaiva temple at Kekind[1] under discussion, is known as Nīlakaṇṭheśvara or Guṇeśvara temple (Pl. 6.1). The temple faces east and consists of a *garbhagṛha* and *sabhāmaṇḍapa* with three porches on the three sides. The fragmentary inscriptions of the *sabhāmaṇḍapa* reveal the name of the deity as Guṇeśvara and the grants given by Rājaputra Rānā Mahipāla and Chāhamāna Rudra of Kiṣkindhā for the maintenance of the temple.

The temple shows a number of sculptures on its exterior and interior. However, the present paper discusses only the Rāmakāthā scenes in the temples. The domical roof of the *sabhāmaṇḍapa* is octagonal and supported by eight pillars, on the top of these pillars are brackets which represent some scenes from the *Rāmāyaṇa*. These are square panels and include the following episodes:

(i) Rāvaṇa seated on a chariot and abducting Sītā; (ii) Lakṣmaṇa hurt by the *śakti* of Rāvaṇa during the fight (Pl. 6.2); (iii) Rāma and Lakṣmaṇa seated while Hanumāna is shown paying obeisance with folded hands (Pl. 6.3); (iv) Hanumāna lifting the mountain with his raised hands while the monkeys are shown in various postures as standing in rows or moving towards one direction suggesting the mobilization of army of monkeys; (v) Building of the bridge by monkeys (*setubandha*), monkeys are shown carrying stones on their heads; (vi) Rāma along with bird Jaṭāyu; (vii) and (viii) panel representing the combat scene between the demons, monkeys and monkey chiefs (Pl. 6.4). In some panels the demon is depicted as seated on the chariot and the monkeys are shown in diminutive form attacking the demon. Besides, the story of Rāma has been depicted on the lintels supporting the domical roof, and the lintels of the *samatala* ceiling of the *Raṅgamaṇḍapa*. The domical *maṇḍapa* is connected on three sides with porches. It has four half pillars supporting a *samatala* square ceiling. The lintels of this part of the *maṇḍapa* have long horizontal panels with motifs of pillars and *caitya* arches and between every two pillars the episodes from the *Rāmāyaṇa* or from the life of Kṛṣṇa are carved.

These lintel panels start from left side with the figures of Rāma, Lakṣmaṇa and Sītā in separate niches going towards forest. Again they are shown seated in *pañcavaṭī*.

Then the golden deer is carved and Sītā is shown indicating towards it. In another niche Rāma and Lakṣmaṇa are standing. The gesture indicates that Rāma is going towards the forest asking Lakṣmaṇa to stay. Next niche shows Rāma in *ālīdha mudrā* wielding the bow and arrow. Further the niche shows Mārīca whose head is cut off with the arrow of Rāma. The demon is emanating out of the deer's head. The next panel pertains to Sītā-*haraṇa* episode. It starts with the meeting of bird Jaṭāyu with Rāma and Lakṣmaṇa followed by Rāvaṇa taking away Sītā in his chariot. Rāma's meeting with Sugrīva and killing of Vāli. These seen are represented in nine small niches. The next panel which is on the upper side of the entrance porch depicts the fight between the demon and monkeys. Similarly, the panels on the right side of the *maṇḍapa* mainly depict the life and exploits of Kṛṣṇa. The inner side of the dome of the *Sabhāmaṇḍapa* has circular panel on the lintel. It has many episodes, every episode is separated from the other by a pillar and *caitya* window motif. This circular panel represents scenes from the life of *Kṛṣṇa*. Among these some are identified as Gajāsura-*vadha,* Śakaṭāsura-*vadha,* Pūtanā-*vadha,* killing of *Vṛṣabha*, horse and donkey demons by Kṛṣṇa, Kṛṣṇa playing flute, depiction of the life of Vraja and Mathurā, killing the mad elephant and wrestling competition in the court of Kaṁsa.

Generally, these panels are carved in relief and in diminutive form. The episodes depict some of the important and selective episodes of the narrative rather than showing the whole narrative in serial order. The selection of the episodes depends upon the dramatic appeal, emotions of pathos and surprise and vigorous action. Thus the whole story of the *Rāmāyaṇa* is represented in a nutshell by representing the significant and dramatic events as is discernible in the one verse *Rāmāyaṇa* which reveals the whole story of Rāma by recounting the chief events:

Ādau rāmatapovanādigamanaṁ hatvā mrigaṁ kāñchanaṁ
Vaidehiharaṇaṁ jaṭāyumaraṇaṁ sugrīvasambhāṣaṇam
Vālīnirdalanaṁ saṁudrataraṇaṁ Lankāpurīdāhaṇaṁ
Paśchādrāvaṇakumbhakarṇanaṁ chaitaddhirāmāyaṇam

The sculptures of this temple, pertaining to *Rāmāyaṇa* only represent the golden deer in the forest and Rāma shooting it with an arrow, abduction of Sītā by Rāvaṇa, encounter with Jaṭāyu and death of Jaṭāyu, friendship with the monkey chief Sugrīva, slaying of Vālī, crossing the sea by Hanumān, building of the bridge on the sea by monkeys, burning of Laṅkā and combat between Rāma and demons (Pl. 6.5) - Rāvaṇa and Kumbhakarṇa (Pl. 6.6). Further the sculptural representations in the temple indicate that the theme of the *Rāmāyaṇa* is arranged to suit their artistic features and need of the architecture.

Hence the format of representation and size of the figures are according to the size of lintel and bracket panels. Moreover, the artist has used many symbolic techniques of presentation to overcome this limitation of the architecture. Secondly, the place and size of these representations suggest that the themes from the life of Kṛṣṇa and Rāma were very popular hence they formed the part of the temple decorations of all Brahmanic temples comprising Śaiva, Vaiṣṇava and Śākta, because the story had penetrated into the lives of people and become a living and dynamic tradition.

The popularity of *Rāmakathā* in Rajasthan is also evident from the epigraphical records belonging to fifth and ninth centuries AD.[2] The narrative representations of the epic story are carved in the Vaiṣṇava and Śaiva temples of Rajasthan.[3] It also indicates that the epical narrative had already merged into folk literature and found place among the relief panels of the *Vedibandha,* pillar brackets and lintels of the roof but not in the principal niches as the cult images.

The technique of representation have been adopted according to the format of presentation. For instance, the pillar brackets of the temple at Kekind are square panels which has affected the treatment of the human figures and the composition in many ways. The full human figure could not have stiffly fitted into the size. Instead of reducing the size of all the figures of the composition the sculptor has carved the main figures as bigger in size but always in seated posture. The size of other figures have been reduced and they are inserted in the residual space. Even the episodes showing movement of shooting of arrows, Hanumāna flying with mountain, and building the bridge (*setubandha*) are adjusted to the need of architecture. Many symbolic and suggestive expressions have also been adopted by the artist of these panels to overcome the lack of space. For instance, the building of the bridge by monkeys is represented with several small monkeys holding stones and Rāma is shown in the posture of shooting an arrow. This is an example of simultaneity of action. Both these actions though occurred successively are represented simultaneously as if occurring at the same time.[4]

Similarly, in the animate combat scenes between the prowess of the monkeys against the demons the movement and the attack is suggested by small and flexible figures of monkeys. The main figure seems to be of Meghanāda or Kumbhakarṇa because he is shown in the posture of attack and striking monkeys back. The treatment of the figure of demon, in comparison to monkeys is peculiar. The towering figures of the demons hurling weapons make the reliefs piece of dramatic movement.

Moreover, these representations depict the main figures always seated in order to adjust to the limited size of the stone. The treatment in the carving is totally two-dimensional specially in the carving of the chariot representing one wheel, a running horse in harness in profile with the seated figure of Rāvaṇa facing front and a female figure standing beside the chariot. Even the delineation of the human figures in sculptures is two dimensional and reminds of miniature paintings. Among the representations, the combat scenes are most popular to indicate the idea of continuous struggle between the forces of good and evil.

The analysis of the sculptures of this temple reveals that the epic of Rāma was so popular in Rajasthan that it was assimilated in the folk tradition and found expression in the temples irrespective of their cult affiliations.

Notes and References

1. D.R. Bhandarkar, *Progress Report, Archaeological Survey, Western Circle, 1910-11,* pp. 35-36.
2. D.C. Sircar, *Select Inscriptions,* Vol. I, Calcutta, 1965, p. 400; J.F. Fleet, *Corpus Inscriptionum Indicarum,* Vol. III, Varanasi, pp. 72-78; R.C. Majumdar, Jodhpur Inscription of Pratihara Ruler Bauka, V.S. 894, *Epigraphia Indica*, Vol. XVIII, Calcutta, 1925-26, pp. 87-88.
3. Margabandhu, Rāmāyaṇa Reliefs in Stones in Rajasthan Temples, *Asian Variations of Rāmāyaṇa* (ed. R.S. Iyengar), Madras, 1983, pp. 168-182.
4. P. Jayakar, *Earthen Drum,* Delhi, 1983, p. 150.

7

Objects of Beauty, Not Art Objects

Harsha V. Dehejia

It is not without reason that the Indian linguistic tradition of Sanskrit does not have a specific word for art, art objects, art activity or even artists. Neither does it set up a dichotomy within human creativity of the classical and the folk or art from craft or artists from artisans, all of these taxonomies being modern art historical constructs. Rather, the tradition subsumes under the rubric of *sundara* or beautiful, everything that human creativity encompasses, whether it is language or music, dance or sculpture, painting or architecture, ritual and even everyday objects. The creation of what was sensually beautiful, and equally incorporating that into one's everyday life and experiencing the sense of beauty from that creation, was considered an integral part of radiant life and noble living. Even the word *Sanskrit,* understood generally as culture or refinement, carries with it the concept of something that is well created or nobly crafted and is therefore not far from beauty as it is commonly understood today. To be cultured was to uphold beauty in many different ways. While relating human creativity to *sundara* or what is objectively and sensually beautiful is fundamental to the Indian world view. The subjective, contemplative and inward experience of that beautiful creation or *saundarya* is equally important as a philosophic principle. In emphasizing both *sundara* and *saundarya,* we in the Indian tradition recognize that there is an inner reality of beautiful objects, a reality that is dismissed or overlooked by modern sociologists and art historians. These modern custodians of the arts seem to be carried away by forces such as patronage and market value of these art objects. While not denying the importance of these socio-economic forces that play on human creativity, there is however, a still centre, a *bindu,* of beauty and an inner reality at the core of the object which is homologous to *brahman* or what is ultimately real, emphasizing that human creativity is similar to cosmic creativity, and that mankind approaches the divine because of his creativity.

The adjective *sundara* or beautiful is intimately related to the abstract noun *saundarya* or beauty just as *sabda* or a word is related to its *artha* or its meaning or as Śiva is tied to Śakti. And still within the domain of linguistics, it is worth remembering that traditionally the adjective *sundara* was never used as a metaphor; thus in Sanskrit one never said *iti sundara-*

vicaraha, this thought is beautiful, once again emphasizing that the beautiful is what is sensually appealing and attractive. The concept of *sundara* or what is beautiful is not only purely sensuous but even importantly secular, and it occurs predominantly in *kāvya* or poetry rather than in *śāstras* or doctrinal literature. While what is beautiful is available to the *sāmājika* or the proletariat one and all, the subjective experience of beauty stemming from the beautiful object requires contemplative analysis and therefore is a prerogative of the *rasika* or the cultivated aesthete. It is worth pointing out that in Sanskrit there is no verb for the predication of beauty suggesting that the creation of beauty is an unknown or perhaps an unknowable process, a creative act akin to cosmic creation that is to be kept sacrosanct and not open to meddlesome probing, and even if probed will yield only psychological insights. It is important to give this preamble from the stand point of language to understand the Indian concept of what is beautiful, for language is the ultimate foundation and the first expression of not only all our doctrines and ideas, but even more importantly our enunciation of the beautiful and the decorative and it is therefore that *nādabrahman* or primal sound is quintessentially the repository of beauty. *Vāk* or exalted speech is not just uttered but sung with melody and rhythm and this gives vocal music a primacy and makes it the foundation of the edifice of all our creations, and all that we consider beautiful rests on the perfect creation and enunciation of sound. That uttered sound or *śabda* is an active performance not a passive creation, it requires participation and not mere idle involvement.

Participation thus becomes the first order of what is beautiful in the Indian tradition and one must go beyond the modern art historian's inability to interrelate beauty and usefulness. The primal objects of beauty for us in India, are objects that we can see and touch, objects of daily living such as kitchen utensils and toys, accessories for adornment such as toilet boxes and mirrors, terracotta and metal pots and textile wraps and coverings and many others. These objects of daily living are neither art objects in the conventional sense nor industrial objects in the modern sense and obey no rules or formulae, and do not answer to any *śāstra* or *mantra,* but arise from the sheer pleasure of the hands of the creator, be he a potter or weaver, a blacksmith or a woodworker. In creating objects of daily living where utility and the beautiful coexist, there is the oneness of the creator, the created and participant in that joyful creative process. These beautifully made daily objects enhance life and are evocative of the magnificence and meaning of gracious living, where the immediate and the ultimate are connected by the living reality of beautiful objects, where the beautiful is received by direct participation and not by detached observation, and joy and delight are not reserved for a later contemplative moment but are in the here and now. Through these objects the common becomes the cherished and joy giving and the beautiful is not only what the eyes can see but what the hands can feel. Colour and texture, shape and form all participate in that sensual experience. The making of these daily objects was considered a noble act and the creator of these objects traced their origins to Viśvakarman or the divine architect. In traditional society these makers of objects were also considered social leaders and given a pride of place.

If utility is the first order of beauty, ritual is the second. Through ritual a correspondence is established between the microcosm and the macrocosm, between the world of humans and that of gods, between chaos and order, between temporality and eternality and between death and immortality. Ritual action is an ancient way of knowing and since water is the basis and substratum of life and creation, many ritual objects were connected with water, objects such as a *kalaśa* or the ritual pot, the ritual spoon, a container for ritual water (Pl. 7.1) and a dispenser for sacred water. These ritual objects were beautifully and decoratively made with one or more metals, with spouts that resembled the mouth of a cow and motifs of snakes and turtles. Fire and light are equally important in rituals and a variety of beautifully made oil lamps are an important part of every ritual. What is beautiful in ritual defines itself not through a refined aesthetic sensibility but through its ability to create that living correspondence between the basic elements of the macro-cosmos on the one hand and the same elements of the world of mankind on the other. These rituals are an attempt of primal man to control a mysterious environment and render it tangible through the visible and the palpable. Ritual also includes votive objects such as clay horses (Pl. 7.2) that form so much a part of tribal and folk worship, and the making of these horses is an important function of the village potter. These votive horses are offered to the deity and left at the shrine, where they stand and perish with time and return to the soil from which they were made and when the potter makes another horse he takes this soil and a horse is created again.

After utility and ritual come adornment where once again beauty is realized through participation. Adornment is a special activity which operates at more than one level. Adornment starts with one's own body then moves on to the home and then ends with adorning the deity in the home shrine. A woman adorns herself with the traditional sixteen adornments and all her oils and unguents, perfumes and pastes are held in beautifully made containers (Pl. 7.3). Her clothes are a special part of that adornment and not only the texture but the colour and the decorative motifs of what she wraps and drapes constitute an integral part of beauty. An important part of adornment is the self-assurance that comes through the mirror and mirrors therefore become an important part of the paraphernalia of adornment. For the romantic heroine adornment is an offering to the beloved for ultimately it for his eyes that she adorns herself and when she sees that glint of pleasure in his eyes she feels truly fulfilled. If personal adornment is the expression of a woman's self-assured beauty, adorning the home converts one's dwelling into a cherished space. Every part of the home from the threshold to the kitchen, outer and inner walls are decorated with designs and motifs that are not only beautiful but which are as it were visual prayers as they invite divine presence, express a certain world view and sanctify the home. Of special importance are doors and windows as they are at the border of the limited space within and the vast space outside and no Indian door is complete without motifs sacred or secular, marks of vermillion and festoons of flowers and decorative banners or *toraṇas.* Adorning the deity in the home shrine is a special part of daily worship and binds the devotee and the deity in a personal relationship and makes the icon come alive and creates a living presence of one's chosen god in one's home. A number of objects for adorning the deity are part of every household.

And finally after deriving the joy of daily living from objects that surrounded them and the strength that was derived from a beautiful ritual, came the pleasure of a good story.

Itinerant story-tellers are very much a part of the Indian tradition and function even today. Most commonly they used a scroll which provided the visual component to the story, whether these were stories from ancient myths or legends of folk heros or chieftains. The scroll was lovingly and carefully made by members of the family of the story-tellers and each part of India had its unique tradition of scroll making. There were the *jādū paṭuās* of Bengal, the *kathā vācakas* of Maharashtra, the *kalamkārīs* of Andhra and the *phaḍa* paintings of Rajasthan (Pl. 7.4). The beautiful objects in this instance, namely the scrolls, were once again intertwined with the story itself in what was a multi-sensory theatre with singing and dancing and as the story unfolds, the listener and the narrator were spell bound in this living theatre. When these scrolls were old and frayed they were lovingly deposited in the river and a new one made and welcomed by the story-teller as one would a newborn child.

These objects of beauty which enrich daily life and living are part of the many living traditions of India. Despite the inroads of urbanization and the supremacy of machines many of these still continue to be made and used. In fact with the advent of post-modernism and the nostalgia that has come in its wake, the value and appreciation of these traditional objects is enjoying a come back. These simple objects of beauty seem to provide a respite from the fatigue of modernity. It must be admitted, however that the post-modernist approach tends to needlessly romanticise these objects and take them out of context and make them into art objects which they are really not. It must not be forgotten that quintessentially these were objects of daily living that the maker of the objects was very much a part of the society in which these objects and their users lived and it is important they not be considered as art objects but regarded as objects of beauty. For the concept of art brings with it its own baggage, its biased and historical discourse, its hierarchies of art and craft, its view of what is art and what is not, its museums and curators and all of this would needlessly distance these objects from their unique position as objects of beauty in the everyday life of traditional and present day India. To call them art objects would draw attention to the objects, take them out of context and fragment the wholeness of life but to consider them as objects of beauty would underscore the fact that the creation and enjoyment of beauty through these objects was an ancient way of knowing and of realizing, of being and becoming through conferring dignity and nobility to daily living.

There are two valid questions however that should be asked about these objects, questions that would take us into the domain of aesthetics and away from art history, cultural anthropology and sociology. First, why do we consider these objects beautiful and second how does the beauty that inheres in those objects become *saundarya* and lead to *ātmajñāna* or ultimate knowledge. Unless these questions are answered, a proper aesthetic discourse cannot develop and these objects will stay relegated to the folk or the craft. To claim that these objects are beautiful for purely post-modern nostalgic reasons is not enough. To reconstruct the times and the methods which led to their creation is interesting but does not take us to the core of the aestheticians's concern which is epistemology. These objects and our enjoyment and celebration of them needs to be brought into the investigation of what constitutes beauty for us in the Indian tradition. These objects suffer from a double misfortune. In the times in which they were made and used, they were an integral part of beautiful and gracious living and therefore did not have an elevated status of their own. With modernity they were downgraded to the status of folk art and craft and as with other features of the little tradition did not generate an aesthetic discourse. The time has come to move away from both these positions, even though the patronage for such objects has changed, but those who are concerned with *saundarya* or beauty and not just the *sundara* or the beautiful, must bring them into the mainstream of Indian aesthetics. In their time these objects were sold in bazaars or traded within the prevailing barter system but today, especially in urban India, they adorn urban homes and have moved to the living room and on coffee tables. The making of these objects whether it is a pot or a door, a toilet box or adornments for a home, does not follow any canons or doctrines, nor does it arise from prescribed methods or the dictates of a royal patron. It stems from that uninhibited joy of creation, spontaneous craftsmanship, the desire to cater to the needs of the ordinary people amidst whom the creator lives, the freedom to follow the heart rather than the mind and a well-honed skill that has developed over many years by observation and practice passed down orally and visually from father to son and mother to daughter. It is that joy and pleasure of creation that passes from the maker to the user through the object, it is that satisfaction that utility has not constrained creativity and a rejoicing from the realization that form has exceeded function that makes these objects beautiful in the first instance. Secondly beauty resides objectively in the physical and sensual form of the object and when that beauty results in the subjective feeling of joy and self-assurance through the sensuality of the object, it is then that the joy of sensuality is converted into knowledge understood as *ānanda.* It is an ancient way of knowing and results in the knowledge of being integrated in the world of everyday objects around oneself, a joyous self-awareness of one's place in that world, and ultimately a realization of the nobility, beauty and dignity of life itself. There is in the creativity of these objects for the creator and the recreativity of the same object for the user, a sense of *purnatva,* wholeness and fullness, a breakdown of the dualities of the human ratiocinative mind, an integration of the fragmentation of the mind that inevitably results in dealing with modern life and living. A third way in which these objects bring home the concept of beauty is by bridging the sacred and the secular and in so doing connect the microcosm to the macrocosm. The living objects of beauty in incorporating motifs from the world of trees and blossoms, birds and rivers suggest in its typically non-doctrinaire style the inter-connection of the world in which we live, reminding us that the sap that flows through the vegetative world resonates with what animates us. Many examples of this can be cited. A kitchen shredder or grater shaped in the form of a tortoise is not very far from the *kūrma* of Viṣṇu, a cup for making medicines with Gaṇeśa and Kārttikeya as its handles invokes the presence of Śiva, a vessel for pouring sacred water shaped like the human *yoni* reminds one that just as life begins in the *garbha* of the mother one is reborn in the sanctum of the temple, the *kalaśa* for storing water becomes special with the image of Gaṇeśa inscribed on it and countless such objects which move us from the sacred to the secular and the other way around emphasizing that the sacred and the secular are one continuum and not two opposites ends of the human experience. The fourth way by which these objects lead us to an experience of beauty is through the motifs it employs such as the circle which represents the sun, the vine, mango or the leaf which come from the tree of life, the parrot and the fish which suggest fertility, the checkered pattern which is none other than the sacrificial *vedi* and many such motifs which when understood are not mere decorative but lead us to a greater vision and reveal a world view and thus become sources of beauty. And finally in the words of Octavio Paz these daily objects of beauty not only "teach us how to live but also how to die". For these objects have no pretense to be immortal or everlasting, they are time bound and eventually they do perish and decay, and when they do so they return to the elements that they came from, and it from the same elements that another object will be lovingly made, and thus the cycle of creation, death and recreation continues through these objects, and the humble but beautiful object reminds us and teaches us in a simple but elegant way of that cycle of life and death of which we must all be a part.

In fostering a sense of beauty through its unpretentious but self-assured presence, these objects assert that beauty exists even outside what are conventionally called art objects and there is a *rasa* in them even beyond the prescriptive canons of Bharat in the *Nāṭyaśāstra.* These objects of beauty are in the end a celebration of the creativity of human hands and seem to resonate the primal Upaniṣadic thought that creativity arises from joy and into joy it leads us.

8

Decorated Bricks from Sarnath Museum

Niharika

Sarnath is one of the foremost centre of art and culture where Buddha gave his first sermon *(dharmacakrapravartan)*. The centre is well known for its sculptures and other archaeological antiquities. The present paper aims at discussing the details and features of ancient bricks found from Sarnath and at present in the collection of Sarnath Museum. The use of mud and terracotta for plain bricks (unbaked and baked) was prevalent since Indus valley civilization where it was used to build rampart walls, house walls, drains, bathroom floors, wells, great bath of Mohenjo-daro and Harappa and great dockyard of Lothal, etc. Bricks were used for builiding Piprahava *stūpa* (3rd - 2nd cent. BC) and temple at Bhitargaon in Gupta period. Decorated terracotta bricks were used to build temples and *vihāras* at Sarnath, the more important being Mauryan temple near Aśokan pillar (3rd cent. BC), main shrine of Gupta period (4th - 5th cent. AD), model of *Pancāyatana* temple (5th cent. AD) and *Dharmacakra Jina vihāra* of Gahadwala period (12th cent. AD). Many votive *stūpas* were also built with terracotta bricks in different periods. These bricks are rectangular and circular in shape and are sometimes decorated too. The bricks at Sarnath show artistic patterns on them, which are generally noticed on stone architectural fragments of the same periods. These bricks, though not well emphasized, are the parameters of artistry of the artisans, their skill and attitude towards their profession. They throw light on the social and religious conditions and beliefs of the place.

Mostly bricks from Sarnath were collected from the excavations of 1904-05 by F.O. Ortel and B.B. Chakravarti and of 1907-08 by J.H. Marshall. These bricks, circular and rectangular in shape are decorated with lotus, vase and palmette, floral, chequer, bead, cross, bow-arrow, quiver and many more patterns. It may be noted that all circular bricks and few of the rectangular ones are plain (undecorated). The plain bricks are porous, thus ascertaining the use of husk as an admixture. They are not finely made, except a few, which are made with well-kneaded clay, resulting in a smooth and even surface. The bricks with different motifs are described in the following pages.

Bricks with Different Motifs in Sarnath Museum

S. No.		*Mauryan*	*Gupta*	*Medieval*	*Undated*
1.	Lotus		33	3	15
2.	Vase & Palmette		25	1	—
3.	Floral		20	2	8
4.	Palm Leaf		6	—	—
5.	Cross		8	—	1
6.	Chequer		12	—	—
7.	Beaded		3	—	—
8.	Quiver with Arrow & Bow		3	—	2
9.	Lion and *Kīrtimukha*		2	—	3
10.	Human Figure		—	1	4

Lotus Pattern

The most common pattern on bricks and brick capitals is lotus. It is depicted as a full blown flower or a half flower arranged in a semi-circle or square. The lotus, its petals (often in inverted position) and stalk were very popular designs for the bricks. This pattern was carved independently or with some patterns like wavy or plain lines (Pl. 8.1), frieze of dots or dentils, square beads, triangles, rectangles and insignificant ornamentation and ornamented border. The petals of this flower is hollowed to give them extra depth and their outer ends are made pointed, though some of the bricks show inverted ends, which make the flower more realistic, natural and as if freshly plucked from water.

More than 50 bricks with this motif are reported from Sarnath Museum. Mostly they belong to the Gupta period, three of them are of medieval period and a few are of unassigned period. The number of bricks reported in the catalogue of Sarnath Museum (by D.R. Sahni) is more than hundred but all are not available at present.

The Gupta bricks show lotus (25 × 20 cm), lotus petals (8.75 × 8.75 × 6 cm), lotus with alternate squares (2.5 × 21.25 cm), lotus and its stalk with two leaves (13 × 10 × 5 cm and 12.5 × 7.5 × 5 cm), lotus with plain lines (12 × 8.5 × 6.5 cm and 23.5 × 11 cm), with ornamentation (5 × 3.75 cm) and floral pattern (16.25 × 10 cm), lotus petals arranged in squares, with raised ornamented border of triangles as a circle around the lotus (22 × 23 cm), and garland pattern (30.5 × 23.5 × 5 cm). There are thirteen brick capitals showing lotus pattern with wavy lines, frieze of dentils or dots (19 × 19 × 8 cm) and frieze of dots between a row of double lines (14 × 12.5 × 3.5 cm). One brick capital (20 × 19 × 10 cm) shows ornamentation divided into two layers-the upper portion with lotus pattern and the lower with a floral design.

A beautifully carved bricks tile is also known in 'L' shape. The vertical arm of the 'L' is decorated with lotus petals in squares and the horizontal arm is endowed with plain lines (23.5 × 11 cm).

The bricks with lotus pattern are sometimes used above the bricks carved with reel and palmette designs. Such examples can be seen in the temple near Aśoken pillar at Sarnath. Apart from Gupta period, three bricks belonging to medieval period, show lotus design. In one example lotus petals are surrounding a circle while petals and floral designs are seen on the corner. Such examples are noticed in the *Pancāyatana* temple (Fig. 1). Another brick of the same period shows a lotus on its one edge (21.5 × 19 × 4.5 cm). The third example is carved with a lotus design (2.5 × 5.6 cm). It also has a inscription in Gupta script read as '*sarana*'.

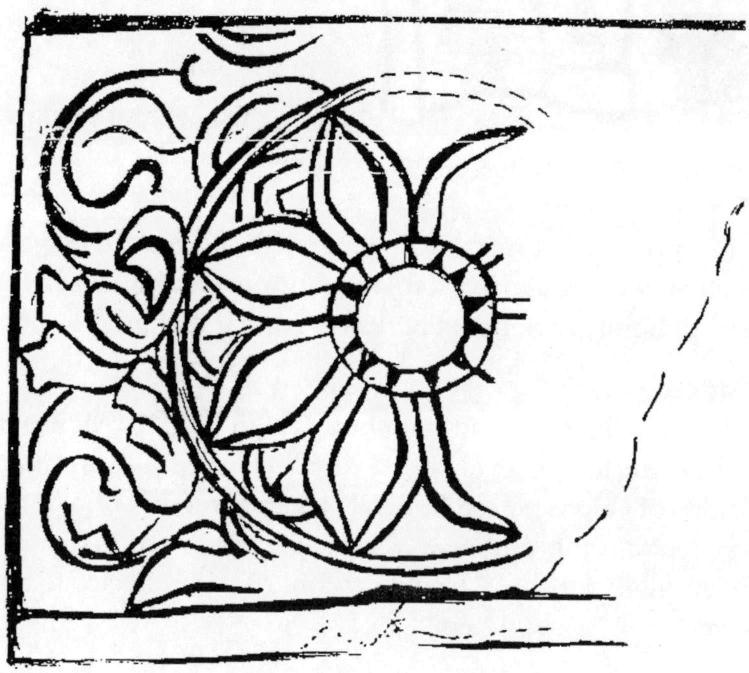

Fig. 1. Brick with lotus pattern, *Pancāyatna* temple, Sarnath.

There are a number of undated bricks showing lotus design with a border of square beads (12 × 18.75 cm, 28.75 × 12.5 cm), with plain lines (15 × 8.75 × 17.5 cm) and plain lines and triangles (23.75 × 23.75 cm). There are some examples with lotus petals in the upper portion and a four petalled flower. The upper and lower patterns are divided with a rectangular design (20 × 20 cm). There are examples of brick capitals showing different design and shape on both sides. One side of the brick is round and another is rectangular. The round side is finely carved with lotus petals and a three sided box like pattern with holes. The rounded side shows a large floral pattern, though not very fine. It seems that both sides were carved either in different periods or by different artisans because they are widely different from each other in execution, fineness and skill.

Floral Pattern

Thirty bricks are decorated with floral pattern. Among these twenty are dated to Gupta period, two to medieval period and eight are undated. Gupta period specimens show four petalled decoration with a circle in the centre (21.5 × 14 × 6 cm) (Fig. 2). Four petalled flowers

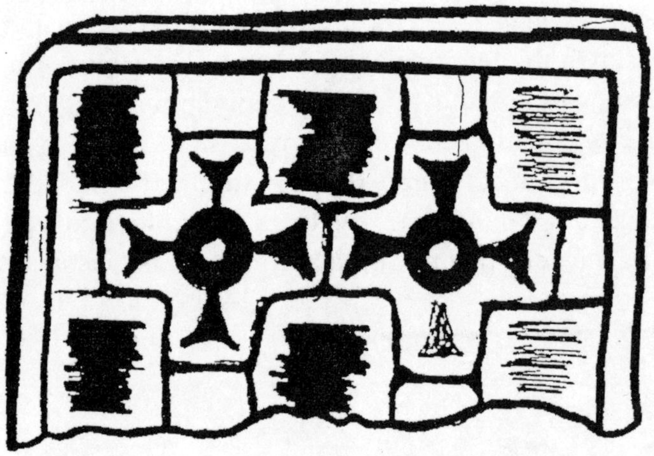

Fig. 2. Brick with floral pattern, Sarnath Museum.

with floral design surrounded by a border of zig-zag pattern, a wavy line, (the deeper portion of the line is filled with floral pattern), floral pattern with inverted pyramid, geometrical designs, four petalled flower surrounded with beaded garland and border of rosettes and other floral patterns (17.5 × 14 × 10 cm) are also noteworthy.

One example of medieval period shows a rose in the corner and four leaves along with other floral patterns.

Among undated examples, one brick (21.2 × 6.2 cm) shows leaves in a row, rectangular blocks in the lower portion and circular pattern at the upper corner. However, others show flowers and other floral patterns, two identical flowers and a few incised lines.

Vase and Palmette Pattern

There are 26 bricks showing vase and palmette design (Fig. 3). All are dated to Gupta period except one which belong to medieval period (16.5 × 11 × 6 cm). This pattern is commonly used on the stone columns of Gupta period.[1] Such bricks are mostly pilaster capitals. Apart from bricks and pilaster capitals, this pattern is also visible on terracotta tiles. In measurement few of them are 3.7 cm in length and 10-27.5 cm in width, 25 × 24 × 12 cm, 16.5 × 11 × 6 cm and 14 × 12 × 6 cm approximately 12.5 cm, 12 cm.

Palm Leaf Pattern

There are six bricks decorated with palm leaf design (Fig. 4). They measure 12.5 × 11.2 cm, 2.7 × 22.5 cm, 25.62 × 16.2 cm, 22.5 × 13.7 cm and 14.37 cm and belong to the Gupta period.

Cross Pattern

Eight bricks, decorated with cross design are attributed to Gupta period while one is undated. The Gupta specimens are carved with parallel rows of ornamental crosses. One of them shows filled up blocks while two others show half at the block filled as triangles which sometimes look like alternating floral petals. One brick shows topped cross pattern where each hand of the cross is topped with a semi circle. These bricks measure 6.25 × 5 cm, 12.5 × 12.4 × 5 cm, 14.5 × 12 × 5.4 cm, 18 × 9 × 5 cm, 9 × 7.5 × 5 cm and 20 × 15 cm. The undated specimen is 23.75 × 7.5 cm, in measurement. It is a slightly rounded brick with cross pattern in floral style. The cross pattern looks like four rhombus petalled flower between parallel lines.

Fig. 3. Brick with palmette design, Sarnath Museum, Gupta period.

Chequer Pattern

Twelve Gupta period bricks are decorated with chequer design (Fig. 4). They show alternate hollow and filled blocks to make a chequer pattern. Their average size is 20-21 × 13-14 × 5-7 cm, while a few are smaller than this.

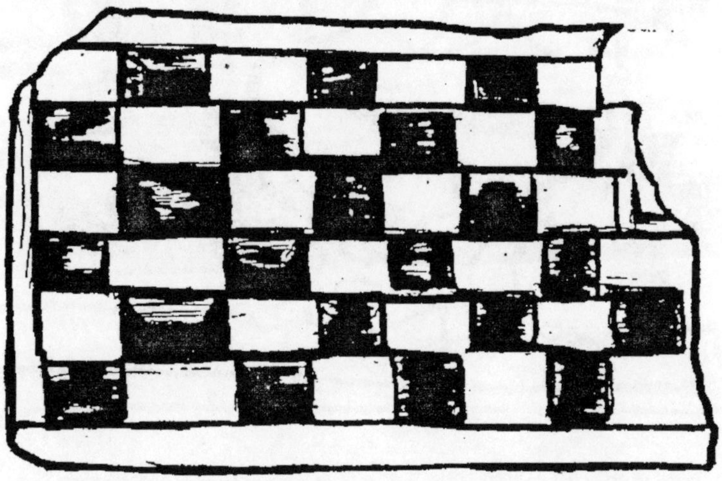

Fig. 4. Brick with chequer pattern, Sarnath Museum, Gupta period.

Beaded Pattern

There are three bricks of Gupta period with beaded design. The beaded rows are separated with square channels. This 30 × 26.5 × 5.5 cm measuring brick is unusual in shape. Another brick (16.2 × 14.4 × 3.7) shows beaded border in surrounding lines, with diamonds or some geometrical pattern. However, the beads are not even in size and shape.

Quiver with Arrow and Bow Pattern

There are bricks which show decorated quiver with three or four arrows, half portion of bow and half lotus design. The Sarnath Museum catalogue wrongly describes this brick as 'brick fragment', carved on one side with two embossed lines becoming narrow upwards, one hanging vertically and the other is a garland pattern with square beads design between incised lines and lotus motif at extreme right.

Similar pattern is found on a few more bricks of Gupta period. Some of them show quiver and bow decorated with triangular pattern and a lotus in the bow (22.5 × 21.2 cm). One example has square beads instead of triangles.

Bricks with Lion and Kīrtimukha

There are bricks carved with a lion's head (Fig. 5). One Gupta example of capital (13.7 × 18.7) is decorated with lion's head and a foliated crest over his forehead. Another fragmentary brick (21.2 × 25 cm) of the same period also show lion's head spitting out foliage. This motif was apparently copied from the stone columns of Gupta period.[4] One example (13.7 × 26.2 cm) shows a couchant lion with its turned head on back and spitting pearls on its front. This beautiful piece is a moulded example. These lions are sometimes reported as *kīrtimukha* can

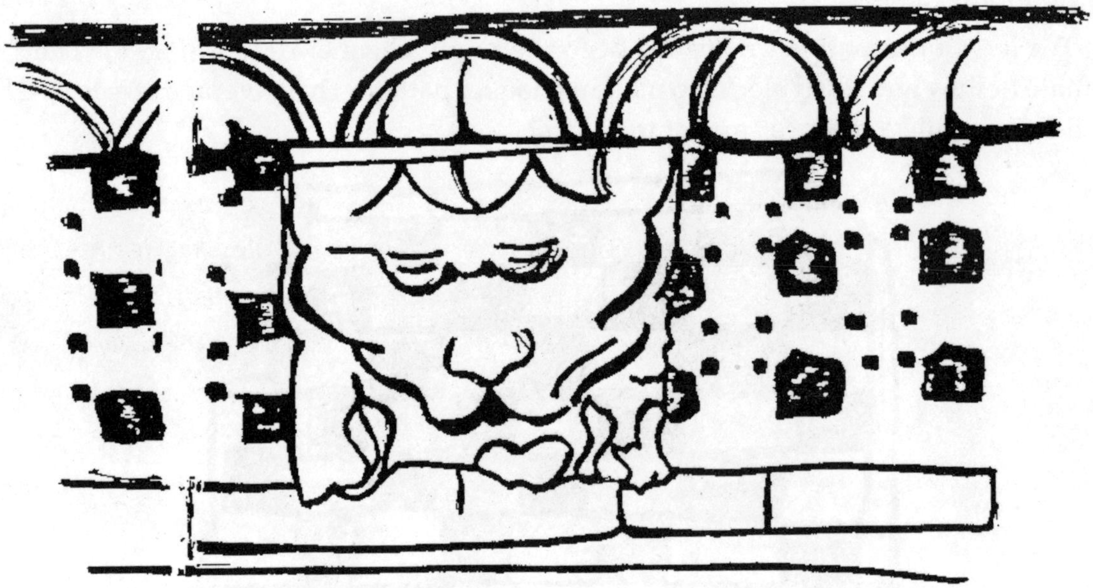

Fig. 5. Brick with lion head, *Pancāyatana* temple, Sarnath.

be seen in the *Pancāyatana* temple.

Human Figurines as Pattern

There are a few bricks endowed with human figurines and the figure of Kubera. One example (27.5 × 2.5 cm) shows three standing male figures with transparent drapery. At the proper right, the figure is probably holding *vīṇā*.

One more undated brick shows a standing female figure. The left part of the figure is broken. The portion below the breast, except right hand, is also missing. Two fragmentary examples also show human figures. Both figures are broken from their knees and their one hand is also missing (Pl. 8.2). One medieval brick (14.4 × 14.4 × 6.2 cm) shows a defaced seated figure of Kubera. Two examples are inscribed one measuring 2.5 × 7.5 × 15 cm inscribed with eastern variety of northern Gupta script which reads *'Prakulasya'* while another reads *'Sarana'*

Other Patterns

Apart from the above, Sarnath bricks are decorated with several other motifs like step (Pl. 8.3), *āmalaka,* scroll, chain, grill, *stūpa* and shrine. Nine examples are decorated with inverted pyramid like design[5]. These motifs can also be seen in the art of Bodhgaya temples, *stūpas* of Sāñchi and Bharhut in India and in Percipolice, Susa, Iran and Mesopotamia. One fragmentary brick shows an incised *stūpa* (6.2 × 6.2 cm) while another brick is shaped like a *stūpa.*

One Gupta period brick is shaped like a temple with chequer pattern at the lower portion while the upper portion shows temple shape and decorated with rectangular beads, scrolls and floral pattern. Three examples show scroll pattern, two are shaped like *āmalaka* measuring

12.5 cm and 16.2 × 16.2 cm. One shows an *āmalaka* in the middle surrounded with four fan shaped design. These bricks are dated to Gupta period.

Notes and References

1. D.R. Sahni, *Catalogue of Archaeology at Sarnath*, F (c) 62-82.
2. Sarnath Museum Catalogue, Acc. No. 6355.
3. *Ibid.*, Acc. No. 6355, 6356, 6357.
4. D.R. Sahni, *op. cit.*, p. 300, F (c) 19.
5. *Ibid.*, p. 304, F (c) 212-214.

9

A Forgotten Jaina Centre: Bhālki

Hampa Nagarajaiah

Bhālki, a *taluka* headquarters, is about 40 km to the north-west of Bīdar, in Karnataka. It once prospered as a major Jaina centre from the early medieval period. Available archaeological vestiges, corroborated by epigraphical evidence, indicate that the place was a nerve centre of Jaina settlement from ancient times which rose to greater prominence in the early Chālukya and the Rāṣṭrakūṭa period. Bhālki had not less than three Jaina houses of worship dedicated to Ādinātha, Neminātha and Mahāvīra *Tīrthaṅkaras*. The Ādinatha Basadi was popular as *'Brahmā Jinālya'*, which has been recorded in a later inscription dated 1113 CE, when Tribhuvanamalla Vikramāditya VI (1076-1125 CE), emperor of the imperial Chālukyan dynasty, was ruling from Kalyāṇa, *Vijaya-skandhāvāra,* the main capital, about 35 km to the south-west of Bhālki.[1]

The surviving Jaina sculptures, loose and displaced images, are found near the Māruti *alias* Hanumān *Kaṭṭe,* a raised platform, in the south-west outskirt of Bhālki town and in the small museum of Śri Cannabasaveśvara College. In the museum a broken image of Jina seated in *padmāsana,* a pillar of a destroyed Jaina temple and sculpture of standing Jaina couple, etc., are preserved.

There are three more sculptures of Jaina affiliation near Māruti (Hanumān) *Kaṭṭe (Jagatī),* which are unique and significant in the context of Jaina iconography. This article aims at a detailed discussion of these art pieces.

1. An image of *Tīrthaṅkara* seated in *dhyāna-mudrā* with *śrīvatsa* symbol, prominently carved on the broad chest as a *mahāpuruṣa-lakṣaṇa* is significant (Pl. 9.1). The image is a matchless example of *śrīvatsa* sign on the chest of *Tīrthaṅkara* which is rarely found in Karnataka. However, with two examples, *śrīvatsa* sign are also found. One is an eighth century figure of a Jina with *śrīvatsa* mark on the chest from Śravaṇabeḷagoḷa, which is in the Government Museum, Bangalore. Other one with *śrīvatsa* mark is from Bāpaṭla in Andhra Pradesh (Guntur Dist.). The image of *c.* early eighth century is housed in the Hyderabad Museum.

Both the above mentioned images with the *śrīvatsa* symbol belong to eighth century. The mark on the chest connotates that the highest knowledge is manifested from the heart of Jina. Some of the *Āyāgapaṭas,* the tablets of homage obtained from Mathura, also contain the symbol of *śrīvatsa.* It may be recalled that the mark was common to images of gods in all Indian religion, including Jainism, as an important stamp of great men on the chest. In the North the catchet is prominently found from second century, the early Kushāna period. Albeit, it did not become popular in the Digamabara Jaina tradition of the south.

The seated Jina image (height 1.24 m, width 0.85m) of Bhālki is highly polished and severely damaged. Curiously, the palms placed one above the other, placing the right palm on the stretched left plam in *dhyāna-mudrā,* are intact. In the centre of the right palm is shown lotus. The sole of the squatted feet are unimpaired. The oval face and the half-closed eyes propose that Jina is engrossed in deep meditation. The eyebrow, frizzy hair on the head, the slim waist and broad chest are neatly executed. The image must have been the *mūlanāyaka* of one of the extinct Jaina temples. The image can be assigned to late eighth century, i.e. last decades of the (Vātāpi) Chālukyas and beginning period of the Rāṣṭrakūṭas.

Second image of (Jina) height: 56 cm, width: 42 cm in *kāyotsarga* posture of meditation is headless image and the relics of its broken head are missing (Pl. 9.2). Except for the missing head, the image with lion cognizance is intact to suggest the identification with Mahāvīra. Mahāvīra, flanked by fly whisk bearers at the bottom, place usually devoted to the attendant deities called *Jinaśāsanadevatās* or *Yakṣa* and *Yakṣī.* Stylistically the image is datable to late eighth century, the period of the Rāṣṭrakūṭas.

The third image of Ambikā from Bhālki, frontally carved with her face slightly leaning towards right, is one of the peerless images that richly deserves special treatment (Pl. 9.3). The hallmark of this figure is its distinctive and uncommon features. The nuances of its iconographic characteristic attributes are worth pondering.

The two-armed figure of Ambikā, of about four feet high and more than two feet wide, with smiling countenances is flanked by two of her attendants (their modelling is somewhat crude and not benign in appearance), resting on an architectural device of *makara-paṭṭī.* Ambikā is seated on a *bhadra pīṭha.* She bears an *āmra-lumbi* (a bunch of mangoes) in her right hand and a fruit in her left hand. Her elder son Subhaṅkara (Siddha in the Śvetāmbara tradition), is standing nude to her left while Prabhaṅkara (Buddha in the Śvetāmbara belief) is mounted the lion shown on the right corner of the pedestal. The lion mount of Ambikā is shown with bulging eyes and protruded tongue. Ambikā, thus reveals concordance with the textual and traditional prescriptions. The image is datable between *c.* 750-800 AD.

A diminutive figure of seated Jina is enshrined in the centre of the delicately decorated and nicely finished *karnada-mukuṭa.* Ambikā is bejewelled with *kanṭha-hāra,* or a broad necklace, *stana-hāra* or *suvarṇa-vaikakṣaka,* pearl-necklace passing between her breasts and gracefully going round her breasts, *maṅgalamālā* with a bell at its end, *mekhalā*-beaded waist-belt, *keyūra* or *tōḷabandhi* armlet worn on the upper arm, *padakas*-medallion, *ratna karṇakuṇḍala* heavy earring worn in the lobe, *nūpura*-anklet-*kāl-kaḍaga*-bracelet, *uṅgura*-rings for the fingers and *valaya*-

bangles. Full grown lofty breasts, and *talōdara,* the slim waist, adds to the grace of the deity. Her oval shaped serene face is smiling-*ānandamaya.* The long and elegant nose is mutilated. Broad eyes with bow shaped eyebrows, soft cheek, pretty jaw and tender lips are all chiselled to perfection.

Apart from a small sized seated Jina in the centre of Ambikā's crest, one more Jina in *padmāsana,* a little bigger in size is enshrined in the middle of the branches of *āmra-vṛkṣa*-mango-trees, spread over the Ambikā's head like a canopy shown above the crown. Luxuriant tree top is carved as a floriated canopy, a pleasing device. Jina seated in the centre can be identified as Arhat Pārśva, though much of the canopy of snake-hoods, over his head is nebulous. Gandharvas, hovering *mālādharas,* drummers and bunch of managos could be identified with difficulty. These details at the top, roughly analogous with Ambikā images at Deogarh, indicate that the deity sitting under the mango-tree, has attained the state of a superior goddess and has been accorded the status of Jina-*śāsana devatā,* guardian deity of the Order of Jina.

Ambā, Āmrā, Kuṣmāṇḍinī, Agnila and Siṁhavāhanī are the other appellations of Ambikā, the mother goddess.[2] Available archaeological and literary evidences establish that Ambikā cult which originated in the Girnār (Ūrjayanta, Raivataka) region in Gujarat, in the fifth century, slowly picking up, had gradually reached all the cardinal directions of India by the end of seventh century. In the context of Karnataka, it started very early in the reign of the Chālukyas of Bādāmī with its manifestation first at Aihoḷe. The early and independent sculptures of Ambikā from Karnataka exhibit the extraordinary dexterity of the artists and royal patronisation of the period.

The foregoing account makes it amply clear that Bhālki was an important Jaina *tīrtha-kṣētra,* pilgrim place till the end of medieval period. The images discovered and described above are revealing. Iconographically Jina with *śrivatsa* mark and Ambikā with Arhat Pārśva overhead are most important characteristic features which have been rarely witnessed at other places.

Acknowledgement

The author is grateful of D.N. Akki of Gogi and Dr. G.B. Visaji of Bhālki for their co-operation in the fieldwork.

Notes and References

1. Hampa Nagarajaiah, *A History of the Rāṣṭrakūṭas of Maḷkhēḍ and Jainism,* Bangalore, 2000 and R.M. Shadaksharaiah, Two Jaina Sculptures from Bhālki: A Note, *QJMS,* Vol. LXXI, No. 1 & 2, January - June 1980, pp. 69-70, Bidar Jilleya Devi Śilapagaḷu (Kannada) in- *Ithihāsa Darshana,* Vol. 8 (1993), p. 76.
2. M.N.P. Tiwari, *Ambikā in Jina Art and Literature,* New Delhi, 1989; U.P. Shah, *Akoṭās, Bronzes,* Bombay, 1959.

10

Apsaras Figures from Kaṅkālī Mound, Mathura

S.D. Trivedi

The feminine beauty has always been given a special place in Indian art[1]. But for the Didarganj Yakṣī taken usually to be of Mauryan age[2], from Śunga period onwards we come across continuous portrayal of beautiful females in gayful moods and in various modes. These representations are termed as *Yakṣī*[3], *Devatā*[4], *Śālabhañjikā*[5], *Apsaras*[6], *Vṛkṣakā*[7], *Nāyikā*[8], *Ramaṇī*[9] (damsel) and so forth. Though a woman plays a variety of roles in life, her place is determined in the society in an entirely different context[10]. The central point of attraction has almost been always been her physical charm and festive youth.

The artists of Mathura and their masters were also fascinated by the joyous feminine beauty. The artist experimented with all innovations to highlight the feminine elegance in a variety of representations. Kaṅkālī mound of Mathura has yielded many such marvellous sculptures representing the female figures. In-depth study of these offers many propositions, re-appraisal of which is intended in the present paper.

Before we discuss some of the related problems, it would be appropriate to enumerate some facts about such illustrations.

(*i*) These are carved generally on upright pillars and brackets used in the *Stūpas.*

(*ii*) Such sculptures were found from several mounds of Mathura and adjoining areas where Jaina and Buddhist *Stūpas* were erected. The Kaṅkālī mound has also yielded a large number of architectural remains of a Jaina *Stūpa.*

(*iii*) Majority of the female figures are naked or semi-naked. Through their look, postures, and body language, they all speak the language of sensuousness. An erotic projection, implied or explicit, is conceived in their portrayal. One cannot resist the attraction of their richness.

(*iv*) They are all in standing position, either slightly bending or standing cross-legged.

(*v*) There is always a mount under their feet which is either a grotesque dwarf or an animal. Sometimes they are mounted on a throne or a footstool like thing.

(*vi*) Sometimes the top portion depicts a scene of drinking revelry or a loving couple, which is separated from the figure below by a decorative motif of railing.

(*vii*) In appearance, the scheme of presentation seems to be more or less the same. But a close examination reveals many changes in the presentation of the top portion, the portion below her feet, as well as in the dress and ornamentation of the principal female figure.

(*viii*) The expression on their faces is always very pleasing.

(*ix*) There is not much difference in the size of all these female figures.

(*x*) A majority of railing pillars are carved on both the faces. The reverse side has half and full medallions containing lotus rosettes.

(*xi*) All such examples with the exception of two[11], belong to Kushana period.

Among other things, the State Museum, Lucknow, received a large number of upright pillars carved with a variety of subjects, from the excavated site of Kaṅkālī mound at Mathura[12]. Some of them depict lovely figures of exceptional grace and beauty. In order to understand the connected problems, the details of some important figures are given here.

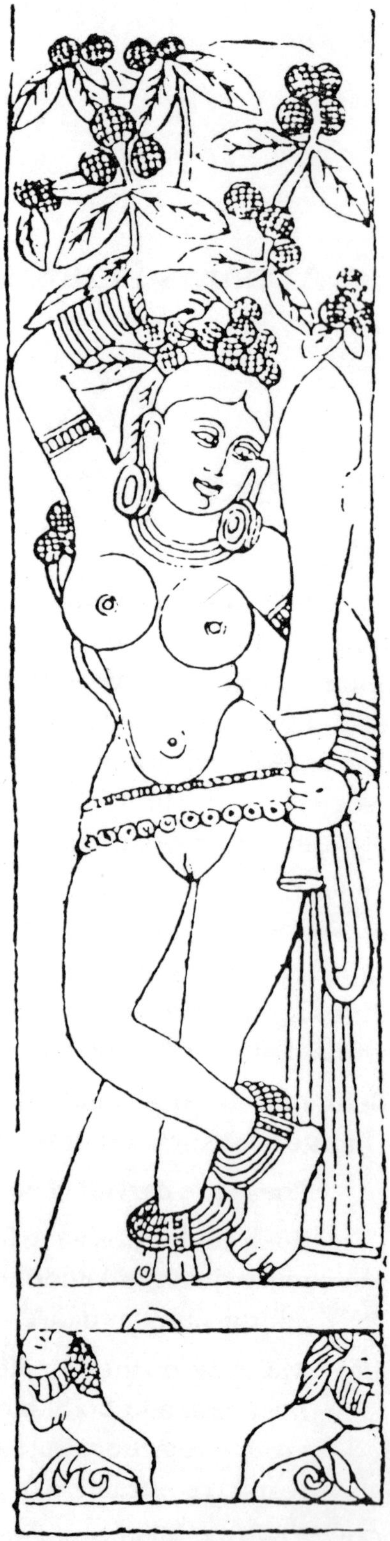

Fig. 1. Woman with sword, Kaṅkālī Ṭīlā, Mathura. National Museum, New Delhi.

A railing pillar[13] of red sandstone, carved on both faces is now in the National Museum, New Delhi[14]. This shows a woman (Fig. 1) Standing on a lion-throne[15] under a *Kadamba* tree in flower. She is holding a short broad sword[16] in her left hand and is touching the cluster of flowers overhead with her raised right hand. Her hair is parted in the middle and combed back from the front, and she is bedecked with usual ornaments. The lions

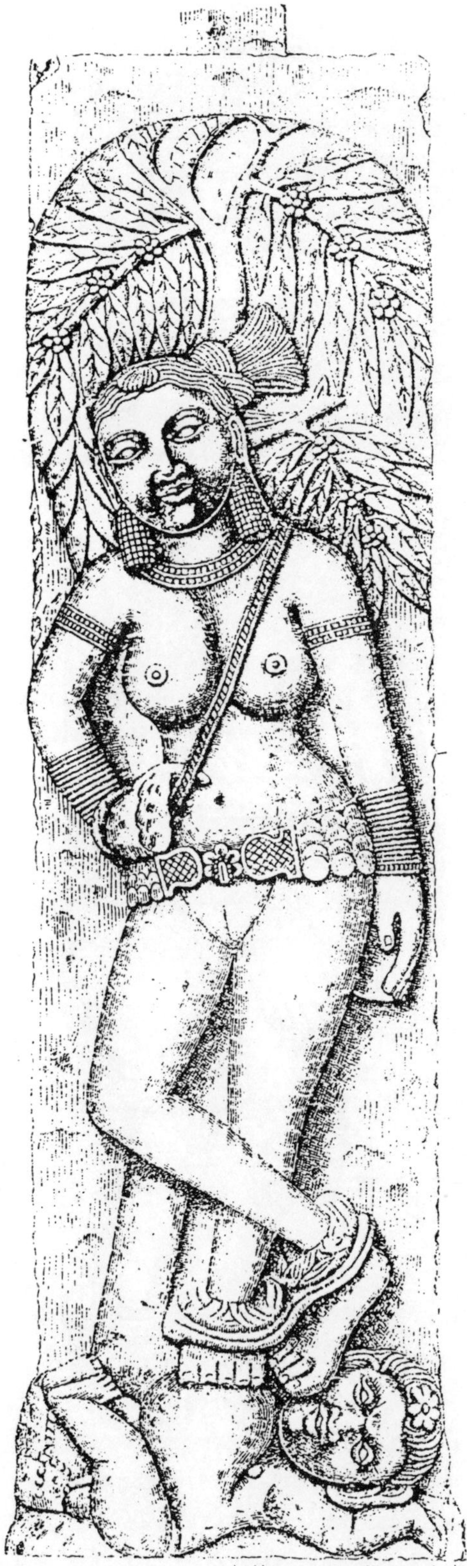

Fig. 2. A female under Aśoka tree, Kaṅkālī Ṭīlā.

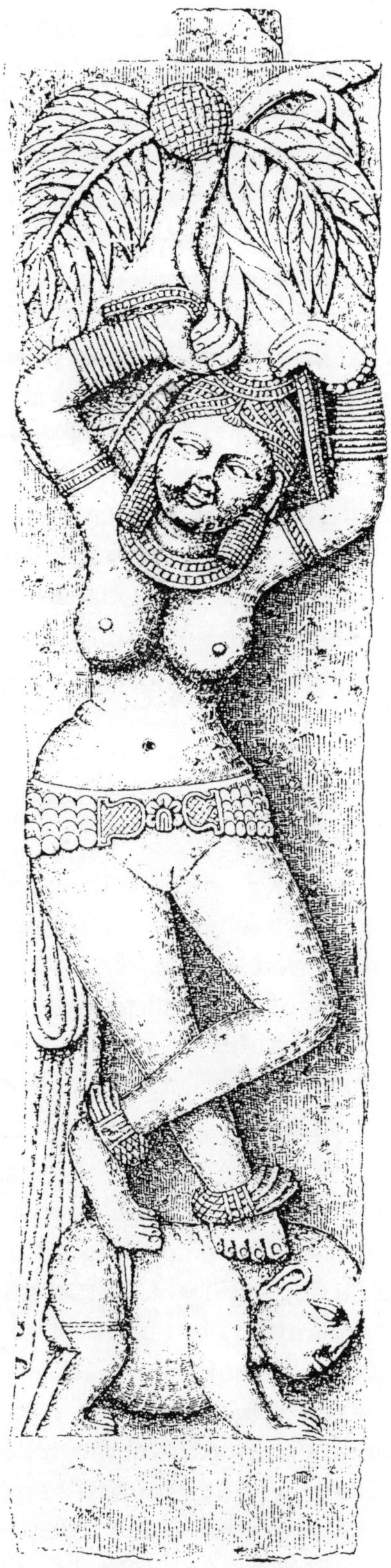

Fig. 3. A lady busy in beautifying her coiffure, Kaṅkālī Ṭīlā.

bearing the throne are careering in different directions, a corrugated leafy decoration appearing between them.

The other rail-post[17] is also carved on both sides. The obverse (Fig. 2) shows a female figure, standing cross-legged on a dwarf crouching on his back. She stands under a blossoming tree, her hair combed back from the front and tied in a fantastic knot at the back of the head. She has got the thumb of her right hand hooked in a peculiar chain-like ornament, may be a sort of big necklace *(hāra yaṣṭi)* passing across her body in *Yañjopavīta* fashion[18]. She is looking at someone or something on her left and smiling coquettishly. Here the dwarf too is not crouching in the usual manner. Instead she seems to be standing on his stomach with the dwarf throwing up his legs and hands in obvious mirth. Another unusual feature is the hairstyle of the dwarf. They are carefully combed back and beautified with a flower placed in the centre. His face is purposely highlighted.

Another railing pillar[19] from the same site depicts a naked figure of a female (Fig. 3) standing with crossed legs under a flowering Aśoka tree on the back of a corpulent male. Apparently she is busy in beautifying her coiffure by fastening the chain-like ornament into her headdress[20].

The next specimen[21] portrays a quite different mood of a lady who is doing nothing but enjoying a bath *(nirjhara-snāna)* under a waterfall descending from a rocky region (Fig. 4). Her three-quarter profile from the right, a little bend in the body, and the posture of her hands, all features convey the message of a satisfying bath in a very natural way. Her face is beaming with pleasure[22]. The trefoil decoration appears on the pedestal. It may be an indication of water drops. Its back shows beautiful lotus flowers in full and half medallions (Fig. 5).

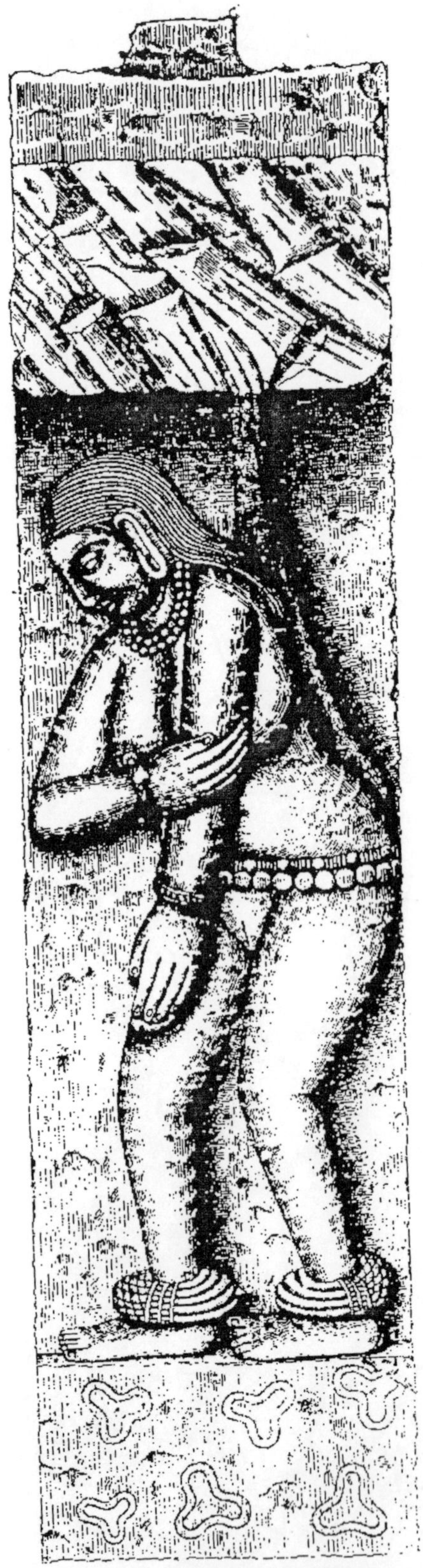

Fig. 4. Woman bathing under a waterfall, Kaṅkālī Ṭīlā.

The bracket[23] of a *Toraṇa* (beam lintel) shows a standing female figure, carved in the round, under a flowering tree, which she holds with both of her hands (Pl. 10.1). The master artist chiselled the minute details of front and back of a curved figure so marvellously that one can appreciate both – her physical beauty and her rich embellishment. On the reverse of the piece we notice two plaits of her hair intricately intertwined, which fell down on her back. Her right foot rests on the head of a seated elephant and the left on its uplifted trunk.

There is another bracket[24] showing a female (Pl. 10.2) in round with almost similar decorations. She stands on a kneeling dwarf[25]. Her double-striped braid is seen hanging down on her back. The other details are also minutely carved out on front and back. There is change in her ornaments and the faces of the two are also treated differently. On the basis of stylistic features both bracket-figures may be assigned the date of 1st century BC. The Kaṅkālī mound yielded some more fragments of brackets where either lower part or upper portion remain intact. They show the usual posture of Mathura female figures standing on their *vāhanas.* The *Toraṇa* brackets are carved on both faces with females, complete with their back details. A couple of fragments also indicate that they were standing on scaly crocodiles[25a].

It has been established that the upright pillars and brackets bearing such figures were the architectural members of railing and gateway respectively. Now the question arises about their actual placement. What purpose did they serve by their presence on a religious shrine where the people throng to worship the deity with full concentration and devotion?

The perusal of their description clearly shows that they were placed there to emphasize an element of happiness and beauty. They also exude sensuality, conveyed through their gestures. They have graceful faces, full prominent breasts, deep navel and an extra slim waist. The contours of their hips and thighs are modelled so beautifully that they create a sort of rhythmic effect. The richness

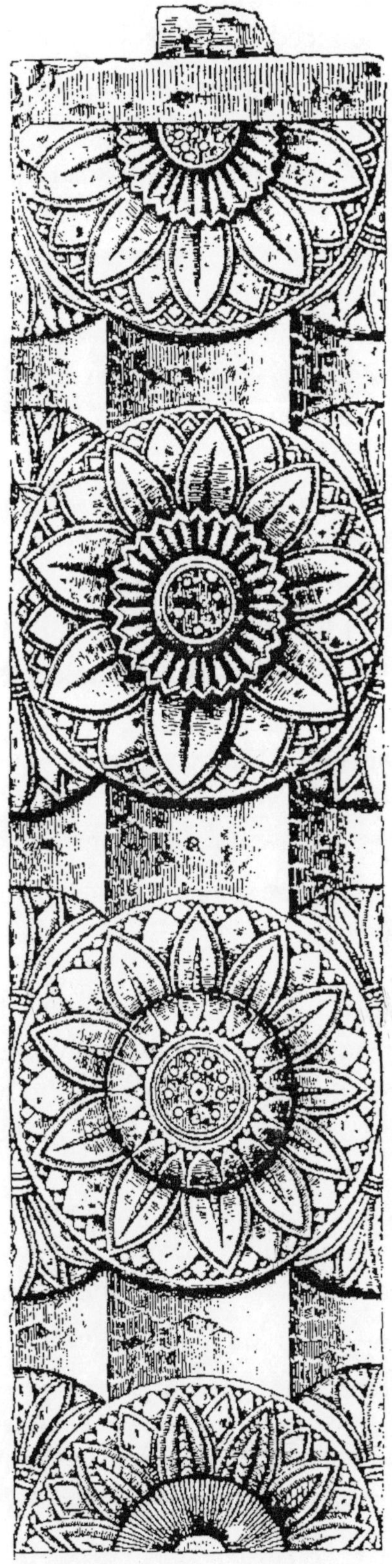

Fig. 5. Lotus medallion (back of Fig. 10), Kaṅkālī Ṭīlā.

of ornaments add luster to the graceful feminine beauty. The nudity, full or partial, establishes the pronounced sex appeal beyond any doubt.

Scholars expressed their views differently about these female figures. V.A. Smith[26] writes,

This series of pillars is more peculiar and interesting than the preceding series, and is, with the exception of plate LXIV undoubtedly Jain. The figures in plate LX to LXIII are indecently naked and could not be Buddhist.

He associates these female figures with Jaina because of their nudity, a *digambara*[27] phenomenon. But this opinion cannot be accepted because the Bhuteśvara railings, which are carved in the same fashion of nakedness have Buddhist subjects on their back.[28] Obviously such naked female figures were an accepted part and parcel of both Buddhist and Jaina *stūpa* decorations.

Because of indicative traces of lower garment in many of the examples, it is undisputedly accepted that the genital organ is exposed because of their transparent drapery. Sivaramamurti[29] affirms that diaphanous apparel of the women is quite clear in the frieze of the cloth prominently shown in the representation of the Bhutesvara *yakṣīs.*

A.K. Coomaraswamy[30] takes them as :

unmistakable descendants of the *yakṣīs* and *Vṛkṣakas* of Bharhut, Bodhgaya and Sāñchī. It is true that the architecture of *Stūpa* was more or less same and the artist and his patron must have received the inspiration from the early art centers where we find the rail post with female figures.

V.S. Agrawala[31] endorses this view pointing out,

......the figures are shown standing on crouching dwarfs *avanmukha guhyaka* by which the artist wished to indicate that the older tradition of these female figures being *yakṣīs* was still accepted in popular belief.

Mulk Raj Anand[32] remarks about the artist of Kushana period : "Apart from the comparison of the Buddha, they seem to have discovered the grace of woman, both mother and object of arching desire in the fullness of her big breasted, large hipped and delicately adorned presence". The fact is that both aspects are admirably represented in Mathura art. The master craftsman attained such a high state of perfection that one can differentiate easily between an aged and ugly woman and a beautiful lady (heroine), both assimilated in the same composition[33]. There is no doubt that the feminine beauty is purposefully highlighted with sensuous features on these railing pillars.

The noted Jaina art historian U.P. Shah expresses his opinion in these words:

The railing pillar figures of *yakṣas* and *yakṣīs* at Bharhut show that they had to be included in places of worship though an interior status of decorative pillar sculptures was assigned to them The same is the case with such figures from the Kaṅkālī Ṭīlā, Mathura. For want of names inscribed below them, it is not possible to recognize them, but it is noteworthy that they have *vāhanas* (dwarf, elephant etc.) below their feet[34].

It has already been stated that the examples of old art centres were there for the artists of Mathura to see. But there is hardly any feature, which may be indicative of their religious leanings[35]. *Yakṣīs* are consorts of *Yakṣas* who are also described as gatekeepers[36] in the *Samavasaraṇa*[37] of a Jina. By virtue of their assignment they are both present on the outer side of the shrine. *Yakṣas* are shown as ugly figures[38] whereas *yakṣīs* are supposed to be epitomes of beauty. They are both vegetal spirits. *Yakṣa* and *yakṣī* are *Śāsanadevatā*[39] of Jaina Tīrthaṅkaras and they have a special place in the Jaina iconography. Their popularity among the ordinary people was considerable.

The context of dancing apsarases the court of Indra, god of gods, is well known. It is said that he had sent the dancer named Nīlāñjanā to King Ṛṣabha. After seeing the dance of Nīlāñjanā, his mind turned away from worldly pleasures[40]. A fragmentary sculpture[41] of the State Museum, Lucknow, depicts the scene beautifully. It is also possible that with this background, these nymphs are suggestive of evanescence of all worldly objects. V.A. Smith also attributes the status of dancing girls to these figures[42].

The subject-matter of crouching grotesque human figures as their *vāhanas* requires a separate study. It is interesting to note that the postures of these kneeling dwarfs are varied and so is their expression. Sometimes one is burdened due to the fall weight of standing female while another one feels happy bearing the beauty queen over his back. They are termed as *Guhyaka, Yakṣa, Vāhana,* or *Vāmana* (diminutive male). A verse from *Chaturbhani*[43] describes the merit of her feet, which is the abode of Kāmadeva (god of love) and at whose touch the Aśoka tree blossoms into flower before time, and it is because of this that a dwarf who crouches under her feet becomes a blessed figure.

In *Meghadūta*[44] of Kālidasa the *Yakṣa* is desirous of the stroke of the left foot of his beloved *(vāmapādabhilaṣi).* "This suggests that the kneeling dwarf figure under the feet of the sensuous beauty in the *Śālabhañjikā* scene is none other than the *Yakṣa* himself, who, being overpowered by the mighty strength of his beloved, is reduced to the size of a short statured person."[45]

It is certain that what the artist had in mind was to provide elevation for these beautiful figures. Therefore the pedestal in any form including grotesque figures was provided to highlight the sumptuous beauty personified in the form of these female figures.

The merrymaking, drinking and love scenes are depicted on the top of sculpture separated with railing motif[46]. Heinrich Zimmer[47] observed in his work that "It depicts the balcony of a palace in the blissful realm in amourous dalliance, enjoying the bliss of that paradise". But this author feels that the *gavākṣa* window carved out at the top of the upright pillar presenting scenes commensurate with the *Surā Sundarī* aspect of female beauties which was an effort at combining the aspect of beauty with the aspect of pleasure which go hand in hand in real life[48].

To sum up, one can definitely admire the creative activity of master craftsmen of Mathura. There must have been an overwhelming response from masses for these magnificent creations[49]. As a matter of fact, the sensual aspect of human beings predominates at all places and ages not only for arousing worldly desires but for the fulfilment of the task intended and commanded by nature for perpetuation of life. These figures convey sensuality and gentle eroticism for the sake of well being of mankind. These delightful female figures radiated sweet fragrance of pleasure and enchanting beauty around the religious edifices, whether Jaina, Buddhist or Brahmanical. So was the case with the Great *Stūpa,* once erected at Kaṅkālī mound of Mathura where the Jaina worshippers must have encountered for the first time the beautiful females appearing on outer face of the railing. They were there for bestowing upon their devotees *(bhaktas)* boons of fertility, abundance and happiness. Above all, these are the best specimens of feminine beauty in the whole gamut of Indian art[50].

Notes and References

1. Female figures are represented in different art mediums, viz., terracottas, metal images, stone sculptures, ivory carvings, etc. The paper is restricted to the stone sculptures only.
2. Niharanjan Ray and many other scholars do not agree on its Mauryan date. The author also holds the same opinion.
3. A good number of female images of 3rd-2nd century BC have been found in different parts of the country and they are termed as *yakṣī*. Even in the later period this word continues to be used for identifying some female figures. *Yakṣī* or *yakṣī* is a consort of *yakṣa,* a folk deity.
4. The word '*Devatā*' occurs in the short epigraphs engraved on some Bharhut sculptures depicting females.
5. The '*Śālabhañjikā*' is very common word, often used for such women standing under a tree. The ancient literature gives an eloquent and graphic description of this motif. Udai Narain Roy, *Śalabhañjikā in Art, Philosophy and Literature,* pp. 1-14.
6. It is also spelt like *apsarā.* They are mentioned in the epics, *Samhitās* and other literary works of later period. They are semi-divinities of celestial region.
7. *Vṛkṣakā* is used for woman and tree motif. In other words, it is synonymous with *śālabhañjikā.* A.K. Coomaraswamy and Stella Kramrisch frequently used this word for such representation. The word *Dohada* also provides the same meaning. A.L. Srivastava, The Śālabhañjikā : A Study in Symbolic Motif, *Kalā*, Vol. VII : 2000-2001, p. 63.
8. It is a poetic word and generally used in the context of paintings. But some scholars used this adjective for the young ladies depicted in sculptural art too, particularly of medieval period.
9. The connotation of *Ramaṇī* underlines the nature of charming beauty. This is also frequently used for beautiful female figures.
10. Pāṇini's *Aṣṭādhyāyī* mentions different categories of woman like *Kumārī, Patnī, Mātā, Chhātrā, Acharyā.* V.Ṣ. Agrawala, *Pāṇinikālīna Bhāratavarṣa,* iv.1.116.
11. A couple of *Toraṇa* brackets with female figures belong to 1st century BC.
12. Dr. A. Fuhrer, the then Curator of the Lucknow Museum conducted excavations in late nineteenth century in three consecutive sessions. He brought the antiquarian wealth en block to his Institution from the excavated site. V.A. Smith published this treasure in his book titled *Jain Stūpa and Other Antiquities of Mathura.*
13. J.275, Originally the sculpture was in the Lucknow Museum and later on it was given to the National Museum, New Delhi.
14. Shashi Prabha Asthana (Late), *Mathurā Kalā,* p. 98, Fig. 103.

15. This is one of the rare examples. A lion throne is usually provided to the divine figures.
16. V.A. Smith identifies it as a mace, *op. cit,* p. 38; some scholars suggest that she is going to perform sword-dance (*khaḍga-nṛtya*).
17. J.276, State Museum, Lucknow.
18. Prof. Udai Narain Roy identifies this ornament as Vaikaṣa or Vaikakṣaka. The *Pādatāḍitakem* refers to a such garland-shaped ornament, made of gold *(Hemavaikākṣyaka)* used by the ladies for displaying fine rounded breasts looking like jars. *Śalabhañjikā in Art, Philosophy and Literature,* p. 51.
19. J. 277, State Museum, Lucknow.
20. Prof. Roy described the lady holding the branch of the tree with her both hands. This is not correct, *op. cit.* p. 50, Fig. 30. V.S. Agrawala describes the female in the act of beautifying her coiffure by fastening to it a lotus garland. But it does not seem to be a lotus garland. *A Short Guide-Book to the Archaeological Section of the Provincial Museum, Lucknow,* p. 10, Fig. 11.
21. J. 278, National Museum, New Delhi. Actually it was in the Provincial Museum, Lucknow from where it was transferred there. V.S. Agrawala, *ibid,* p. 10, Fig. 10.
22. Shashi Prabha Asthana, *op. cit,* p. 99, Fig. 104.
23. J. 595a, State Museum, Lucknow, A.K Coormaraswamy, *op. cit.*, Fig. 75.
24. J. 595b, State Museum, Lucknow.
25. Prof. Roy mistakenly mentions a swan *(Rājahaṁsa)* as her *vāhana, op. cit.,* p. 52, Fig. 33 (back view).

25a. V.A. Smith, *op. cit.*, Pl. XXXVI, Figs. 1 & 2.

26. V.A. Smith, *ibid.*, p. 38.
27. Jaina *Tīrthaṅkaras* are shown naked but not the females.
28. R.C. Sharma, *The Splendour of Mathura Art of Museum,* p. 125.
29. C. Sivaramamurti, *Sri Lakshmi in Indian Art and Thought,* p. 20.
30. A.K. Coomaraswamy, *op. cit.,* p. 65.
31. V.S·Agrawala, *Indian Art,* p. 226.
32. *Marg,* Special number on Mathura, March 1962, p. 3.
33. Accn. No. 2800, National Museum, New Delhi; *Mathura Art,* Fig. 100.
34. Umakant P. Shah, *Jaina-Rūpa-Maṇḍana: Jaina Iconography,* p. 207.
35. R.C. Sharma also holds the same opinion, *op.cit.*, p. 125.
36. U.P. Shah, *op. cit.,* p. 207.
37. *Samavasarana* literally means assemblage and refers to the sermon-hall. As discussed by D.R. Bhandarkar, Jaina Iconography, *Indian Antiquary,* Vol. XL (1911), pp. 125-30,153-161.
38. A.K. Coomaraswamy, *Yakṣas,* p. 11.
39. The *Yakṣa* Statues are considered as the examples of folk art. In appearance they are colossal and pot bellied. V.S. Agrawala, *Indian Art,* p. 113.
40. U.P. Shah, *op. cit.*, p. 112.
41. S.D. Trivedi, *A Guide Book to the Archaeological Section State Museum, Lucknow,* p. 15, Fig. 14.
42. V.A. Smith, *op. cit.*, p. 38.

43. Motichandra (ed.). *Chaturbhāṇī,* Verse 130, p. 249.
44. *Meghadūta,* 2, verse 18.
45. U.N. Roy, *op. cit.,* p. 57.
46. Stanislaw Czuma *Kusana Sculpture : Images from Early India,* figs. 28, 29 & 30.
47. Heinrich Zimmer, *The Art of Indian Asia,* p. 115.
48. Women in intoxication or engaged in drinking has been a favourite subject of Mathura art.
49. Strangely, this important segment of Mathura art and culture is entirely omitted in the *Mathura: The Cultural Heritage* (Collection of seminar papers), AIIS publication.
50. The author gratefully utilized the sketches of relevant figures from the *Jain Stūpa and Other Antiquities of Mathura* by V.A. Smith.

11

Identification of Pitcher Carriers in Gaja-Lakṣmī Reliefs

A.L. Srivastava

R.C. Agrawala, Former Director of the Department of Archaeology & Museums, Rajasthan, and a well-known name in the world of scholars has recently drawn our attention to quite a new subject in Gaja-Lakṣmī panels.

Gaja-Lakṣmī has been a favourite motif of Indian artists from the Śuṅga period onwards. The goddess is normally shown as seated or standing on a full-blown lotus and holding lotus stalk in both the hands. She is being anointed by flanking elephants. Later on, flanking maidens holding *cāmara* or flywhisk, *chatra* or parasol and *kalaśa* or water-vessel have also been shown.[1]

Flanking maidens attending to the goddess Śrī-Lakṣmī and holding flywhisk and parasol are found in many panels including a medallion on the railing pillar (no. 26b) of the Stūpa No. 2 at Sāñchī in which the maiden on the right of the goddess holds a *kamaṇḍalu* or water-vessel in her right hand and a parasol in her left and that on the left waives the flywhisk (Fig. 1).[2] Similar composition is seen on a terracotta plaque from Kauśāmbī, now in the private collection of late G.K. Kanodia, Patna (Fig. 2).[3] Fragments of similar terracotta plaques from Kauśāmbī are also housed in the Allahabad Museum (Figs. 3-5)[4] and from Lauriya-Nandangarh in the Indian Museum, Calcutta.[5] The *cāmara*-bearer maidens flanking Gaja-Lakṣmī are also present on the sanctum door-lintel of the Muktesvara temple at Bhubaneśwar (Fig. 6)[6] and on the eastern doorway of *jagamohana* of the famous Sun temple at Konark.[7] This feature of the flanking *cāmara*-bearing maidens continued up to the eighteenth century and is found on a wooden door-lintel of a household Jaina shrine, now in the National Museum collection, wherein a four-armed seated Śrī-Lakṣmī is flanked by standing *cāmara*-bearing maidens along with elephant riders (Fig. 7)[8] and on a Baroda Museum rectangular panel, probably from the top of a similar wooden door frame (Fig. 8).[9]

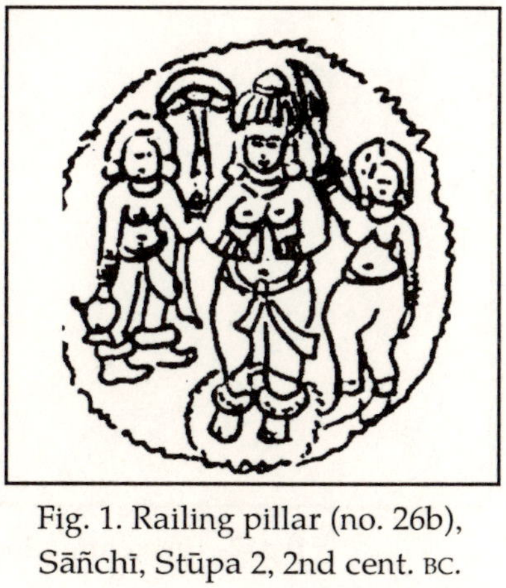

Fig. 1. Railing pillar (no. 26b), Sāñchī, Stūpa 2, 2nd cent. BC.

The flanking maidens carrying flywhisk have textual sanction.[10] But no such literary injunction about the attendants holding parasol and pitcher has been found so far and as such the maidens carrying pitcher in the Gaja-Lakṣmī panels have so far not been satisfactorily identified.

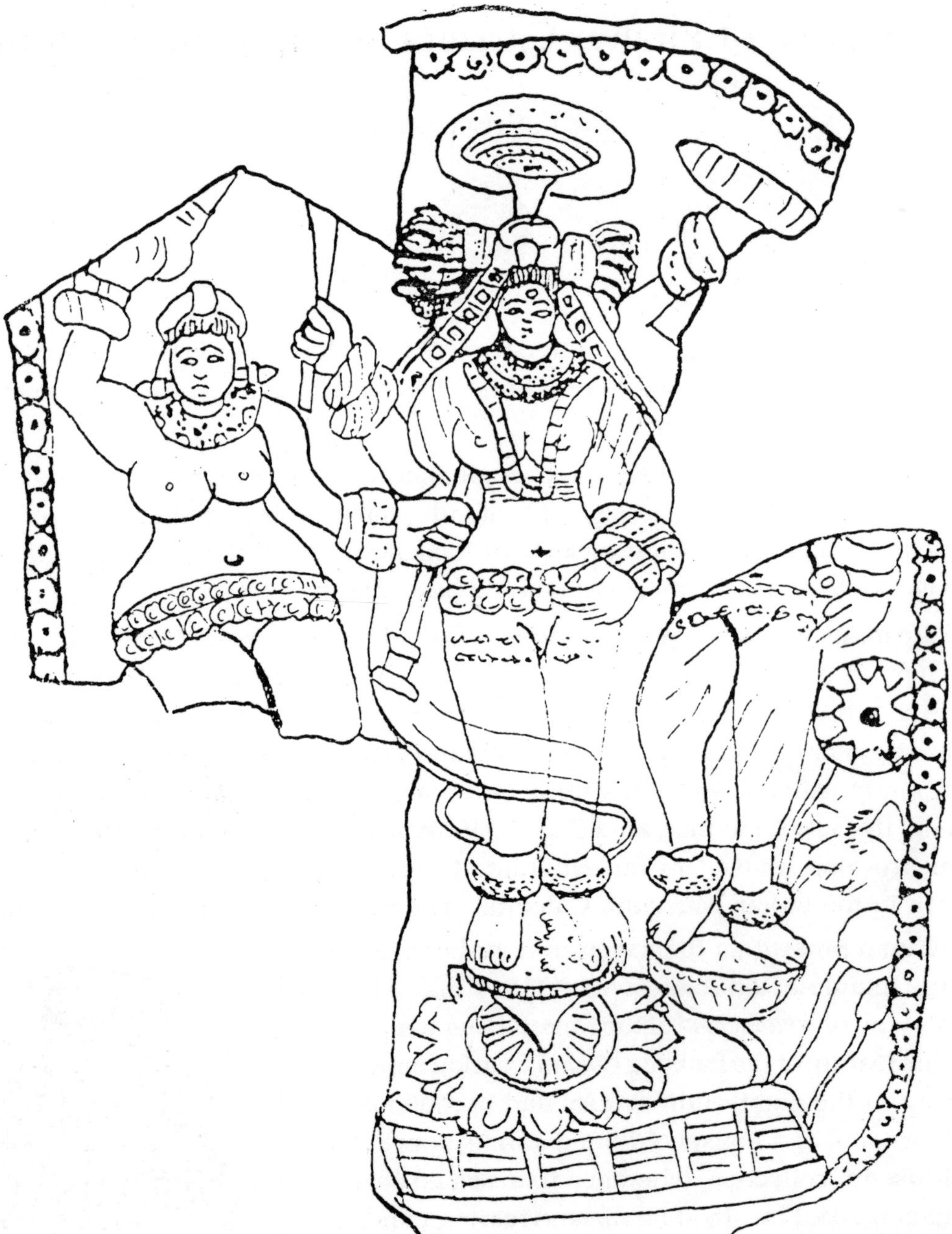

Fig. 2. Terracotta plaque, Kauśāmbī, 1st cent. BC (G.K. Kanodia collection, Patna).

Flanking maidens holding pitchers in the Gaja-Lakṣmī panels from Mahābalīpuram, Ellorā, Amjharā and Indragarh have now been brought to our notice by R.C. Agrawala. In absence of any literary evidence these maidens could not be exactly identified but they were taken by scholars as celestial nymphs holding the holy water in pitchers for anointing the goddess.

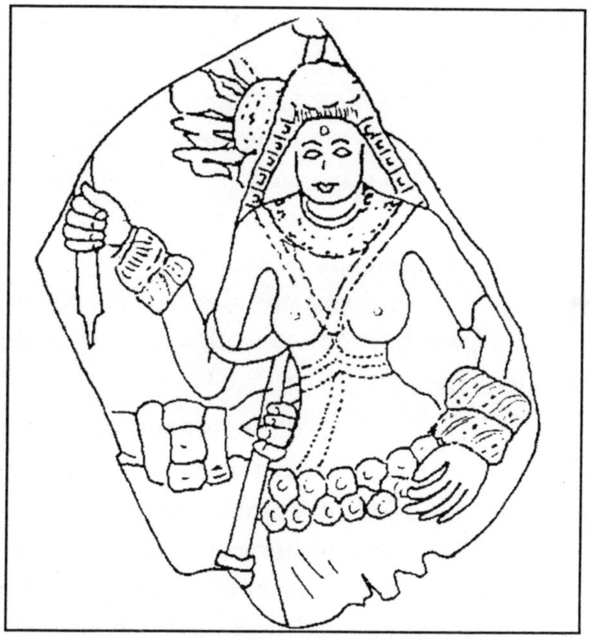

Fig. 3. Terracotta plaque, Kauśāmbī, 1st cent. BC, Allahabad Museum.

However, the Indragarh panel in the Central Museum, Indore, is a rather rare example as regards the representation of the flanking pitcher-carrier maidens. It is the only panel of Gaja-Lakṣmī in our knowledge, in which these pitcher-carrier female attendants are shown with their *vāhanas*. Although the upper part of these flanking maidens is broken, their lower half provides a clear clue for their correct identification. The maiden on the left of the goddess stands on a crocodile and that on the right on a tortoise. Since *makara* and *kacchapa* are well-known *vāhanas* of the *nadī-devīs*, Gaṅgā and Yamunā respectively, R.C. Agrawala rightly identifies these pitcher-carrying maidens with these river goddesses. He also expresses the need for their close scrutiny and corroboration by literary texts.[11]

After going through his articles on the Indragarh panel published in *Kalā,* vols. VII and VIII, we have all along been searching for a literary evidence to corroborate the above-cited representation of the pitcher-carrying maidens flanking Gaja-Lakṣmī. We are happy to have found two such literary evidences, which corroborate the close association of Gaja-Lakṣmī with Gaṅga and Yamunā, the holy river-goddesses. These evidences are taken from the *Viṣṇu Purāṇa* and *Śrīmad Bhāgavata Purāṇa* in the context of the churning of the *Kṣīrasāgara,* the Ocean of Milk, by the gods and demons. According to the *Viṣṇu Purāṇa, Kāmadhenu, Vāruṇī, Kalpavṛkṣa, Candramā, Viṣa* and Dhanvantari with his *kamaṇḍalu* of nectar were churned out of the ocean. After that the lustrous goddess Śrī-Lakṣmī seated on a full-blown lotus flower and holding lotus-stalk in her hands came out.[12]

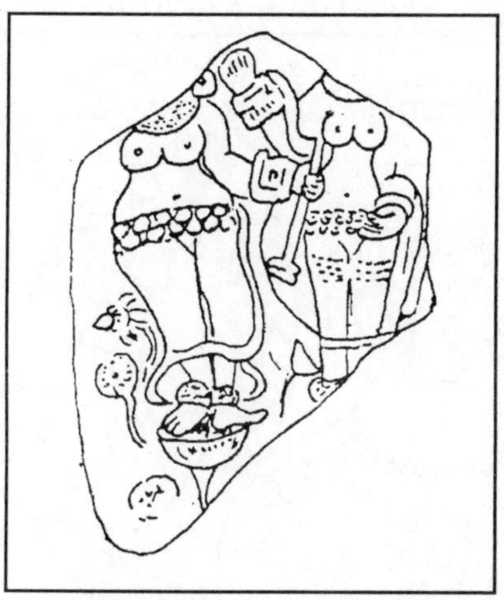

Fig. 4. Terracotta plaque, Kauśāmbī, 1st cent. BC, Allahabad Museum.

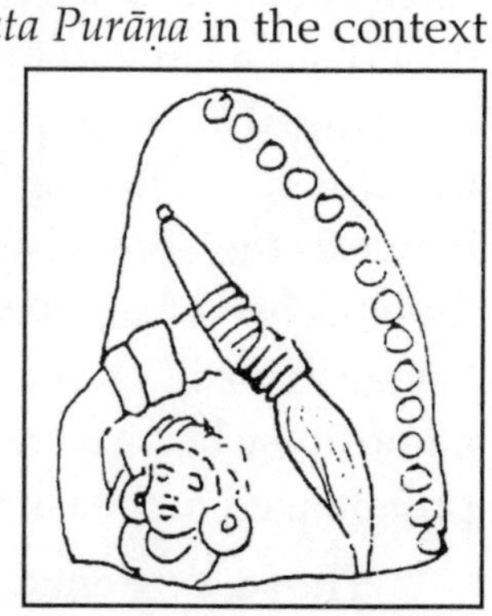

Fig. 5. Terracotta plaque, Kauśāmbī, 1st cent. BC, Allahabad Museum.

Delighted with heavenly and pleasant presence of Śrī-Lakṣmī, sages began to pray her with *Śrī-sūkta,* Gandharvas began to enthral her with their sweet and melodious singing and Apsarases began dancing to please her. At that moment rivers, Gaṅgā, etc., presented themselves with their holy water to anoint Śrī-Lakṣmī and the *dikgajas* bathed her by pouring that sacred water from the golden jars.[13]

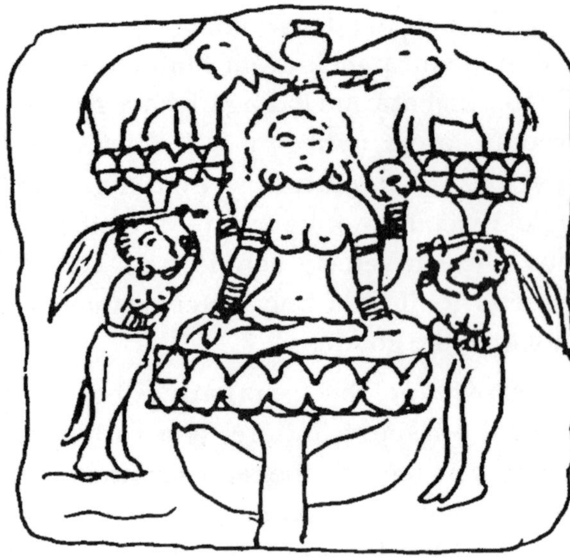

Fig. 6. Gaja-Lakṣmī, Mukteśvara temple, Bhubaneswar, 7th cent. AD.

Almost similar description is available in the *Bhāgavata Purāṇa,* which speaks: 'then, Śrī, the beloved of Viṣṇu, came out of the ocean. The lustre of her glittering body was radiating brightness and causing all the directions shine. Indra placed a wonderful *āsana* or throne for her. The most excellent rivers, in personified form (*mūrtimatī*), brought their pure water in golden jars for her anointment and *dik-gajas,* the elephants of directions, bathed Śrī, who held lotus flowers in her hands, by pouring jars full of that water over her'.[14] In *Viṣṇu Purāṇa,* Ṛṣis, Gandharvas, Meghas (clouds), Samudra, Varuṇa, Sarasvatī and Nāgas are also described as attending in person and offering different presents to the goddess.[15] The only difference between the above two references is the absence of the name of the river Gaṅgā in the *Bhagavata Purāṇa.* But the name of the holy river-goddess is well pronounced in the narration.

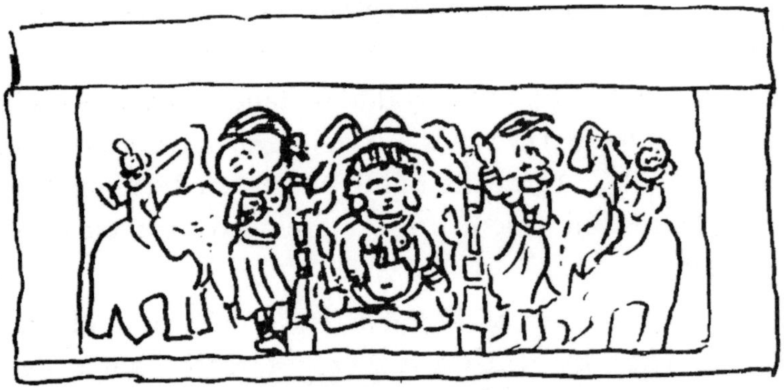

Fig. 7. Lintel of a wooden doorframe, Jain, Western India, 18th cent. National Museum, New Delhi.

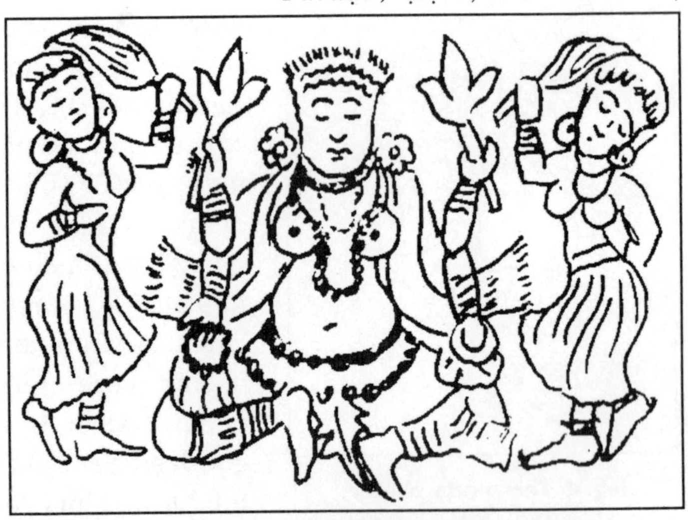

Fig. 8. Fragment of a wooden doorframe, Western India, 18th cent. Baroda Museum

These evidences of the *Viṣṇu Purāṇa* and the *Bhāgavata Purāṇa* certainly corroborate the representation of the flanking pitcher-carrying maidens in Gaja-Lakṣmī panels and leave no doubt in identifying them with the holy river goddesses, Gaṅgā and Yamunā. Thanks to the artist of the Indragarh panel for carving specifically the *vāhanas* of the flanking maidens and thus helping us to identify them.

Pitchers in the hands of the flanking female attendants in the Gaja-Lakṣmī panels were supposed to contain the

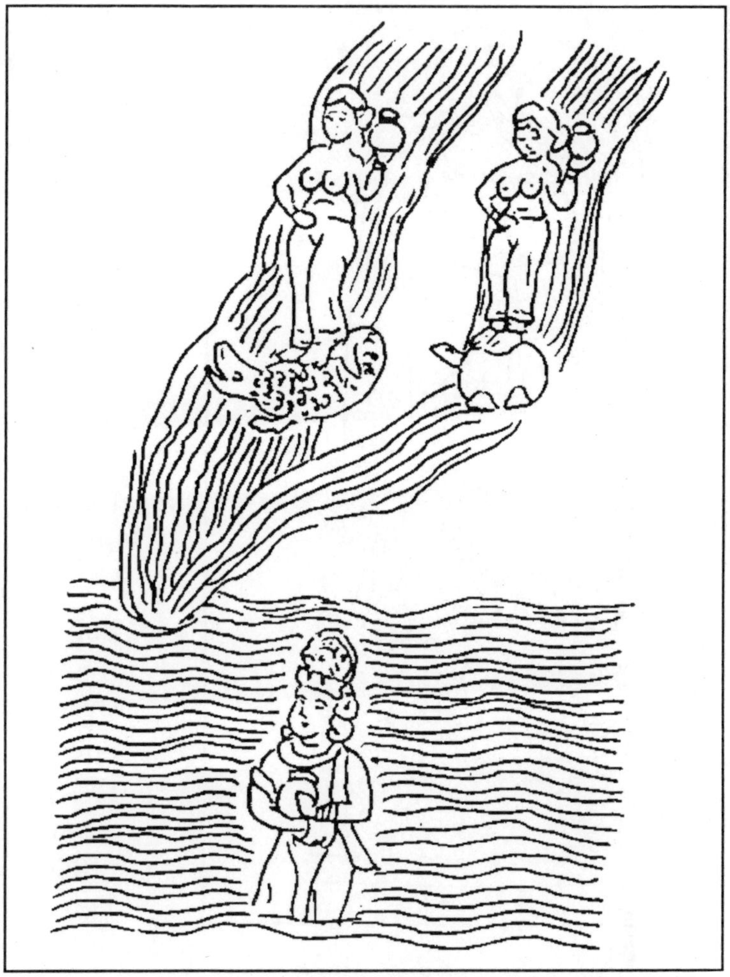

Fig. 9. Gaṅgā-Yamunā, Udaigiri cave, Madhya Pradesh, Gupta period.

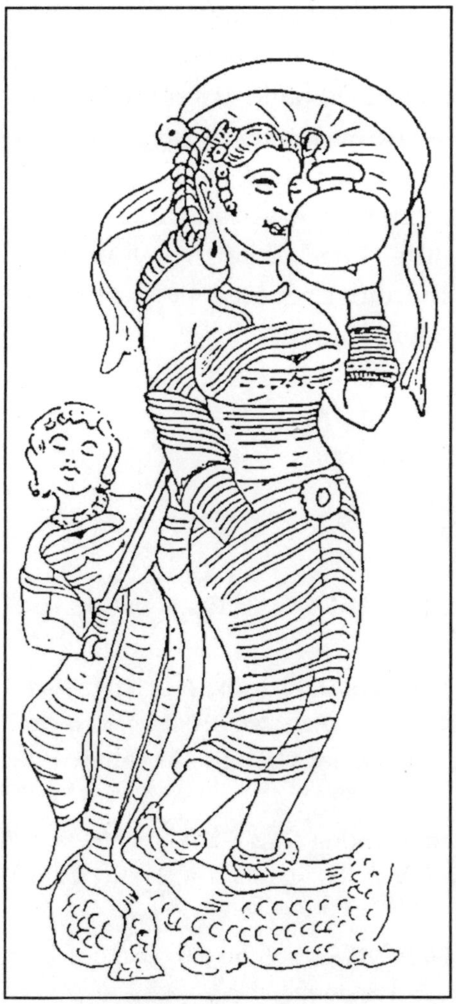

Fig. 10. Gaṅgā (terracotta), Ahicchchatra, Gupta period. National Museum, New Delhi.

holy water and thus symbolized the carriers as *nadī-devīs* or the river goddesses. Now with this singular representation of the *vāhanas, makara* and *kacchapa* below their feet in the panel from Indragarh, these pitcher-carrying maidens in all other panels even without their *vāhanas* are to be taken none other than Gaṅgā and Yamunā.

Moreover, the river goddesses Gaṅgā and Yamunā from the very beginning are shown as holding a *ghaṭa* or vessel in their upraised hand. The representation was started as early as in the Gupta period. The best example may be cited from a cave-wall at Udayagiri in Madhya Pradesh, on which there is a very lively carving of the river goddesses, in natural and personified forms. The meeting of

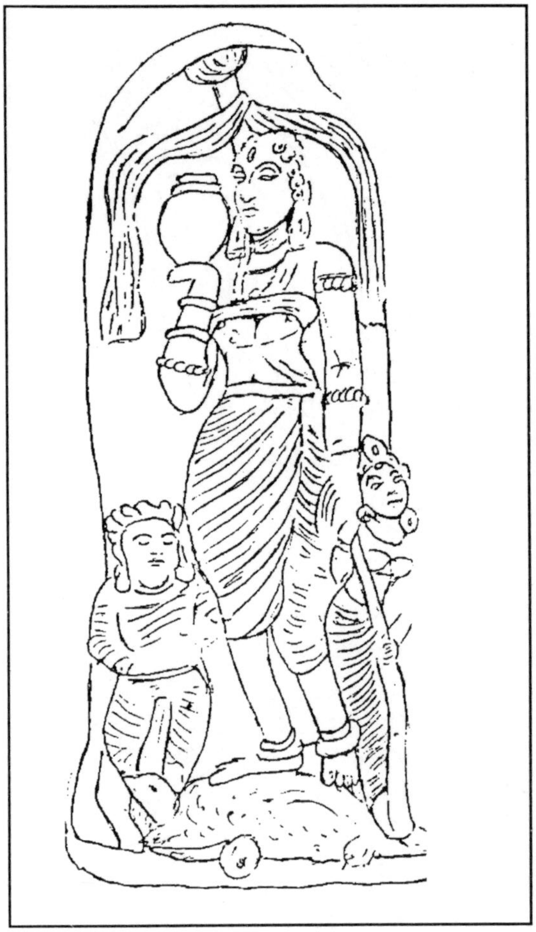

Fig. 11. Yamunā (terracotta), Ahicchchatra, Gupta period. National Museum, New Delhi.

these rivers at Prayāga (Allahabad) and finally with the lord of ocean shown therein is quite picturesque. Gaṅgā on *makara* and Yamunā on *kacchapa* and the ocean-god all have a water-vessel in their hands (Fig. 9). The other similar beautiful examples are the life-size terracotta figures of these river goddesses from Ahicchatrā. Standing majestically on their *vāhanas* and attended by a parasol-bearer maiden, these figures of the river goddesses also hold a *ghaṭa* in their hands (Figs. 10, 11). In subsequent period also, the personified figures of these holy rivers were always shown with a vessel in their upraised hands.

It means the *ghaṭa* or jar is a symbol of holy water and when it is held by a female figure in her upraised hand, it symbolizes the figure as a holy river herself as the embodiment of holy water. And again when the pitcher-carrier maidens are shown attending to the Gaja-Lakṣmī, they are none other than the most revered holy rivers of India, Gaṅgā and Yamunā.

Notes and Reference

1. For all these forms of Gaja-Lakṣmī, see A.L. Srivastava, *Śilpa-Śrī: Studies in Indian Art & Culture,* Delhi, 1990, pp. 96-112, pls. 37-59.
2. Sir John Marshall *et al.*, *Monuments of Sanchi,* London, 1940, Vol. 3, Pl. lxxix; A.L. Srivastava, Conception of Rājya-Lakṣmī and her Plastic Representation in Indian Art, *Abhinandana Bhāratī* (Prof. K.K. Handiqui Felicitation Volume), Kamarupa Anusandhana Samiti, Guwahati, 1982, p. 143, Fig. 5.
3. A.L. Srivastava, A Kauśāmbī Terracotta Plaque Representing Rājya-Lakṣmī, *Journal of Ganganath Jha Kendriya Sanskrit Vidyapeetha,* Allahabad, Vol. xxxvi, nos. 1-4, 1980, pp. 195-199 and Figs.
4. S.C. Kala, *Terracottas in the Allahabad Museum,* New Delhi, 1980, cat. no. 60, acc. no. 4698, Fig. 23; cat. no. 61, Fig. 24 and cat. no. 197, Fig. 92; A.L. Srivastava, *op. cit.*
5. See S.K. Mukhopadhyaya, Terracottas from Lauriya-Nandangarh in the Indian Museum, Calcutta, *Lalit Kalā,* No. 18, 1977, p. 37, Pl. III a and b.

6. K.S. Behera, Lakṣmī in Orissan Art & Literature in D.C. Sircar (ed), *Lakṣmī & Sarasvatī in Art and Literature,* Calcutta (now Kolkata), 1970, p. 93, Pl. IV, Fig. 8.
7. *Ibid.*
8. V.P. Dwivedi, Jaina Wood Carving in the National Museum Collection in U.P. Shah and M.A. Dhaki (ed), *Aspects of Jaina Art &Architecture,* Ahmedabad, 1975, p. 419, Fig. 5.
9. *Ibid.*, p. 420, Fig. 11.
10. *Matsya Purāṇa,* 260, 4.5: पार्श्वे तस्यास्प्रियः कार्याश्चामरव्यग्रपाणयः।

    Mānasollāsa, 1.97: चामरैर्वीज्यमानां च योषिद्रभ्यां पार्श्वयो द्वयोः।

    Dhyānamālā by Srīrāma, MSS, folio 33 (an unpublished work preserved in the Utkal University Library, Cuttack). स्प्रियौ पार्श्वे द्वै कार्ये शुभे चामरहरत्तके।
11. R.C. Agrawala, An Interesting Gaja-Lakṣmī Figure from Indragarh, Madhya Pradesh, *Kalā,* Vol. VII, pp. 15-16, Fig. 2 on; A Note on Pitcher Carriers in Gaja-Lakṣmī Reliefs, *Kalā,* Vol. VIII, pp. 5-8, Figs. 1-2.
12. *Viṣṇu Purāṇa,* I, 92-98 (Gita Press, Gorakhpur, 12th ed., 2045 V.S., p. 43).
13. *Ibid.,* I, 100-103:

    ततः स्फुरत्कान्तिमती विकासिकमले स्थिता।

    श्रीर्देवी पद्मसस्तस्मादुद्भूता धृतपंकजा।। 100

    तां तुष्टुवुर्मुदा युक्ताः श्रीसूक्तेन महर्षय।। 101

    विश्वावसुमुखास्तस्या गन्धर्वाः पुरुतो जगुः।

    घृताचीप्रमुखास्तत्र ननृतुश्चाप्सरोगणाः।। 102

    गंगाद्याः सरितस्तोयैः स्नानार्थमुपतस्थिरे।

    दिग्गजा हेमपात्रमादाय विमलं जलम्।

    स्नापयांचक्रिरे देवीं सर्वलोकमहेश्वरीम्।। 103
14. *Śrīmad Bhāgavata Purāṇa*, VIII, 8.8, 10, 14 (*vide* Indumati Misra, *Pratimā Vijñāna,* 2nd edn., Bhopal, 1987, pp. 158-159, in 2.) .

    ततश्चाविभूत् साक्षाच्छ्री रमा भगवत्परा।

    रंजयन्ती दिशाः कान्त्या विद्युत् सौदामिनी यथा।। 8

    तस्या आसनमानिन्ये महेन्द्रो महदद्भुतम्।

    मूर्तिमत्यः सरिच्छ्रेष्ठा हेमकुम्भैर्जलं शुचि।। 10

    ततोऽभिषिषिचुर्देवीं श्रियं पद्मकरां सतीम्।

    दिगिभाः पूर्णकलशैः................।। 14
15. *Ibid.,* VIII, 8, 12-16.

12

Some Aspects of Inscribed Jaina Images

Krishna Kumari Myneni

Religion always played a major role in the development of art, architecture and the craft works, particularly in carving the metal images. In South India, besides Hinduism, Jainism contributed to the cultural heritage to a great extent. The deep impressions that Jainism has left in the annals of Indian history and its contribution to the Indian thought and culture is considerable. Like the Hindu temples, the Jain *Basadis* were the centres of the fivefold activities, i.e. worship, feeding, medical care, shelter and education. It is quite often observed by the historians that the contribution of Jainism is not only unique but also substantial in terms of both quality and quantity. The art forms created by the artist-sculptors and the craftsmen of different regions of South India display a deep commitment to the Jaina *Dharma,* without sacrificing its inherent aesthetic appeal.[1]

Jainism favoured the worship of *Tīrthaṅkaras* in image form enshrined in the Jaina *Basadis* and in this aspect we do not find much difference between the two religions, i.e. Jainism and Hinduism. As observed and rightly pointed out by Jyoti Prasad Jain as regards the spirit of Jaina art, the master artists not only adopted the architectural and sculptural style prevalent in their places and time but also preferred to include contemporary cultural traits and ideology.[2] In case of building the religious edifices in Jaina faith, it is well noticed that the efforts went through more or less the same stages of development as that of the Brahmanical temples.[3] The Jain temples, since they catered the social, economic and religious needs of the devotees like the Hindu temples, had to be quite large and beautiful enough to attract the large number of devotees and other people. On the other hand, it may be said that they had to foster the religious fervour of the people by the ritual worship of the icons. In image making and image worship Jainism took a lead and it is found that massive stone sculptures of *Tīrthaṅkaras* were consecrated in the sanctum-sanctorum of the Jaina *Basadis.* Besides the main icons, the *kautuka, utsava* and *abhiṣēka mūrtis* or *beras* in metal were also installed in the *Basadis,* majority of which were endowed with the characteristic features of *Jinas.* In the present paper, it is intended to study the inscribed images of the Jaina *Tīrthaṅkaras* of South India in general and the two Jaina icons of 12th century AD preserved and exhibited in the

Victoria & Albert Museum, London in particular, to offer plausible explanations with regard to the basic ideas and intentions of the artists for carving the images in stone and metal with inscriptions as well as their value.

From the *āyagapaṭas* found at Mathura, which are anterior to the Jaina images, we can get the earliest evidence of Jain worship. It is known from the inscriptions on the *āyāgapaṭas* that these slabs were probably placed on the raised platform for worship.[4] The *āyāgapaṭas* are of two types – having symbols and *Tīrthaṅkara* images with inscriptions. Many square stone slabs bearing mostly the figure of Jaina *Tīrthaṅkara* in the centre and some auspicious motifs such as *svastika, śrīvatsa, nandipāda, triratna, kalaśa, puṣpadāma, Vardhamāna, mīna-mithuna* and *vaijayantī,* etc., on its corners or sides have been found from Mathura that contained some inscriptions.[5] It is mentioned in some of the inscriptions found on these slabs that the purpose of setting up of *āyāgapaṭa* was to the worship the *arhat* (*arhat pūjaye).*[6]

In understanding the reasons behind the deliberate encouragement of the laity by the Jaina teachers for performing the image worship and also the erection of the Jina images, the inscribed images throw a welcome light. It is in this perspective the inscribed image of Ādinātha from the village Pervali of Karlapalem Mandal of Guntur district (now placed in Govt. Museum, Guntur) can be studied. The high pedestal of the standing image of Ādinātha contains an inscription-(*Ādināthasvāmy-Pratimāra-makattina-stāpita-Guṇa Nandi Āchāryana-.....)* which states that a certain Guṇa Nandi Āchārya consecrated this Ādināthasvāmī image. Although the inscription is not dated, on the basis of its palaeograhical characters, it can be ascribed to 4th - 5th centuries AD.[7]

Not only the inscribed Jina images provide the information about the cultic practices centred around certain Jina images, but sometimes they also bring to light evidence of unusual historical significance. The three inscribed *Tīrthaṅkara* images are found near Vidiśa, of which two are of Candraprabha (8th Jina) and the third one is that of Puṣpadanta (9th Jina) according to the inscriptions. While mentioning about the name of the Jinas that were consecrated, information is also given about the donor of the images. In this connection, the three inscriptions of the Jina images refer to *Mahārājādhirāja* Rāmagupta as responsible for the carving of these images.[8] K.D. Bajpai has identified this Rāmagupta with the Gupta ruler and the elder brother of Chandragupta Vikramaditya. The label inscriptions of the Jina images thus provide some valuable information of the installation of the Jina images by the Imperial Gupta rulers, whose historicity and identification posed problems till the discovery of the inscribed Jina images.

The inscribed images of Jinas on the hill at Konakondla closely resemble the Jina images reported from Pedatumbulam (No. 2505 of the Madras Museum) and the two images from Vemulavada in their execution and the iconographical details.[9] The Konakondla images carved on red slab stone are about four and a half feet high and have circular *prabhās* round their heads. The triple parasol is found above their heads and the images are in *kāyotsarga* posture. Another interesting thing is that a sketch of a Jina in *kāyotsarga* posture is incised on the hill on horizontal level and rocky ground suggesting the idea of the sanctum of an open Jinālaya to be constructed on the hill. Although S. Gopala Krishna Murtthy has stated that the writing below the Jina figures was a Rashtrakuta habit,[10] it is difficult to agree with him as the archaeological evidences present a different picture. Another important Jaina centre that gave rise to the inscribed Jina images is Danavulapadu (Jammalamadugu Tq of Cuddapah District). From the inscription of the Jina image it can be gathered that the Rashtrakuta king with the title "Nityavarśa" (Indra III or Govinda III ?) was responsible for the installation of the Jina image.[11] Another image inscription mentions the construction of a stone seat for the bath of the image of Śāntinātha by the same Rashtrakuta king who is referred to by his title only.[12] These records provide ample evidence for the royal patronage extended by the Rashtrakutas for the worship of the Jina images.

The image inscription found on the pedestal of a Jina image in the Rajeśvara temple of Vemulavada (Siricilla Tq. Karimnagar District) refers to the construction of a Jaina temple named Subhadama Jinālaya by Baddega for the favour of a scholar Somadeva Sūri of the Gauḍa Saṅgha.[13] The temple referred to in the inscription can be identified with the Subhadāma Jinālaya of Vemulavada and Somadeva Sūri. The image of Pārśvanātha and another Jina image housed in the Hyderabad State Museum, containing the inscriptions on the pedestals inform us that the images were installed and the *maṇḍalika* chiefs constructed the temples for them. The insertion of the Jina images into the walls of the Hindu temples and worshipping them as a god along with the other Hindu divinities can also be noticed from Andhra region. One label inscription on a Jina image in the characters of 8th century AD has been noticed at Kesanapalle (Gurazala Tq. Guntur District) with the word *calēśvara.*[14]

Although label inscriptions of the figures are short and sometimes fragmentary in nature, they rarely provide the details of the names of the sculptor also. The best example is the inscribed image of the 23rd Tirthaṅkara-Pārśvanātha carved in black shale stone that hails from Gulbarga, Karnataka State, which is now exhibited in the Victoria and Albert Museum, London (Pl. 12.1). The Jina is carved as standing in *kāyotsarga.* Above his head the Nāga is shown as protecting him, while the figures of *Yakṣa* Dharaṇēndra and *Yakṣī* Padmāvati are carved on either side. The coils of the serpent can be seen at the back of the image. The hair is done in the shape of ringlets. The figure is nude and the face is serene. The seven-hooded serpent is shown prominently over the head of the Jina. Above his head is carved the three-tiered parasol. The figure is highly polished. The inscription below the pedestal in Telugu-Kannada script of 12th century AD refers to the carving of the image after a period of persecution and that the image was made for a temple after its restoration. It also mentions the name of the sculptor as Chakravati Pāloja and such type of reference to the sculptor is a rare occurrence. Although this image is comparable with the Pārśvanātha images reported from Hyderabad State Museum[15] in iconography, the image under consideration is important since it provides the information about the sculptor and also about the restoration of a Jain temple.

Inscription on the pedestals or below the Jina images are found not only on the stone sculptures but also on the metal images. From the religious and artistic point of view the Jaina metal images are very important. The inscriptions found on the metal images help us in dating the images, and in tracing the stages which metal art underwent in different periods. Sometimes they provide the crucial and important information like the triumph of the Jina over the other gods or religious faiths. The inscribed bronze image of Sāntinātha in seated posture, displayed at the Victoria and Albert Museum, London, is a rare example of bronze casting that bears an inscription referring to Sāntinātha and Vikram year 1224 (AD 1168) (Pl. 12.2). This remarkable large-scale, solid-cast image depicts the 16th Jina enthroned on a jewelled cushion and surrounded by celestial attendants, elephants and musicians. He sits in a yogic meditation posture, with his hands gently resting, one on the other.

Thus the study of the inscribed images of the Jinas has brought to light certain important issues like the idol worship in Jainism, the transitional stage of worshipping the sacred symbols and Jinas on *āyāgapaṭas,* dating of the images on the basis of the label inscriptions, which are either dated or undated and the construction of temples for enshrining the images or indicating the practice of open *Jinālayas* on hill tops or in natural cave shelters. The image inscriptions have also provided useful informations with regard to the identification of the dynastic rulers whose historicity is questionable. The royal patronage extended to the writers and poets of the Cālukyan period by way of installation of Jina images and the construction of the Jaina temples for the merit of the donor is also evident from the image inscriptions. The study also brings to light the names of the sculptors who were responsible for carving the images and the restoration of the Jain temples.

Notes and References

1. Raghunath Bhatt, Jain Contribution to Art and Architecture, in Haripriya Rangarajan *et. al.* ed. *Jainism Art, Architecture, Literature and Philosophy,* Delhi, 2001, p. 216.
2. Jyoti Prasad Jain, "The Genesis and Spirit of Jaina Art", in A. Ghosh ed., *Jaina Art and Architecture,* Vol. II, New Delhi, 1975, pp. 35-40.
3. K.V. Sounder Rajan, Monuments and Sculpture AD 1000 to 1300 South India in A. Ghosh ed., *op. cit.*, pp. 310-34.
4. R.C. Sharma, *Mathura Museum and Art,* Mathura, 2nd ed., Delhi, 1976, p. 36.
5. V.S. Agrawala, "Catalogue of Mathura Museum", *JUPHS,* XXIII, 1950, Pt. 1-2, pp. 69-7; Aniquities Nos. Q2, 569, 1603, 2313, 2563; A. Ghosh, *op. cit.,* Pls. 1, Mathura Museum, Q2, 2B, SML (J255), 14 (SMLJ 250), 15 (MM & 49), 16 (SMLJ 248).
6. D.C. Sircar, *Select Inscriptions,* Calcutta, 1942, Bk. II, No. 25, pp. 118-119.
7. G. Jawaharlal, Ādinātha Worship in Andhra, *Proceedings of Andhra Pradesh History Congress,* XXVIth Section, 2002, Anaparti, p. 40.
8. K.D. Bajpai, Ancient Jaina Art of Madhya Pradesh, R.C. Dwivedi ed., *Contribution of Jainism to Indian Culture,* Patna, 1975, pp. 196-199.
9. S. Gopala Krishna Murtthy, *Jain Vestiges in Andhra,* Hyderabad, 1963, pp. 30-31.
10. *Ibid.,* p. 31.
11. G. Jawaharlal, *Jainism in Andhra,* Hyderabad, 1994, p. 190, No. 18, Dānavulapāḍu Inscription.
12. *S.I.I. IX,* pt. I, No. 63; 83 of *Inscriptions of A.P. Cuddapah District,* Vol. I, p. 92.
13. *Ibid.,* No. 20; pp. 194-195.
14. *Ibid., APGRE* of 1965, No. 93.
15. Kiran Kranth Choudary, Some Pārśvanātha Images from Telangana in Haripriya Rangarajan *et. al.* ed., *op. cit.,* pp. 158-160.

13

Little Known Viśvarūpa Image from Himachal Pradesh

Subhashini Aryan

Bajaurā (ancient Hāṭ) village is located a few metres off the Mandi-Kulu highway, about 14 km from Kulu town. It is well known for its Śiva temple popularly known as Basesara Mahādeva (Viśveśvara) temple, built in the Nāgara style with a tall curvilinear *śikhara*. Today this highly impressive stone temple stands within a compound, enclosed by a boundary wall on all the sides. This structure had been erected on the order of an unknown royal patron sometime around AD 800. Within and outside the compound, and all the way down to the bank of the river Beas, flowing past down below, numerous stray stone sculptures and architectural fragments are seen lying scattered, some in very mutilated condition, others in a slightly better state of preservation. These sculptures convey the impression that this village was an important site in ancient and medieval period, and numerous stone temples dedicated to Śiva and Viṣṇu Vaikuṇṭha (whose statues in the round are still extant) existed here. Some European travellers' narratives inform us that there existed a fortress at this site till the closing years of the 19th century, its crenellated walls enclosed numerous *śikhara* style stone temples[1].

However neither the fort nor its walls are seen any longer.

The special focus of my attention in the present paper is a little known stone statue of Viṣṇu Viśvarūpa that stands apart from the rest of the stray sculptures, and which is the only example of Viṣṇu's cosmic form from this region. One more example of the Viśvarūpa image from Mandi was brought to the notice of the scholars by T.S.Maxwell recently[2] but it is datable to a very late period and does not stand comparison with the image under discussion (Pl. 13.1).

The life-sized free standing Viśvarūpa figure stands on a pedestal near the small opening in the walled enclosure surrounding the Basesara Mahādeva temple. It is still being worshipped by the local villagers. Viśvarūpa or Viṣṇu in his cosmic form had been revealed to Arjuna, one of the Pāṇḍava brothers, by Lord Kṛṣṇa in the battlefield of Kurukṣetra with a view to urge and exhort him to fight with his enemies and vanquish them. A detailed visual imagery of this cosmic form derives from the *Srīmad-Bhāgavata Gītā*, expounded by Śrī Kṛṣṇa Himself (Ch. 11. verse 16) which was concretised in plastic form by the sculptors almost all over northern India. Viṣṇu's central human face is full and overload, with a perfectly serene expression which is further emphasized by his large lotiform half-closed contemplative eyes. He wears a *kirīṭa mukuṭa* engraved with delicate floral patterns, that recalls the identical crown worn by the same god in a Gupta period sculpture from Mathura[3] as well as by the Kārttikeya statue *in situ* at the Chhatrarhi temple of Ādi Śakti Devī. A pair of rosettes above his ears are attached to his crown. This feature is common to all the sculptures from Kashmir and Himachal Pradesh executed between 7th and 13th centuries. His distended earlobes hold large circular beaded earrings, in continuation of the Gupta and post-Gupta sculptural tradition. Flanking the central human head are the Man-lion (Narasiṁha) face in three-quarter view and the Boar (Varāha) head in profile, shown as if emerging from behind the vertical parallel rows of ringlets of hair falling over Viṣṇu's powerful, massive shoulders. The three heads are set on a thickset physique. Two of his four arms are broken, and in the original statue, must have rested on the standing figures of personified *āyudhas, Gadādevī* and *Cakra-puruṣa.* The pedestal of the Viśvarūpa statue still survives, intact with three pairs of feet, broken from ankles, evidently belonging to the god and his *āyudhas.* Between Viṣṇu's foot was carved a tiny figure of Bhūdevī which is also broken. In his other two hands, the Viśvarūpa holds his usual attributes, the *padma* and the *saṅkha.* He sports simple beaded ornaments and an *ardhoruka* covers his upper thighs. In addition to his *yajñopavīta*, he has a large floral *vanamālā* draping his entire body, showing prominently around his shoulders, and decorated with three rosettes. The anatomical modelling is competent. It has remarkable affinities with contemporary images from prominent centres of Gupta sculpture such as Pawaya (Gwalior), Deogarh etc. The anatomical modelling, of our Bajaura Viśvarūpa is not marked by an articulation of chest and pelvic muscles, nor is the torso 'V' shaped, nor do the facial features bear any resemblance to the images chiselled in Chamba-Kashmiri style in our area of study. The figure of the god conveys an illusion of being short, but actually it is not so; it is perfectly well proportioned.

The visual imagery created by the north Indian sculptors to give form to the Cosmic manifestation of the Lord Preserver of the Universe is a large *prabhamaṇḍala* teaming with a profusion of figures carved with in horizontal tiers. Tiny, well-carved figures[4] of Adityas, Vasus, Rudras, Aświnī Kumar, the Maruts, and all the semi-gods in a diversity of postures, engaged in a variety of activities, contribute to the liveliness of the carving. It must be stressed that some of Viṣṇu's incarnations such as Sankarsan, etc., are carved in high relief and portrayed as emanating from both sides of his crown. From the apex of the *kirīṭa mukuṭa* projects the foreshortened form of Hayagrīva.

A curious feature of this *prabhāmaṇḍala* is a series of disembodied heads carved all around the outer rim, nine is profile on each side, with a centrally carved head in fully frontal view at the apex. The peripheral heads forming a series merely by repetition have been termed by T.S.Maxwell "a *rakśāvalī* or ritually protective boundry, with no overlapping suggestive of an emanatory progression."[5] The depiction of such peripheral heads, conceived originally by the Mathura sculptor, had been perpetuated by the sculptors of Śāmalājī in Gujarat, Deogarh and Kannauj in Madhya Pradesh, and Baijnath in Almora in the modern state of Uttaranchal, their number varying from image to image. In all these examples, some effort has been made at differentiating one face from another. The Bajaura sculptor made a departure from the tradition by featuring most of them in an identical manner – they all sport identical *jaṭābhāra* coiffure; their faces have the same cast and expression. A closer examination, however, of the faces carved on the right side reveals that the last two or three sport a beard, and their ferocious expression is conveyed by open mouths and growling eyes. Many *bhadramukhas* depicted in the stone temple *candraśālās* feature the *raudra* aspect of Śiva (the face occupying the right side of the central Śiva head) in the same manner. The Deogarh Viṣṇu Viśvarūpa, chiselled contemporaneouely, with the Bajaura Viśvarūpa has crowned heads of *dvādaśādityas* on the right side distinguishable from those on the left whose hair is tied up in rather flat *jaṭabhāra*. Another striking departure made by our Bajaura artist is the neat symmetrical arrangement of all the figures carved on the *prabhāmaṇḍala* in horizontal registers. The earliest images of Viṣṇu Viśvarūpa were created by the Mathura[6] artists in AD first and second centuries. From iconographic viewpoint, our Bajaura sculpture harks back to the ancient tradition initiated and evolved by the Mathura sculptors during the Kushana and Gupta periods. It also shares numerous features with the Viśvarūpa images chiselled in subsequent centuries by the *śilpīs* from Sāmlājī,[7] Deogarh[8] and Baijnāth in the Almora in Kumaun hills, and looks forward to the well-known images of the God from Kannauj (AD ninth century)[9].

This sculpture is a local version of the sculptural iconography and style developed in the Madhyadesh by accomplished artists. The style is, undoubtedly, provincial, but our Bajaura master was no less competent, imaginative and consummate. Drawing upon the iconographic and stylistic traditions crystalised and perfected by the Gupta and post-Gupta artists, he created a highly impressive image of the Viśvarūpa. Stylistically, it is closer to the Madhyadesh tradition than to the large number of locally carved sculptures that had been executed in a style that was an admixture of Gupta and Chamba-Kashmiri sculptural styles. It seems that, as at Bharmaur and Chhatrarhi in Chamba district, at Bajaura also, two stylistic groups of sculptors were available – one trained in the Madhyadesh tradition, the other at Chamba-Kashmiri style and iconography. The latter group appears to have chiselled the figural sculptures embellishing the Viśveśvara Mahādava temple, the twin Viṣṇu Vaikuṇṭha statues and a few more sculptures. A sculptor from the former group carved the Viṣṇu Viśvarūpa 8th century AD sculpture and numerous image which are lying scattered all over the place around the grandiose Śiva temple of Bajaura.

Notes and References

1. Moorcroft and Trebeck, *Travels in the Himalayan Provinces of Hindustan and the Punjab,* Vol. 2, London, 1841, p. 328.
2. T.S. Maxwell, *Vishvarupa,* OUP, 1988, p. 38.
3. *Ibid.,* This has been discussed in detail by Maxwell.

4. *Ibid.*
5. *Ibid.*, pp. 139-141.
6. *Ibid.*, pls. 10, 49-53, 55.
7. *Ibid.*, pls. 57-58.
8. *Ibid.*, pls. 63-64.
9. *Ibid.*, pls. 66-70.

14

Kapileśvara Temple of Charada

P.K. Nayak

Charada, situated 5 km west of Binka, a *tehsil* headquarter of Suvarnapur district of Orissa, has a temple complex on a rocky outcrop (Pl. 14.1). It has a beautiful legend about the self revelation of the *liṅgam*/Lord Śiva in Charada. It is said that the Gaṅga king Anaṅgabhīmadeva, suffering from an incurable disease was advised to go on a pilgrimage. The king, after consulting his *Rājaguru* and astrologers, decided to start his religious tour towards western Orissa. In course of his tour he reached Charada area and encamped with his retinue at a place called Rahelā. At night the king saw a dream that Lord Śiva is instructing him to take a dip in the river to wipe out his sins and cured the disease. Then he should proceed backwards from the bank . On the way he would find the Lord. The Lord had been established in the form of *liṅgam* by the famous sage Kapila and hence called Lord Kapileśvara. It was a strange dream. The king woke up in the morning and acted upon the divine order of the Lord. He saw the Lord in the form of *liṅgam*. Then the king ordered his officers for the construction of a temple for the god and stayed there till its completion.[1]

The temple facing east consists of a *vimāna* and a *jagamohana*. In between the *vimāna* and *mukhaśālā* there is a vestibule. The sanctum has three prominent parts, viz., *bāḍa* (Pl. 14.2), *gaṇḍī* and *mastaka*. The *vimāna* possesses a *triaṅga bāḍa* namely *pābhāga, jāṅghā* and *baraṇḍa*. The sanctum displays *pancaratha* plan. The vertical segments of the *gaṇḍi* correspond with wall to that of the *bāḍa*. The *pābhāga* has four mouldings. The *jāṅgha* measures 5 feet in altitude. The *baraṇḍa* comprises a large *khura* type moulding above which is noticed a *kanṭhi* (recess). Out of the five *pāgas,* the two *kaṇika pāgas* look like pilasters having moulded base and the top contains hanging festoons from the *kīrtimukha*. The *anuratha* possesses a *Khākhārā muṇḍi*. The niche of the *anuratha* is surmounted by a number of small tiers (*pirḍas),* in succession, gradually receding in size. The niche in the *rāhā* is a simple superstructure crowded by a sloping roof. The *rāhā*-niches contain figures of Gaṇeṣa, Kārttikeya and Pārvatī in southern, western and northern side respectively which was the usual features of Orissan Śiva temples. The *pārśvadevatās* appear to be later in date. The proportionate ratio of the *kaṇika, anuratha*

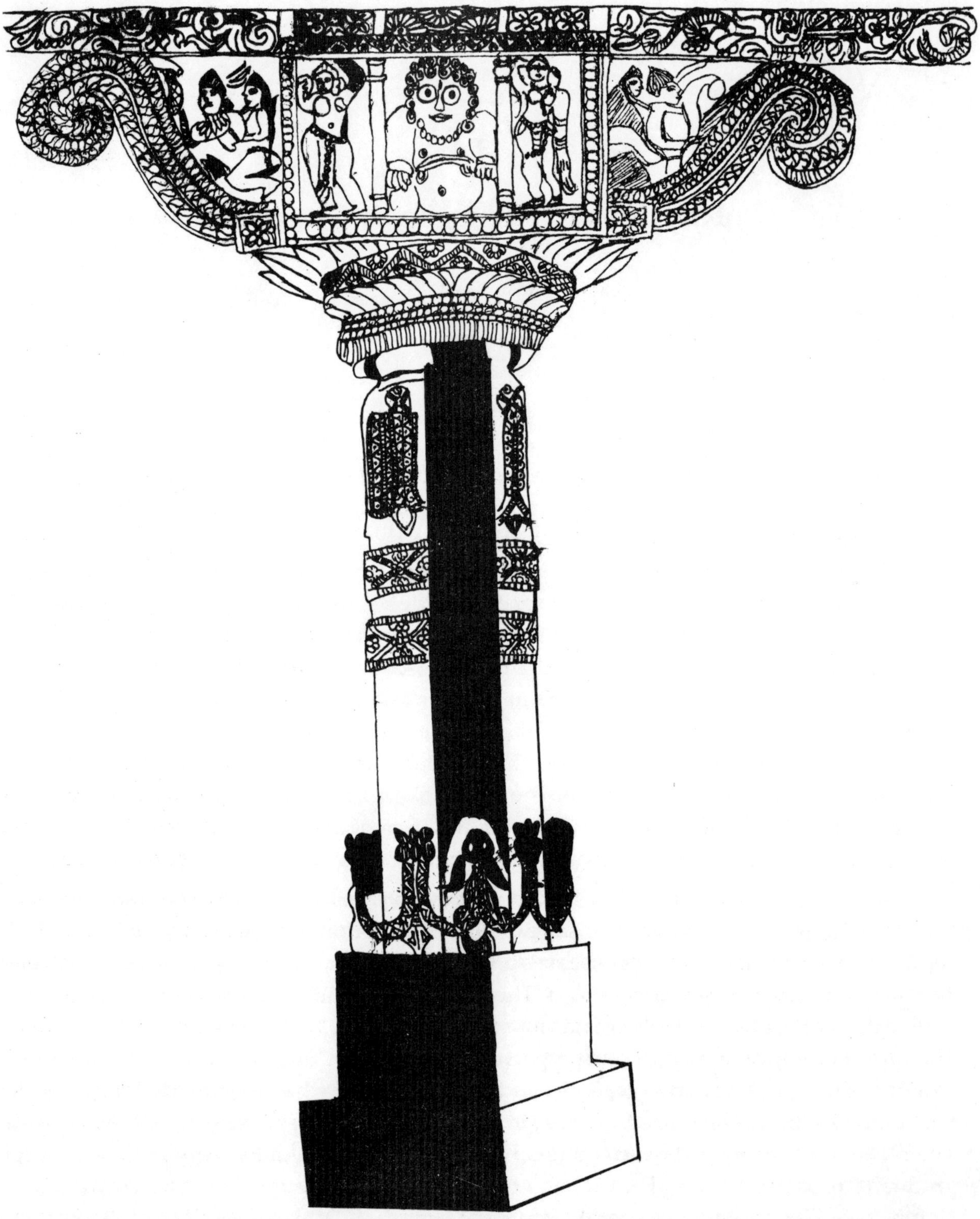

Fig. 1. Pillar, Kapileśvara temple, Charada.

and *rāhā* is 1:2:4.[2] The demarcation between the *pagas* is made by the *dhāra* recesses. In *kaṇika pāgas* is noticed a number of span created by the ribbed right angled structures (*bhūmi āmalakas).* The span (*bhūmi)* is composed of three and a half *bhūmi barandikas.*

The *gaṇḍi* above the *baraṇḍa* rises as a curvilinear spire. The *vimāna* measures about 28' in height. The *gaṇḍi* is heavily plastered and its body contains some erotic figures in stucco, naturally of later date. The *gaṇḍi* ends with the *biṣama* which also exhibits a *pancaratha* plan. The *mastaka* rises from the *biṣama.* It comprises the *beki, āmalaka,* a *khapuri* with a top designed with lotus petals. It is surmounted by a small *āmalaka* above which are metal *kalaśa, Āyudha* (trident) and *dhvaja.* The elements of the *mastaka* above the large *āmalaka* are found in the Chauhan temples of the late medieval period. It suggests that this temple has been repaired whenever necessary during the Chauhan rule. The doorframe like that of the temple of Vaidyanath, does not contain the river goddesses but possesses the Śiva *dvārapalas* at the appropriate places. The sanctum is negotiated by the vestibule which has direct access to the *jagamohana* or *mukhaśālā.*

The *mukhaśālā* has a pillared *maṇḍapa* with twelve engaged pillars and four pillars in the centre. The *mukhaśalā* is square and it measures 24' 10" × 24' 10" externally 19' 3" × 19' 3" internally.[3] It makes a lithic frame very much akin to that of Vaidyanāth. The *mukhamaṇḍapa* has the main entrance in the east between two engaged pillars. On the northern wall of the broad entrance is fixed the image of Kārttikeya and on the south is found the figure of Gaṇeśa. Gaṇesá is represented riding on his mount rat. The rat is an oversize one. Kārttikeya also is shown riding his mount peacock. The *mukhaśālā* possesses two *gavākṣa* projections, one in the north and the other in the south. This has been walled up and plastered. That these two were originally the two balconied porches as at Vaidynāth is clearly evident from its remains existent in the plinth of southern wing. The extended two sides when closed by the brick screen have created an alcove where the *nāyikās* have been placed.

The pillars are highly ornate (Fig. 1). Recently the pillars are burnished with various colours which conceals the minute details of the scroll work. The pillars have three distinct parts, viz., base, shaft and capital. The pillar emerges from a *ghaṭapallava* placed on a square pedestal. The shaft of the pillar is octagonal. The two courses having square cut diamond shaped design surrounding the shaft in the middle which divides it into two halves. The lower portion has in its each facet a *kīrtimukha* and lion figure alternately. The hanging string of pearls are issued from the mouth of the *kīrtimukha.* The facets of upper half preserves the *kīrtimukha* heads and the multistringed garland of pearl beads swinging from the mouth to mouth of these *kīrtimukhas.* A bell suspended from the each garland is noticed in the *ālambas.* The capital is an octagonal slab divided into two having octagonal cross-section. The capital is crowned by a bracket having upward curved ends. It contains *bhāra rakṣakas, caurī* bearers and *vidyādhara.*

The doorframe towards the west which leads to the sanctum is composed of four courses scroll work. The Gajalakṣmī is depicted on the lintel. The flanked pilasters possess entwined *nāga* figures. The second lintel has a beautiful representation of *Śeṣasāyī Viṣṇu.*

In the *mukhaśālā* there are graceful sculptures carved artistically. An image of Harihara is attached to the wall of the *maṇḍapa.* The *samabhaṅga* image carved in high relief is four-armed. Below the slab is depicted the figure of bull to the right and an attendant is sketched to the left. The upper right hand holds a trident while the upper left a conch. A *gaṇa* attendant is noticed on the right side. *Garuḍa,* the vehicle of Viṣṇu, is delineated on the left side. The image is 4 feet 10 inches high and 1 feet 10 inches wide. Another standing image of *Ardhanārīśvara* is also found in the *jagamohana.* It stands in *samabhaṅga* posture. The bull and attendants are found on both the sides. The right upper hand carries a *paraśū* while the lower is in *varada* pose. The left upper catches either a mirror or a *pāsa* and the lower one holds a part of the garment. A *gaṇa* is depicted on the right and the lion on the left. The size of the image is 16 inches by 20 inches. A large size two-armed image of Śiva in *sthānaka* pose is also found here. The right hand is broken and the left is akimbo. He wears *jaṭāmukuṭa* with beautiful *prabhāvalī.*

The bull and an attendant on the sides of the god are carved. The image has an height of 4 feet 10 inches and width of 1 feet 6 inches. Another important figure is of *Naṭarāja*, The ten-armed Śiva is dancing blissfully. The upper most pair of hands hold the snake in an arched form. The next pair to it catches a kettledrum in the right and a spear in the left. Then the normal pair (3rd) of which the left hand is in *gajahasta* while the right is on the chest. The right hand of the fourth pair is raised upward perhaps showing *abhaya* pose and the left is extend downwards displaying *varada* posture. The left hand of the lowest pair moves downward and the right hand also has a similar movement wherein the thumb touches the ring finger. To the right side is carved skeletal figure and to the left a female. A bull is depicted behind the legs. The figures of *alasakanyās ḍālmālikas,* etc., were also noticed in the *mukhamandapa* of Charada as at Vaidyanāth. A standing four-armed image of Gaṇeśa eating *modakas* from the pot is realistically carved sculpture. Donaldson[4] refers to an image of Agni in the temple premises. It is a four armed image standing in *tribhaṅga.* Flames radiate from his head. The head is missing and the right hand is also broken now. There was another four armed image when the author visited it in 1974. The upper pair of hands hold a *khaḍga* in the right and a skull in the left. The lower right carries a knife while left possesses some unidentifiable object. The head radiates flame behind the head. The figure was known there among the local people as that of *Jvālāmukhī.*

At present the temple complex is filled with additional structures of modern times. At present more than of 25 per cent of the population of the villagers are *pūjakas/thanāpati.* It is gathered from the *pūjakas* that there were twenty-two villages which are donated for performance of different kinds of services to the Lord, viz., Phūlmuṭhī was donated for supply of flowers perpetually, Sankara was granted maufi for blowing conches before the lord, Gurdula was given for washing and cleaning of the premises, kitchen, etc. This reminds us of 36 kinds of services (*chatisaniyoga)* arranged by Anaṅgabhīma III for Jagannātha temple at Puri. On epigraphical consideration the date of Vaidyanāth may be fixed in the later half of 11th century AD.[5] As the temple of Charada has close similarities in architectural style and sculptural programme with that of the temples of Vaidyanāth, the time of the former may be placed in the 11th century AD D.R. Das[6] fixes the date of Kapileśvara temple at Charada in between last half of 9th century AD and 1st half of 10th century AD. T.E. Donaldson[7] favours a date of 10th century AD. While Vidya Dehejia[8] assigns a date of 9th century AD.

Acknowledgement

I am thankful to my students – Bharati, Sravani, Sushama and Sujata for the preparation of line drawing.

Notes and References

1. Collected by the author from Late Sri Jagmohan Hota of Papanga.
2. D.R. Das, *Temples of Orissa,* 1982, Delhi, p. 48.
3. T.E. Donaldson, *The Hindu Temple Art of Orissa,* Vol. I, 1985, Lieden, pp. 209-210.
4. *Ibid.,* pp. 211-212.
5. P.K. Nayak, Dating Vaidyanath Temple: The Epigraphic Evidence, *Journal of Orissan History,* Vol. XIII-XIV, Sambalpur, 1995, pp. 61-66; K.C. Panigrahi, *History of Orissa,* Cuttack, 1981, p. 445.
6. D.R. Das, *op. cit.,* p. 42.
7. T.E. Donaldson, *op. cit.,* p. 209.
8. Vidya Dehejia, *Early Stone Temples of Orissa,* New Delhi, 1979, p. 185.

15

Symbols in Indian Art: An Overview

Savita Sharma

Symbols have always been an important and revealing expression of art and beliefs. Whether in concept or form or both, the symbols encompass varied aspects of culture both in terms of time and space. It hardly needs to say that the symbols are not merely the forms in respect of aniconic representations but they are manifestations with deeper meaning. This needs to be explored more and more in order to understand the thought and expression process of mankind. Symbols have frequently been used in different art media. They occupy significant position almost in every kind of artistic expression. The symbols on coins,[1] seals, sculptures, architectures and other objects have their apparent artistic value as well. At the same time they have religious, social and philosophical connotation. Indian art virtually embraced the totality.

The temples were the standing exhibition ground of contemporary life of actuality and imagination in terms of visual language of sculpture and painting.[2] There have always been two parallel factors working separately in art-making in all the media and forms. Firstly, art in terms of beauty (aesthetics) which is pleasing to the senses, has hardly anything to do with the religion. Thus, the representation of *Apsarases* (nymphs) and *nāyikās* in revealing poses, exposing their pulchritude and above all, grossly erotic figures are undoubtedly meant to arouse sensuousness visually. A temple in India was the centre of social life, hence, representation of erotic art gained favour here. The rendering of the endless panorama of life on the ancient temples reveals that this was a world which keeps one glued for long to a life of temporal pleasures and pursuits to which even gods and goddesses were prone.[3] The second and, of course, the more important objective was to get inner pleasure of mind in order to involve the faculties of human consciousness, resulting in a vast galaxy of divine and semi-divine figures, myths and legends. It is, perhaps, here that religion comes in and almost dictates the art.

Through the visual forms of the Indian deities, such as the Buddha, Mahāvira, Viṣṇu, Śiva, etc., though belonging to different faiths, we find expression of the mind and heart of the contemporary people. A.K. Coomaraswamy has explicitly remarked that the formal element in art represents a purely mental activity, *cittā-sanna.*[4] It is worth noticing that the artists depicting the Buddha, Mahāvira and other deities had never seen them, hence, their depictions more or less are the symbolic representations of the divine and supreme reality in anthropomorphic form.[5]

The abstract ideas were also expressed through symbolic language in Indian art from very early times. It dominated the entire realm of Indian art. The language through which art came in a form was that of symbols. The symbols or signs depicting the divine and semi-divine, and the unexpressed concepts represent aspects of paramount truth as seen by man through the ages. The symbols also, however, served the purpose of decoration and space-filling. The symbols which manifest the invisible through the visible form[6] are necessary and helpful intermediaries between the inadequate capacity of the mind of the would-be worshipper and the incommunicable nature and fullness of the unknown whom he adores.[7] A sign or a symbol at the same time is an analogous abbreviated expression of a definitely known things.[8] But, however, the material objects too have been used as symbols. Nature, throughout the Indian art is taken as divine as everything which surrounded the ancient Indian people and, which was impressive by its sublimity, became a direct object of adoration; such as mountains, rivers, springs, plants, animals and birds.[9]

The worship of the Sun was prevalent throughout the world from the times immemorial in different appellations and forms, such as disc, lotus, *svastika*, etc. The warmth and productive power of Sun have always been considered beneficial. Light which dissipates the darkness,[10] was considered by the primitive man as a friend and defender of humanity against evil.[11] In the primitive agriculture world, the livelihood and even destiny, depended upon fertility of the land and domestic animals. Sunshine and rain were considered necessary amidst the threat of drought, flood and storm, etc. These environmental forces which could not be conceived in realistic form, were represented by signs and symbols or personified by certain distinct marks.[12]

The Vedic literature is full of references to the symbolic forms revealing the truth of cosmic realities. The sense of dependence of human welfare on nature, with supposed 'Supernatural' character, led to aniconic, theriomorphic and anthropomorphic forms of worship. The principal environmental forces, represented by Sūrya, Indra, Agni, Vāyu and Varuṇa were given paramount status in the galaxy of deities personifying different elemental aspects of nature and mental status[13] and found depiction in Indian art through symbols and later on in theriomorphic and anthropomorphic forms. These symbols accepted as auspicious symbols such as *Pūrṇaghaṭa* (*Bhadrakalaśa*), *Svastika, Śrīvatsa*, *Cakra, Srivṛkṣa* and *Padma,* find mention in the Vedic literature and later works. These symbols were also associated with different religions with frequent interchanges at a later stage (*c.* 2nd-1st cent. BC). The *Cakra*, for instance, was adopted in Buddhist, Jaina and Brahmanical sects. It is represented by the former two sects on the thrones while in the case of Viṣṇu it comes in the hand. One hundred and eight auspicious symbols are mentioned in the *Harivaṁśa* and *Vāsturatnakoṣa*.[14] These

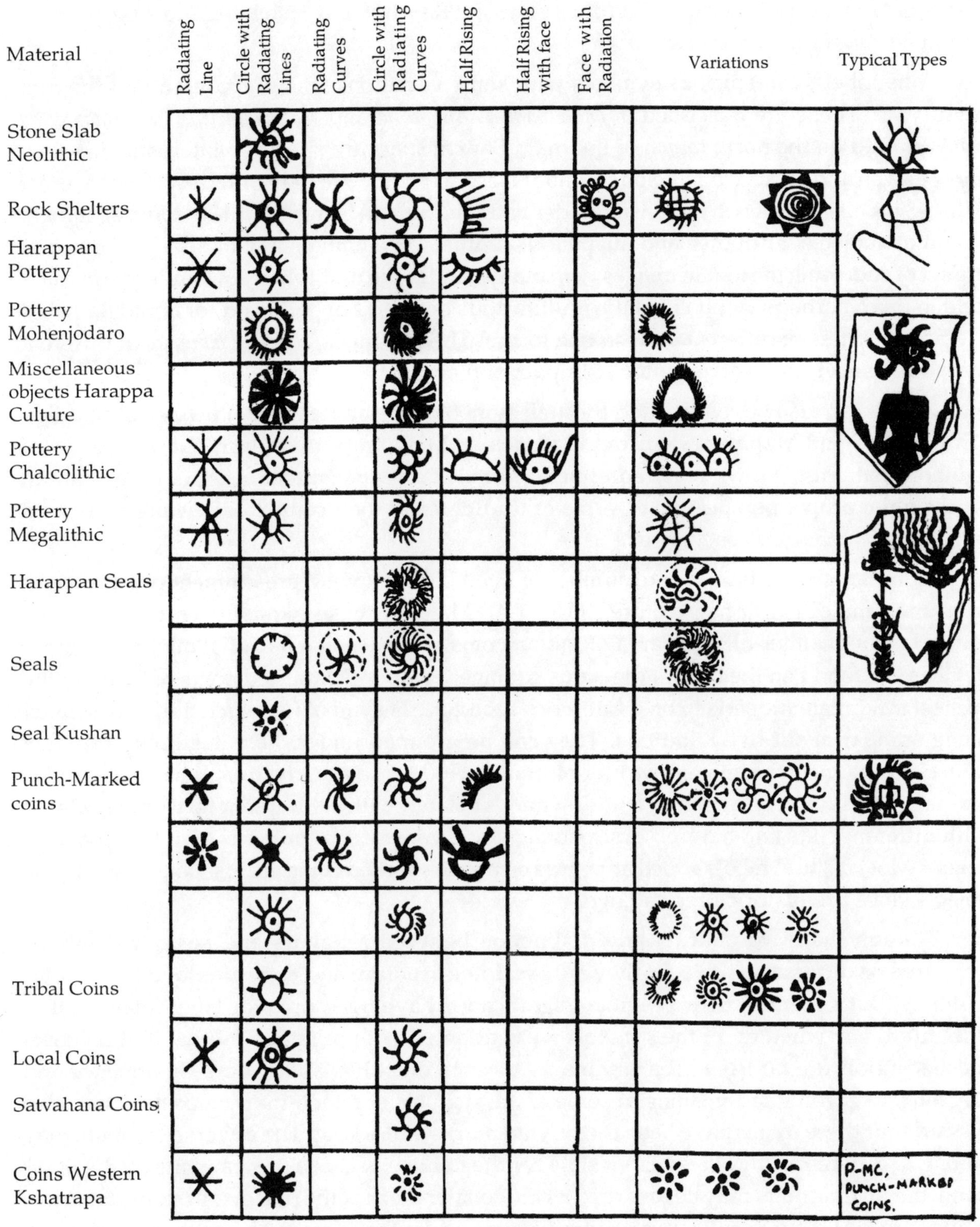
Material
Radiating Line
Circle with Radiating Lines
Radiating Curves
Circle with Radiating Curves
Half Rising
Half Rising with face
Face with Radiation
Variations
Typical Types
Stone Slab Neolithic
Rock Shelters
Harappan Pottery
Pottery Mohenjodaro
Miscellaneous objects Harappa Culture
Pottery Chalcolithic
Pottery Megalithic
Harappan Seals
Seals
Seal Kushan
Punch-Marked coins
Tribal Coins
Local Coins
Satvahana Coins
Coins Western Kshatrapa
P-MC,
PUNCH-MARKED
COINS.

Fig. 1. Sūrya.

symbols are represented on the Buddhist *stūpas* at Bharhut and Sāñchī (*c.* 2nd - 1st cent. BC) and Jaina *Āyāgapaṭas* (*c.* 1st cent. BC)[15]

A list of eight auspicious symbols with some variations was prepared about the first century AD. These are described in *Mahāvaṁśa, Aṅgavijjā* and *Harṣacharita.* Two *māṅgalika mālās* carved on the north *toraṇa* of the main Sāñchī *stūpa* are specially interesting as they show eleven and thirteen auspicious symbols respectively.[16] We may precisely classify most of the symbols accepted in Indian art, under animals, human beings, semi-divine, vegetation, inanimate objects, attributes and auspicious motifs. The symbolism can also be viewed in the act of endowing the Indian images with many hands. The multiplicity of hands and *āyudhas* held in them perhaps symbolized the multifarious activities of gods and/or combination of the potentialities of different gods in one form.[17] The attributes and the *vāhanas* of different Indian deities virtually give symbolic impact of their function or activity.

Myths can also be represented through symbols. The stories from the lives of Buddha, Pārśvanātha and Mahāvira depicted in stones and paintings are woven out of a series of symbolic patterns. The symbols, representing human beings or animals in art, require a careful study in the proper perspective in terms of tradition and their contextual meaning to avoid any hasty or arbitrary conclusions.[18]

In Indian art, we find a large number of symbols occupying pre-eminent position right from the time of Harappan culture. (Figs. 1-4). Many of these persist even today having passed through, inter-alia, the area of Indian coins. An extensive use of symbols and other devices are found on the early indigenous coinage. The punch-marked coins, which are the earliest in numismatic series, constitute a rich repertoire of symbols in which the basic symbol alone number about five hundreds. They can be grouped under the categories of human figures, implements, arms and works of man, including *stūpas*, *chaityas*, bow and arrows, animals, trees or their branches, fruits, symbols related with solar, planetary or associated with different cults and nature.[19] Astronomical and geomatrical patterns also find place on coins.[20] Most of the symbols which appeared on punch-marked coins are also found on various objects since pre-historic times all over the world.

Though there was hardly any distinction between religious and secular symbols, appeared on different art objects, they are heralding in nature and were employed as secular symbols. But generally their religious significance have been upheld. Nevertheless, it is difficult to say whether all the symbols were adopted with religious motive. But on coins these symbols are far from arbitrary marks as each must have had some significance and meaning. Regarding the meaning of some of the symbols of punch-marked coins, it can also be said that these might have been the private marks of the king. The obverse symbols may belong to different authorities responsible for the minting of these pieces while on the other hand, the reverse mark may be regarded as the counter mark of the moneyers (sharoff marks). It appears that the symbols were primarily selected for their familiarity with the populace. Undoubtedly, the coins were to be used as a medium of exchange for inland and foreign trade hence the purpose of these symbols was probably also to reflect their standard weight

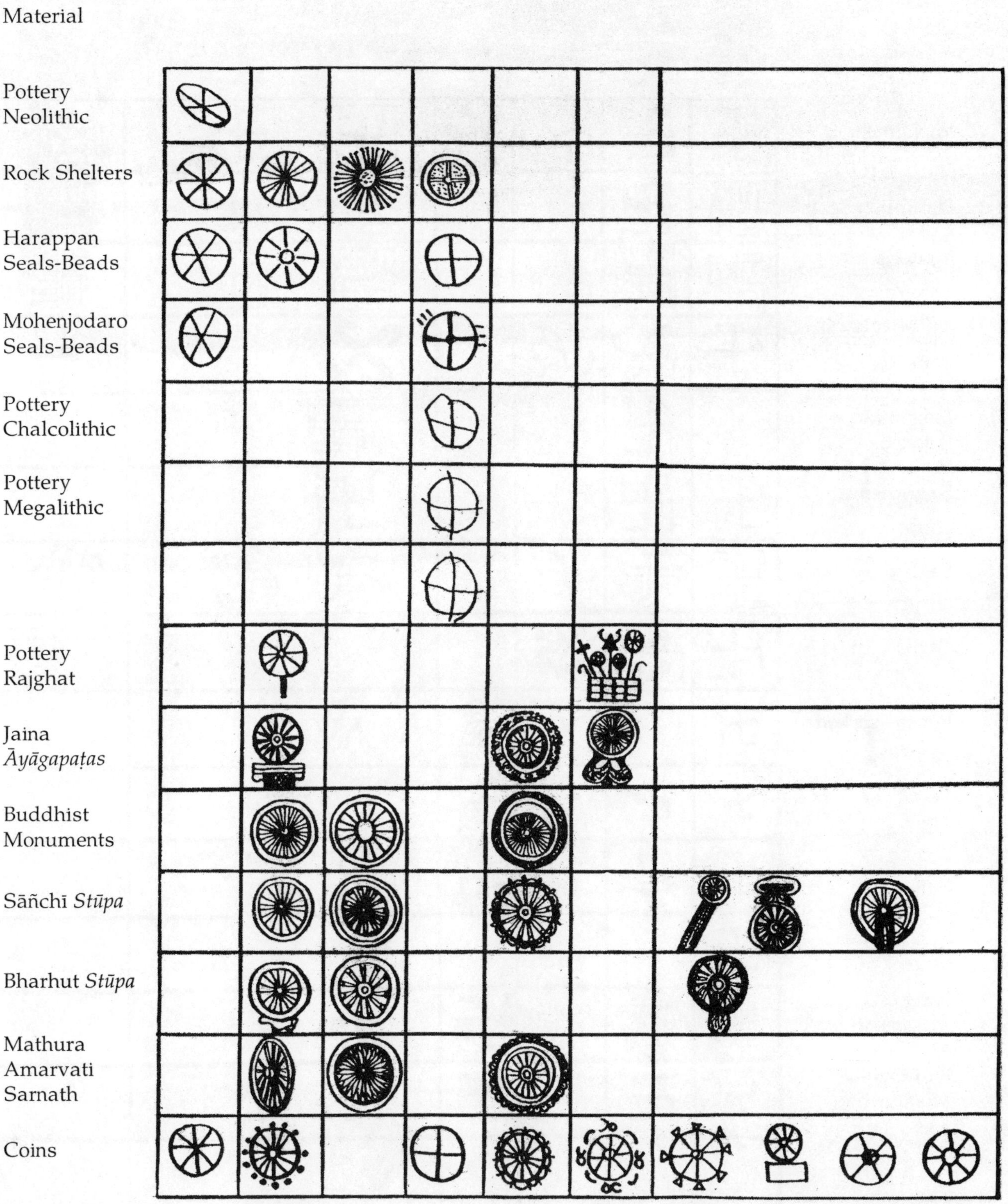
Material
Pottery
Neolithic
Rock Shelters
Harappan
Seals-Beads
Mohenjodaro
Seals-Beads
Pottery
Chalcolithic
Pottery
Megalithic
Pottery
Rajghat
Jaina
Āyāgapaṭas
Buddhist
Monuments
Sāñchī *Stūpa*
Bharhut *Stūpa*
Mathura
Amarvati
Sarnath
Coins

Fig. 2. *Cakra.*

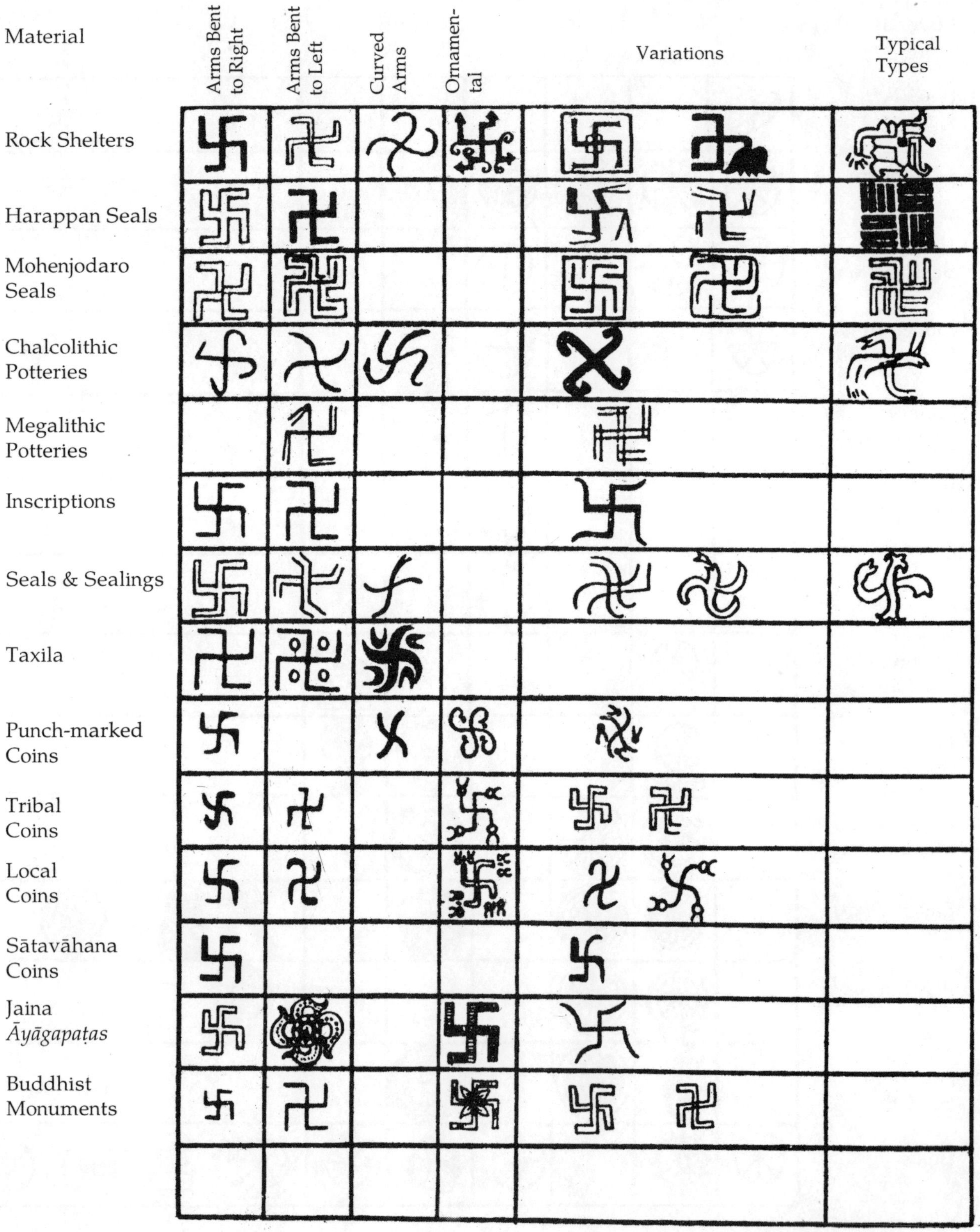

Fig. 3. *Svastika*.

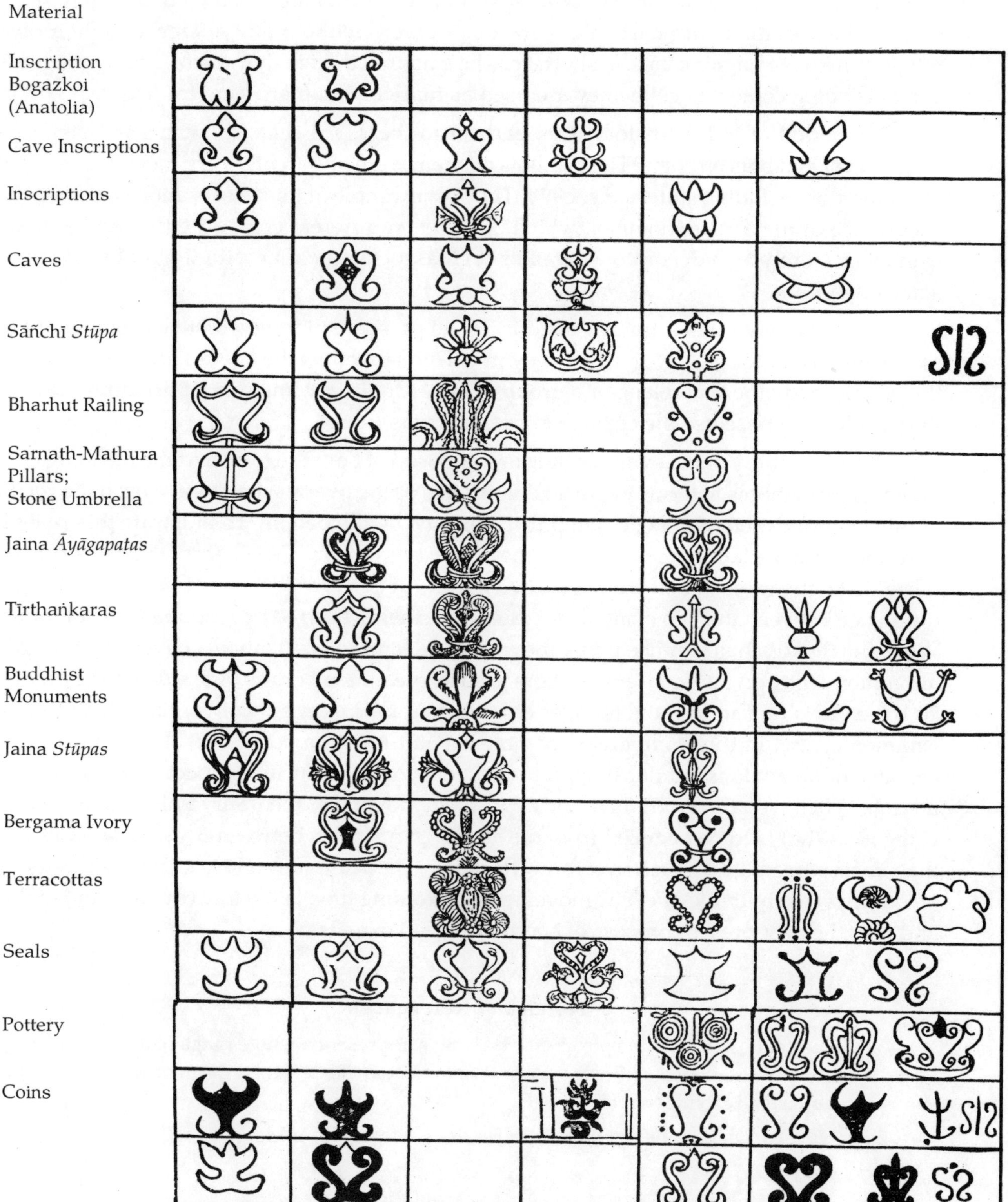

Fig. 4. *Śrīvatsa.*

and money value as the identity of issuing authority was not inscribed on them. They seem to have their relation with particular persons or places without any reference to their own religious merits or significance. In short it can be said that though they are originally religious symbols but in context of coins they are used as mark of commerce and trade also.

The period of Indian history from earliest to the *c.* 3rd cent. AD, witnessed vigorous depiction of symbols on coins. The symbols on them were apparently very much meaningful to contemporary Indian state and society. The best example of this observation would be the occurrence of the *Svastika* symbol, which is found on different coinage, either as the main symbol or merely as a decorative detail or even associated either with the Brahmanical or some other faith.

Secondly, what has attracted me during the present study is a distinct personality of each symbol and the ease with which a symbol tends to reflect the overall life-view of either the issuing body (be that a king or a group of individuals governing in a particular area) or the people for whose use the coinage in question was issued.

The personality of the symbols thus is composed of both the form and the meaning. The depiction of symbols in terms of particular strokes or the overall shape have been the result of fullest application of thought at a particular time by the people. To illustrate this point it may not be out of place here to compare the *Svastika* with *Cakra* in respect of their form alone. It can distinctly be seen that whatever the variants of *Svastika* or those of *Cakra* may be, the difference between the two symbols in general has never blurred beyond ready recognition. While the *Svastika* has four linear members (with all kinds of stylization) converging towards a common centre giving equal elbow-room to such linear members on both sides (to be precise 90°), the *Cakra* has an unequal number of 'spokes' or strokes, but converging likewise to a common centre. In this comparison one more point must be noted that the *Cakra* symbol because of its obvious similarity with the wheel acquires a further aspect of movement or motion. When we talk about their one aspect, i.e. movement then Sūrya also comes to the category. What is to be deduced from the above comparison between *Svastika* and *Cakra* is their basic personalities in terms of form. The başic characteristic in Sūrya, *Cakra* and *Svastika* ofcourse is the rhythmic or cyclic movements, unfolding time in the form of days and nights and also the ever present process of contraction and expansions.

Notes and References

1. The coins, specially the punch-marked coins, represent a whole range of symbols, though do not present themselves in very neat patterns but indicate their meaning and significance upto some extent if not fully.
2. Niharranjan Ray, *An Approach to Indian Art,* Chandigarh, 1974, pp. 250-258.
3. *Ibid.,* p. 257.
4. A.K. Coomaraswamy, *Transformation of Nature in Art* (*TNA*), p. 5.
5. The images are only hypothesis *(avasthā)* of God, who is in the last analysis without likeness *(amūrta),* not determined by form *(arūpa)* and transform *Pararūpa.* His various form or

emanations are conceived by a process of symbolic affiliation. See *TNA*, p. 157; V.S. Agrawala, *Indian Art,* Varanasi, 1965, p. 7.

6. V.S. Agrawala, *Studies in Indian Art,* Varanasi, 1965, p. 3.
7. H.R. Zimmer, *Myths and Symbols in Indian Art and Civilization,* (ed. by Joseph Cambell), New York, 1953, p. 11.
8. *TNA.*, pp. 126-27.
9. A.K. Coomaraswamy, *A History of Indian and Indonesian Art,* London, 1929, p. 41, A. Barth, *The Religions of India,* Delhi, 1978, Introduction.
10. The dawn expelled the shadows from both the poles (umentemque Aurora polo dimoverat umbram). *The Aeneid,* IV, 7. The Aeneid Virgil, edited by T.E. Page, Macmillan and Co. Ltd., London (1931).
11. *The Encyclopaedia Americana,* p. 361; In the Vedic literature, Sūrya, is the great life principal or *Prāṇa* moving to whole cosmos.
12. *The Encyclopaedia Britanica,* Vol. 2, p. 491.
13. The Vedic deities on the basis of their nature are classified under the groups: (1) The Celestial Gods, (2) The atmospheric gods, and (3) The terrestial gods. See V.M. Apte, *The Vedic Age,* Ch. XVIII, pp. 362-76.
14. V.S. Agrawala, *Indian Art,* pp. 336-37.
15. The list usually included *Svastika, Śrīvatsa.* A pair of fish, *Bhadrāsana, Nandyāvarta, Vardhamānaka, Kalaśa* and *Darpaṇa.* However, *Dharmacakra,* lotus and a few other symbols are also included. See U.P. Shah, *Studies in Jain Art,* Benaras, 1945, pp. 109-12.
16. V.S. Agrawala, *Indian Art.*, p. 71, Figs. 254-55.
17. J.N. Banerjea, *The Development of Hindu Iconography,* Calcutta, 3rd ed., Delhi, 1974, pp. 81-82.
18. Nemichandra Shastri in his paper 'Jaina Sikke', No. 6, Vol. IV, pt. II, pp. 116-26, has attributed several religious symbols to Jainism. This has been refuted. See M.N.P. Tiwari and Chandra Deo Singh, "So-called Jaina Coins", *The Journal of Numismatic Society of India (JNSI)*, Vol. XLIII, Varanasi, 1981, pt. I, pp. 81-87, also C.S. Upasak, "Some Buddhist Symbols on Punch-marked Coins", *JNSI,* Vol. XXXIX, pt. I-II, pp. 18-26.
19. Savita Sharma, *Early Indian Symbols: Numismatic Evidence,* Delhi, 1990. pp. 10-23.
20. *Ibid.*, pp. 20-21.

16

A Study of Two Vaiṣṇava Manuscripts in the Western Indian Style: Harilīlā-Ṣoḍaśa-Kalā and Prabodha-Candrodaya

Rashmi Kala Agrawal

The *Bālagopāla Stuti* and *Gīta Govinda* illustrations were the only examples of Vaiṣṇavite origin in the western Indian or Apabhramsha style until recently when two other Vaiṣṇavite illustrated manuscripts, *Harilīlā-Ṣoḍaśa-Kalā* and *Prabodha-Candrodaya* were discovered. These two were originally bound in one book form, and this fact gave rise to certain misunderstandings in their dating. The first one, according to U.P. Shah, is the *Prabodha-Prakāśa,* a loose translation in Gujarātī of the well-known Sanskrit allegorical play *Prabodha-Candrodaya* by Krsna Miśra (1050-1100). The present adaptation in Gujarātī was by one poet Bhīma.[1] Bhīma's other known Gujarātī version of the Sanskrit *Harilīlā-Ṣoḍaśa-Kalā* (the Bharat Kala Bhavan folio states as *Harilīlā-Ṣola-Kalā)* is the other manuscript bound between these covers. The folios later on, were separated and sold. Fortunately, the colophon page of *Harilīlā-Ṣoḍaśa-Kalā,* is now in the Bharat Kala Bhavan, Varanasi collection and is dated in V.S. 1586=1529 AD.[2] The *Prabodha-Prakāśa* has no date since the colophon page is missing, therefore it is hard to accept its date as AD 1526 as suggested by U.P. Shah.[3] However, as already pointed out, these are two different manuscripts, each having distinct text, calligraphy and illustrations, but are just bound in one volume. Since the date appears on the very last page, i.e. at the end of the *Harilīlā-Ṣoḍaśa-Kalā* text, the above scholars mistakenly took it to be the colophone of both the manuscripts.

From the stylistic point of view, the *Prabodha-Prakāśa* illustrated manuscript appears to be of late 15th century instead of the date suggested by U.P. Shah. The western Indian style in the late 15th century was quite washed out, which is evident from the present illustration (Pl. 16.1). As in Jain illustrations, the figures are lifeless having three quarter profile face and protruding eyes. The postures are stiff and the treatment of drapery or ornaments is stylized, and there is practically no landscape. The colours fail to make any impact. The illustrator is more concerned with visualizing iconographic forms or episodes. The concepts like *Śānti,*

Karuṇā and *Śraddhā* are treated like common women folk, and they are distinguished through labels. This reflects the condition of the western Indian style in the late 15th and early 16th centuries when the great tradition was already lost, but dragged on. Later characteristics of this western Indian tradition are present in these illustrations like squat figures, lack of compositional varieties, restricted landscape and even suggestive use of architecture.

Harilīlā-Ṣoḍaśa-Kalā illustrations show a variety of scenes (Pl. 16.2) and a manner of folkish expression (though not exactly folk style). In other words, the *Harilīlā-Ṣoḍaśa-Kalā* illustrations to an extent compensate for their stylistic limitations by numerous types of compositions sometimes giving impression of almost free-hand drawing. A leaf with Gujarātī-text in the Goenka collection depicts the popular episode of Kṛṣṇa killing Śakāṭāsura, i.e. the demon in the form of a push-cart. This composition is conceived as a full length panel; at the right corner a man sits within an arched pavilion, this is separated by a dividing wall. The left portion shows baby Kṛṣṇa lying on a hammock. In the right corner, a tiny tortured human figure is shown collapsing within the ruins of the push-cart. Vacant portions are filled with bold Gujarātī floral designs. This scene is a good example of a rarified narrative in the present manuscript. Another full length scene from the same collection shows the dying Ajāmil on a richly decorated bed while two animal faced *yamadūtas* (messengers of the god of Death) have appeared "to take him away", i.e. to take his spirit and leave him dead. The scene is quite simple, yet the dying man has lifeless limbs, while the *yamadūtas* appear with a degree of authoritativeness. The present scene clearly shows that in spite of the erosion of the western Indian painting tradition and rather sketchy style, the painter could express himself with simple representations.

The stealing of butter which shows Kṛṣṇa tied to a mortar, is portrayed in one of the paintings from Bharat Kala Bhavan, Varanasi (Acc. No. 10950). There is no barrier between the two sceneṣ. In the first instance, we find Yaśodā, assisted by a *gopī,* vigourously churning the buttermilk, while baby Kṛṣṇa puts his arm into pot to get the butter. Next we find the punishment episode where baby Kṛṣṇa appears helpless, with his arms tied. These two scenes in one horizontal register is very near to the *Bālagopāla Stuti* illustrations of the fifteenth century.[4] Though we have several instances in the *Bālagopāla Stuti* illustrations where the same compositional arrangements of a particular theme are repeated in different versions,[5] it is quite interesting that even in the early sixteenth century, i.e. in the present *Harilīlā-Ṣoḍaśa-Kalā* AD 1529 the two incidents of *Kṛṣṇa-līlā,* showing subtle emotions, are painted in the same earlier fashion, irrespective of the change of text. The background is plain except for the right corner. There we find a patch of cloud with a semi-circular rim fringed by serrated marks at the edge and two or three concentric curving bands. This reminds us of similar treatment in the *Caurapancāśikā* style.[6] Some other scenes from this manuscript are also indebted to the established scenes of the *Bālagopāla Stuti* of fifteenth century. For example, a panel of the *Bālagopāla Stuti*, now in the collection of the Oriental Institute, Baroda[7] shows Indra surrendering to Kṛṣṇa where the latter defies the former by lifting Mount Govardhana. It has close similarities with *Harilīlā-Ṣoḍaśa-Kalā*, especially in the dancing attitude of Kṛṣṇa or the happy cows in the foreground (shown in the lower register). In many of the illustrations

Kṛṣṇa appears with four arms in his Lordly aspect, this very posture is clearly borrowed from the *Bālagopāla Stuti* scenes. Not only the specific postures and motifs, but the overall symbolic and conceptual treatment of the events with minimal figures and landscapes are indebted to the earlier Kṛṣṇa *līlā* scenes.

Another interesting feature of this manuscript is individual representation of trees of India, almost like a botanical compilation. These are obviously nature studies to an extent, yet the overall impression is of a highly traditionalized and ornamental treatment. The most striking example is the frontispiece in the collection of the Bharat Kala Bhavan, Varanasi, a full page illustration showing a stately tree infested by birds and frolicking monkeys, reminding us of certain *Vasanta Vilāsa* landscape treatments, but at this stage in its simplified and folkish form. This attributes a rare fluency to the brushwork. Similarly in the *Prabodha-Candrodaya,* there was in the art market, a postage stamp size illustration of Gopī and Kṛṣṇa on a swing like bed, a miniaturized version of similar composition popularly found in the *Bālagopāla Stuti* manuscripts.[8]

As far as provenance is concerned, there are reasons in favour of ascribing the *Prabodha-Prakāśa* manuscript to Gujarat. Before we take the points in favour of Gujarat we must not forget that the painter uses a special eye type which is not found in Gujarātī manuscripts, at least not from known evidences. The broad eyes, taking almost lozenge form, to some extent, may be related to later (*c.* 17th century) Mewarī paintings. This however does not necessarily imply that the manuscript originated from Mewar. It is only indicative of a wider connotation of the western India style. Bhīma's present text in Gujaratī dialect also does not help us in locating geographical parameters of the style since we know that such Gujaratī texts were popularily copied almost all over Rajasthan and its adjoining parts. It is best to leave the question open while suggesting certain possibilities for its regional provenance. For example, a flat turban is sometimes used in context with 'middle class' people. This is a close fitting flat turban, rather unostentatious, which has some correspondence with the type used in the manuscripts prepared at Mātar (Gujarat) by the atelier of Govinda, son of Nārada.[9] In view of the above discussion with some degree of Mewarī traits and other features of Mātar style, it can be presumed that this manuscript, *Prabodha-Candrodaya,* is a borderline case, produced somewhere between Gujarat and Mewar.

Notes and References

1. U.P. Shah, *More Documents of Jaina Paintings and Gujarati Paintings of Sixteenth and Later Centuries,* 1976, p. 13, Figs. 37-38.
2. Anand Krishna informs that it is the same colophon page which once belonged to Shri Jagdish Mittal who subsequently sold it to the Bharat Kala Bhavan. At that point Shri Mittal was a bit mixed up in attributing this date to *Prabodha-Prakāsā (Prabodha-Candrodaya)* whose colophon page is missing.

   The colophon of *Harilīlā-Ṣodaśa-Kalā* clearly lays down:

   इति श्री हरिलीला सोल कला समाप्ता।।छ।। शुभं भवतु।। श्री कृष्णार्पण मस्तु।। संवत 1586 वर्षे शाके 1451 प्रवर्त्तमाने। कार्तिक श्रुदि 5 गुरू।। लेखक पाठकयो: शुभं भवतु।।छ।।

Thus the date in Christian era is doubly confirmed as AD 1529/V.S. 1586, Śaka 1451. Consequently I humbly differ with U.P. Shah in giving the date as AD 1526. In his book in the illustration (Fig. 37) he gives the date as AD 1520 which obviously is a printing mistake since in the text he gives the date as AD 1526.

U.P. Shah's above datings were based on Jagdish Mittal's information and most probably he never examined the colophon leaf itself. Thus the dating of *Harilīlā-Ṣoḍaśa-Kalā* is AD 1526.

However, in case there was another colophon page for the *Prabodha-Prakāsa* manuscript which Jagdish Mittal had (now its whereabouts not known) and gave another date for that manuscript, the matter is open to discussion.

3. U.P. Shah, *op. cit.,* vide the description of his Fig. 38.

4. W. Norman Brown, Early Vaishnava Miniature Paintings from Western India, *Eastern Art,* Vol. 2, 1930, Figs. 5, 7, 33.

5. *Kṛṣṇa līlā* scenes in different versions, such as, the Baroda version, the Boston version, the Wellcome Institute, London version, the B.K.B. version, etc. and the loose folios in various collections, are very similar to each other in style as well as in their compositional arrangements. It appears as if there was an original copy (most probably the Boston version) and the last manuscripts were copied from that. See:

   M.R. Majomudar, The Gujarati School of Painting and Some Newly Discovered Vaishnava Miniatures, *JISOA,* Vol. 10, 1942, pp. 1-31.

   M.R. Majomudar, Illustrated Manuscripts of Bilvamangala's Balagopala Stuti, *JISOA,* Vol. 16, 1947-58, pp. 33-61.

   Rashmi Kala Agrawal, Gujarati Painting of the Sixteenth Century with Special Reference to the Bālagopala Stuti Illustrations, *Kalā,* Vol. 5, 1998-99, pp. 145-152.

6. Karl Khandalavala and Moti Chandra, *New Documents of Indian Painting,* 1969, Figs. 186-187, Pl. 20.

7. U.P. Shah, *op. cit.,* Fig. 37.

8. W. Norman Brown, *op. cit.,* Fig. 26.

9. U.P. Shah, *op. cit.,* p. 21, Figs. 51-54.

17

Feminine Beauty in Divine Figures in Indian Art

Haripriya Rangarajan

From the early times of human civilization, the artists had focussed on the specific characteristic beauty of women with regard to 'fertility and procreation' which emphatically suggested the veneration of the motherhood as a divine principle. Archaeological excavations across Europe and West Asia have shown how ancient artists carved women with exaggerated feminine features to emphasize her role in the creative process. As a mother she was explicitly represented with round and full grown breasts, with big pot belly to indicate her nurturing the foetus in the womb and the vulva region for the procreation. She was depicted with a child touching her breast or as feeding the child. More than that she was being represented in squatting position to indicate the action of child birth. She was thus seen in the early societies as an extension of the earth, another mysterious manifestation of cosmic fecundity. In the early periods, in the name of Earth Goddess, she was being represented in the form of *yoni*.

Over a period of time the artists realized her underlying multiaspects and multipowers hidden in her supreme beauty and regarded her as universal Mother *Jagadambā*. The artists were very ambitious to exhibit her unique beauty along with multifacet qualities in sculptural form. To exhibit her in such form, in the first place, they beautified her in the manner of her sitting and standing postures. They depicted her in *lalitāsana, ardhalalitāsana, yogāsana* and *āliḍhāsana* postures. She is depicted standing in *samabhaṅga* and *tribhaṅga* postures. Then they added her different *vāhanas* like, *garuḍa,* elephant, lion, buffalo, owl, ass, horse, tiger, etc., to indicate her mighty power. Secondly in addition to her natural feminine beauty, the artists brought out the *navarasa bhāva* in her eyes, limbs and the way of holding the attributes in the hands. For example, in the representation of mother and child, the artist explained motherly love, affection, compassion and care in the eyes and in holding the child. Similarly in the depiction of corn mother, her expressive eyes indicate satisfaction and grace for human being in supplying food. This is supplemented by the figure of corn in her hand. While coming to the sphere of learning and wisdom, the artist completely changed the expression of the eyes of the goddess in accordance to the particular aspect. For this, the image is sculptured with closed eyes or half-closed eyes or fully opened eyes with the expression of knowledge and meditation. Her attributes such as *pustaka, vīṇā,* etc., are depicted mainly related to learning, knowledge and wisdom. Thirdly, they decorated her with different kinds of *mukuṭas,* differently designed *karṇakuṇḍalas* with beautiful workmanship, necklaces, *mālās* with ornate pendant, *keyūras, hastavalayas* and *nūpuras.* Her ornamentation from head to foot was taken care of by the artists. Fourthly, they dressed her in sārī, skirt, *pyjāmā kurtā* and thin layered upper garment. Fifthly, the artists represented her with respective *āyudhas* and attributes in the hands according to her form and name. These attributes include *śaṅkha, cakra, gadā, padma, hala, musala, śūla,* bell, harp, *vīṇā, pustaka, pāśa, aṅkuśa, mātsya, māmsa, kapāla, kamala,* etc. In addition to these the artists introduced their innovative depiction of female divinity corresponding to the mythology prescribed in the Purāṇas, Śilpaśāstras and Tantras. The result was the emergence of exquisite feminine divine images with unique features and artistic beauty.

In this paper an attempt has been made to explain how the artists had visualized five aspects of feminine divine beauty and personified them very realistically in sculptural forms.

1. Vārāhī - to represent motherhood
2. Vasudharā - goddess of food
3. Vāgdevī - goddess of speech (Personification of Speech)
4. Sarasvatī - goddess of learning (Personification of Learning)
5. Tārā - goddess of wisdom (Personification of Wisdom)

Vārāhī

In this world mother goddess is a special mother to every child. To signify her important role as a symbol of motherhood, the artist has depicted her with a child on her lap. There is a special sculptural representation entitled Seven Mothers (*Sapta Mātṛkā*) which have been found in every Śaiva and Śākta temples of India. These mothers include Brahmāṇī, Māheśvarī, Kaumārī, Vaiṣṇavī, Vārāhī, Indrāṇī, Nārasiṁhī and Cāmuṇḍā. All of them are portrayed with a child on their lap. A realistic and artistic piece of Vārāhī with a child on her lap is preserved in British Museum, London [No.22, ACC. No. 1872-7- 1-47]. The child is identified by the *Paraśurāma Kalpa Sūtra* (Vārāhī Krama sl. 29) and the *Mantramahodadhi* as her *suputra* Caṇḍoccaṇḍa. The image of Vārāhī seated in *lalitāsāna* posture is made of sandstone and is datable to 9th century AD. As a mother, she is looking down with full of love, affection and compassion in her eyes and also holding the child with her left lower hand. The four-armed goddess is very peculiarly shown with the lower right hand turning back and holding the *Kapāla.* The upper right hand is broken. The corresponding hand on the left holds a bell which is an ideal example of the only Śilpa text *Rūpamaṇḍana* and *Vārāhī Kavaca* in the *Śrīvidyāmaharṇava* of Śrīvidyā Upāsana.

Vārāhī is beautifully and neatly decorated with single plait shown on the shoulder. She is elegantly dressed with tight garment from top to bottom which looks like *kurtā-pyjāmā.* The ornaments like *kaṇṭhahāra* with coin shaped design and with a pendant and the necklace with a pendant falling on the stomach are shown neatly. The unique feature of this image lies in the depiction of a long fish which is held by Vārāhī firmly between the teeth. It is seen straight and Vārāhī supports it with her left heel (foot) for its balance of position. The depiction of the figure of fish in this image has nothing to do with *Pañcamakāra* of Tāntric Śakti cult. It is exclusively a symbolic depiction of earth which is brought by Vārāhī from nether region by holding it between her teeth. The *Mantramahodadhi* (Taranga 10, sl. 39) says that Svapna Vārāhī should be meditated as shining with the earth placed on her teeth. The depiction of the figure of fish indicates the fertility aspect of Vārāhī.

Regarding the provenance of this image, R.C. Agrawala has suggested that it could be either from Rajasthan or Madhya Pradesh.[1] But its thin long face, long and striking snout, wide open eyes, and its holding the fish between the teeth, and also distinctly shown ears, slim contour of the body and style of sitting, her garment, unique ornamentation, bell in the hand, and her hairstyle and beautifully designed back slab suggest that it is a masterpiece of a sculptor of Katyuri art from the Almora region (Uttaranchal). It belongs to the Paurava kings of Almora region datable to the 9th century AD. It is very important to note that the author has examined many images of Vārāhī from Tamil Nadu, Andhra Pradesh, Karnataka, Maharashtra, Gujarat, West Bengal, Madhya Pradesh, Rajasthan and Orissa but from no where such an image of Vārāhī is found which holds fish between her teeth. In all the images she is shown holding the fish only in her hand. In fact, in the southern States the fish concept does not seem to have any impact on the sculptors. In other States the artists concentrated on the idea of 'fish' related to *Pañcamakāra* of *Vāmācāra* rituals. Interestingly, the 'fish aspect' was connected exclusively with Vārāhī among the *Sapta Matṛkas*. This image is identified as Svapna Vārāhī in the *Mantramahodadhi* (Taranga 10, sl.39) (Pl. 17.1).

Vasudhārā

The image of goddess Vasudhārā or the personification of goddess of food (*annadā*) datable to the 9th century AD and found from Bihar (the exact place is not given) belongs to Pāla period. It is preserved in India Museum, Kolkata (Acc. No. 3822. A 25138). The goddess is seated in *lalitāsana* on double lotus (*Viśva Padma*) pīṭha. The four-armed Vasudhārā holds *akṣamālā* in the upper right hand while the corresponding left hand is realistically depicted with corn stalk to exhibit her *annadā* aspect (producer of food). In this form she is called Vasudhārā or Dhānya Lakṣmī. The lower right hand has citric fruit while the corresponding hand holds full blown lotus. The image of Vasudhārā is ornamented with big *karṇabhūṣaṇa*, beaded necklace in two rows, long beaded ornament touching the breast and hanging upto the thigh, hipband, studded *hastavalavas, keyūras* and studded pādajālas. Her hair is tied in tribal style and locks are shown falling very stylistically on both shoulders. There is a medallion shown in the centre of her *mukuṭa*. A thin drapery is shown covering the body (Pl. 17.2).

Vāgdevī

A unique image of Vāgdevī preserved in Indian Museum, Kolkata, is a par excellent sculptural specimen of Goddess of Speech or speech personified. According to this author, such kind of representation of Vāgdevī has not been found from anywhere else in India.

Seated in *lalitāsana,* by resting the right foot on lotus she is accompanied by the figure of a lion at the bottom of the pedestal. The depiction of figure of lion is the indication of Vāgdevī as *Jagadambā.* She is four armed. The upper right hand holds a *paraśu* (?) and the left hand holds a harp (instrument). Interestingly both the lower right and left hands hold an object which is identified as the feather end (Quil). Holding in her hands Vāgdevī is shown writing the *bījamantra* on the tongues of the devotees who are seated in kneel down position on either side and looking at her. This articulating representation suggests that Vāgdevī as Mantra-mother bestowing her devotees the great power of speech by writing the *mantra* on their tongues with quil. Her third eye is artistically shown. Her tender and slender body along with gracefully modelled breasts and hip indicate the pulsation of life. It is very much according to the *sūkta* said by Vāgdevī herself in the *Ṛgveda,* 10th Maṇḍala, sūkti 125, verse 5, under the title of 'Vāk'. It says that Vāk is the Mantra-mother and utter the word that gods and men alike welcome it.

> अहमेव स्वयमिदं वदामि जुष्टं देवोभिरुत मानुषेभिः
> यं कामये तं तमुग्रं कृष्णोमि तं ब्रह्माणं तमृर्षिं त सुमेधाम्'

Ṛgveda, 10th Maṇḍala, 125, 5.

Vāgdevī is decorated with *karaṇḍamukuṭa* with a medallion in the centre. Her body contour is proportionate and the face is very calm and peaceful. She is three eyed and the eyes are shown in such a manner that one gets the feeling that she is concentrating in the action of mantra *upadeśa* to her devotees. She is decorated with *karṇakuṇḍalas.* necklaces, *skandhasūtra, keyūras, hastavalayas, kaṭibandha* and *pādajālas.* There is a halo on the back slab. Above her shoulders on either side, a figure of four armed *vidyādhara* is represented to witness the event. It is made of black basalt stone and datable to the 1st regnal year of Gopāla II in Bihar (*c.* AD 952-969) (Pl. 17.3).

Sarasvatī

A beautifully ornate image of Sarasvatī of Hoysala art found from Halebid is preserved in Indian Museum, Kolkata (N.S. 2244/A 25230.). It is datable to the 12th century AD. The four-armed Sarasvatī is seated in *yogāsana* on a double lotus *pīṭha.* The upper right and left hands hold *aṅkuśa* and *pāśa* respectively. The lower right is broken and the left hand holds a *pustaka.* She is richly decorated from head to foot. She has three eyes. Her wide open eyes suggest that she is with full of grace ready to impart knowledge to her devotee. There is a halo behind her *kirīṭa mukuṭa.* It is very interesting to note that her ear ornament is much different from other *karṇakuṇḍalas* (Pl. 17.4).

Tārā

Tārā is the goddess of wisdom or wisdom personified. An exquisite image of Tārā seated on a double lotus (*viśva padma*) *pīṭha* found from Java and datable to the 9th-10th century AD, is preserved in the Indian Museum, Kolkata. (Acc. No.J.3/A, 26258). To indicate that she is a Siddhi devī, Tārā is represented in *yogāsana* on a full blown double lotus in the meditative pose, the soles of both feet are turned upwards. Similarly her both hands are also kept in *yogamudrā.* She is adorned with a necklace with pendants, *skandha sūtra, keyūras, hastavalayas, kaṭibandha, karṇakuṇḍalas* and *jaṭāmukuṭa.* In the centre of *jaṭā* one can see the design of a *stūpa.* It is to be noted that the goddess Tārā is worshipped both in Hinduism and Buddhism. In both religions she is worshipped for attaining *siddhis.* In Hinduism she is worshipped in *Daśamāhavidyā* in which she occupies second place. In Buddhism the form of Tārā is identified with universe (Pl. 17.5).

The *Sādhanamālā* (*sādhanā* no. 98) informs us that those who meditate on the form of Tārā in a proper manner which is identified with the universe, they will be endowed with all the eight great *siddhis.* In fact all the eight great *siddhis* fall at their feet. It clearly shows that Tārā in Buddhism is the goddess of *siddhi.* It also says that if a devotee is not able to meditate then he can mutter the mantra *"Oṁ Tāre Tuttāre Tūre Svāhā". Sādhanamālā* further says that by meditating Tārā (Bhagavatī) in a lonely mountain cave and by having the vision of her with own eyes, she herself gives him breath, even the Buddhahood which is very difficult to achieve. It remains as if it is in the palm of his hand[2]. Usually the images of goddesses in Buddhism are decorated with the figure of the parental Dhyānī Buddha in their crown. In the image of Tārā, in Indian Museum, Kolkata, the centre of the *jaṭā* is decorated with the figure of a *stūpa.* Interestingly a figure of a male deity is represented in the centre of a triangle shown in a corner above her left shoulder. The figure is seated in *padmāsana* keeping the hands in *yogamudrā.* The triangle is fixed on a blossomed lotus *piṭha.* In the image of Tārā, two factors have been examined in the following pages, (i) the reason for replacing a figure of stūpa against a male figure in the centre of *jaṭā,* (ii) the significance of the depiction of a triangle and the presence of the male figure in the centre of it.

From the *Toḍala Tantra* we understand that Tārā is the Śakti of Akṣobhya who is then Lord Śiva. It says that while in the process of churning the milky ocean, the *halāhala* emerged first and Lord Śiva was the only deity who was not agitated to accept it (*akṣobhya*) and at the instance of his Śakti, he swallowed the poison. That 'Sakti' is Eternal Tārā, the *'Saviour'* who always carries the human being to the path of safety. She is the goddess who saves people from disasters, ferrying them across waters of troubles and tribulations. In this form, she is called *Ugra Tārā.* The same Tārā is named *Nīla Tārā* when she is connected with speech and acquisition of knowledge.[3]

Besides these, in the cosmic function Tārā is mentioned as the personification of the sound force or sound symbol 'OM'. While the Vedic seers called this sound force as *'Nitva Vāk', 'Eternal Word'* and *'Akṣara'*, the Upaniṣadic sages regarded as *'Praṇava - the sound symbol OM'.* The Puranic bards named it *'White Gourī'* and the Tantrics called the same sound force as Tārā'. Therefore, in the *Daśa Mahāvidyā,* Tārā, the second goddess in the worship is the primordial *nāda, Paśvanti Vāk,* the source of all speech and knowledge.[4]

In the Buddhist pantheon, Tārā is described as the 'Śakti of Avalokiteśvara, the Lord of Compassion whose eyes are shown downward to symbolize compassion'. At the same time, Tārā is described as having Akṣobhya posited on her head. It is the name of the Buddha who stood unagitated against the onslaughts of Māra. In Buddhism she is called *Prajña Pāramitā.* It is the appellation given to her in Buddhism. The etymology of the word *"Prajñā Pāramitā"* is "the enlightening wisdom". "The perfection of the virture (*pāramitā*) of the enlightening transcendental wisdom (*prañā*) or according to another rendering of the term, equally warranted by the sacred texts, "the enlightening wisdom (*prajñā*) that has gone (*itā*) to the far shore (*pāram*), the shore of the transcendental void where that wisdom eternally abides."[5]

The Tantras describe three of her significant forms or personalities. They are (1) Ugra Tārā, (2) Nīla Sarasvatī, (3) Ekajaṭā Tārā.

Iconographically Ugra Tārā is represented in a fierce form and is mounted on a corpse. Nīla Sarasvatī is the personification of the power of the word and shown standing on the *Piṭha.* In both forms, her hair is shown falling loose to symbolize that her energies scattered. In these forms she is *'muktakesi'.* In both forms, she is attributed with four and eight hands. On the other hand, in the form of Ekajaṭā, the goddess Tārā is shown with single matted hair to indicate that all the scattered vibrations of the sound are fully being channelized in the act of creation. The image of Tārā preserved in the Indian Museum, Kolkata is not just Tārā, she is Ekajaṭā Tārā.

Ekajaṭā

The image of Tārā preserved in the Indian Museum, Kolkata has a graceful form endowed with superb elegance. The eyes are lowered and the fingers are touching each other to suggest the chain of the cycle of birth and death. The slim and erect body is perfectly balanced and exhibits the lines of an equilateral triangle. It is just like that of a yogi who has completely discarded sensual enjoyments and lives on the light diet. The image is an ideal specimen of quietish, most stable and most self-contained. It is endowed with quality of spiritual poise, mental equilibrium, absolute serenity in concentration. The image amazingly attracts the scholars by its delicate physical beauty and its composed serene posture and expression. The scholars may note that the image of Tārā from Java preserved in the Indian Museum, Kolkata may not belong to Buddhism. It may be an ideal specimen of the Vedic Nitya Vāk, Upaniṣadic Praṇava OM, Purāṇic White Gouri and Tāntric Tārā. The reason could be two fold : (1) her *jaṭamukuṭa* does not hold the parental Buddha Akṣobhya. (2) secondly the separate triangle and a figure of some deity in human form in the centre is not at all practised in Buddhism. Triangle in downward shape indicates *yoni* concept and the male figure in the centre suggests the Kāmeśvara *tattva.* If we accept this formula, she may be taken as the representation of Tārā of Daśa Mahāvidyā.

Notes and References

1. R.C. Agrawala, A Rare Image of Vārāhī in British Museum, *Oriental Art,* p. 167, London, 1963.
2. B. Bhattacharyya, *An Introduction to Buddhist Esoterism,* p. 108.
3. S. Sankaranarayanan, *The Ten Cosmic Powers,* p. 21.
4. *Ibid.,* p. 24.
5. H. Zimmer, *The Art of Indian Asia: Its Mythology and Transformation.* Vol. I, p. 102, New York, 1960.

18

A Note on a Rare Viṣṇu Image from Varanasi

Kamal Giri & Pramod Giri

Varanasi, besides being the city of antiquity and continuity, has been a city of multifarious activities of art and culture. The city has yielded a number of stone sculptures, datable from *c.* third century BC through the 20th century. These sculptures exhibit different regional art styles, specially during the early medieval and medieval periods (*c.* 8th-13th cent. CE) and project the cultural and religious harmony and assimilation which was the core of culture of this great city. Some of these sculptures have special importance for their plastic and artistic excellence and peculiar iconographic features. The present paper aims at discussing one of such rare and so far unpublished stone image of Viṣṇu procured from the heart of city near the locality known as Godowlia.

The four-armed black basalt image represents Viṣṇu in *samabhaṅga* with conventional as well as with some peculiar features in respect of attributes and the *parikara* figures (Pl. 18.1). The image, presently in domestic worship has lost its original stone colour since the main figure of Viṣṇu is painted in black (*śyāma*) while his attributes, ornaments, attendant figures, incarnatory forms and also the trinity – Brahmā, Viṣṇu and Śiva carved at top, are in golden colour. The image under thick coating of paint is still intact and well preserved. Its aesthetic and decorative features are distinctly discernible. On the basis of style, composition and ornaments, the image may be assigned to the Kalchuri idiom and could be dated to 11th century CE. The face, ornate necklace and attributes like mace, disk and conch has close similarity with Kalchuri style. The four-armed Viṣṇu shows mace and disc in two upper hands while conch is clear in the lower left hand. Surprisingly the lower right hand showing *varada-mudrā* carries both the rosary and lotus which is something rare and not to be noticed elsewhere.

Through this note we wish to bring this unique unpublished image to the notice of the scholars. This particular Viṣṇu image with other Viṣṇu images and other sculptures prove that Varanasi, apart from Sarnath, was a great centre of art during the early medieval and medieval times. The main features of the present Viṣṇu image are:

1. The ornate *parikara* exhibit two parrots carved at the top which has special significance in reference to the wall paintings of Varanasi which is still in vogue.
2. The rendering of small figure of four-armed, one-faced Brahmā (with *varada, śruk, pustaka* and *kamaṇḍalu*), four-armed Viṣṇu (with *varada, gadā, cakra* and *śaṅkha*) and four-armed Śiva (with *varada, triśūla, sarpa* and water-vessel) is also worth noticing. All these three figures are seated under the canopy of temple *śikhara* which is noteworthy. The beautiful *toraṇa* motif in between these figures are very impressive and artistic.
3. The main figure of Viṣṇu is flanked by the figures of *āyudhapuruṣas* which reveal the continuity of Gupta tradition at Varanasi in 11th century. The figures of both the *āyudhapuruṣas* are highly ornate and wear tall *mukuṭas.* The figure to the right of Viṣṇu is *cakrapuruṣa* with a wheel in hand while the figure to the left is *śaṅkhapuruṣa* showing conch in the hand. Besides *āyudhapuruṣas,* the figure is accompanied by two other figures, probably Jaya and Vijaya, respectively on right and left.
4. On both the sides of main figure in vertical composition, we find the rendering of ten incarnatory forms of Viṣṇu in traditional order. These, starting from the bottom are Matsya, Kūrma (both in theriomorphic form), Varāha, Nṛsiṁha, Vāmana, Paraśurāma, Rāma, Balarāma, Buddha and Kalki. Apparently Kṛṣṇa is dropped here. The figure of Bhūdevī is absent with Varāha who is holding *śaṅkha, gadā, cakra* and *padma.* However, the face of the Varāha is facing front which is a peculiar feature. The Sthauṇa Nṛsiṁha is shown killing the demon Hiraṇyakaśipu with his two hands while his two upper hands are raised holding the upper portion. Except Varāha and Nṛsiṁha all other figures are two-armed. Vāmana with *chatra* and *kamaṇḍalu,* Paraśurāma with *paraśu* and water-vessel, Dāśarathī Rāma with arrow and bow and Balarāma with *hala* and *musala* are represented on right and left. At the top on right is shown seated Buddha in *dhyāna-mudrā.* His right hand is in *vyākhyāna-mudrā* which also shows *akṣamālā* while left hand is placed in lap in meditation posture. Instead of *dhyāna-mudrā* (both hands in lap) or *dharmacakrapravartana,* with Buddha only *vyākhyāna-mudrā* and that too with rosary is a peculiar feature. Surprisingly Buddha wears the ornaments also. At the left of Viṣṇu there appears Kalki with sword and shield and riding on a galloping horse.

Thus the present image has a number of such features which makes it unique.

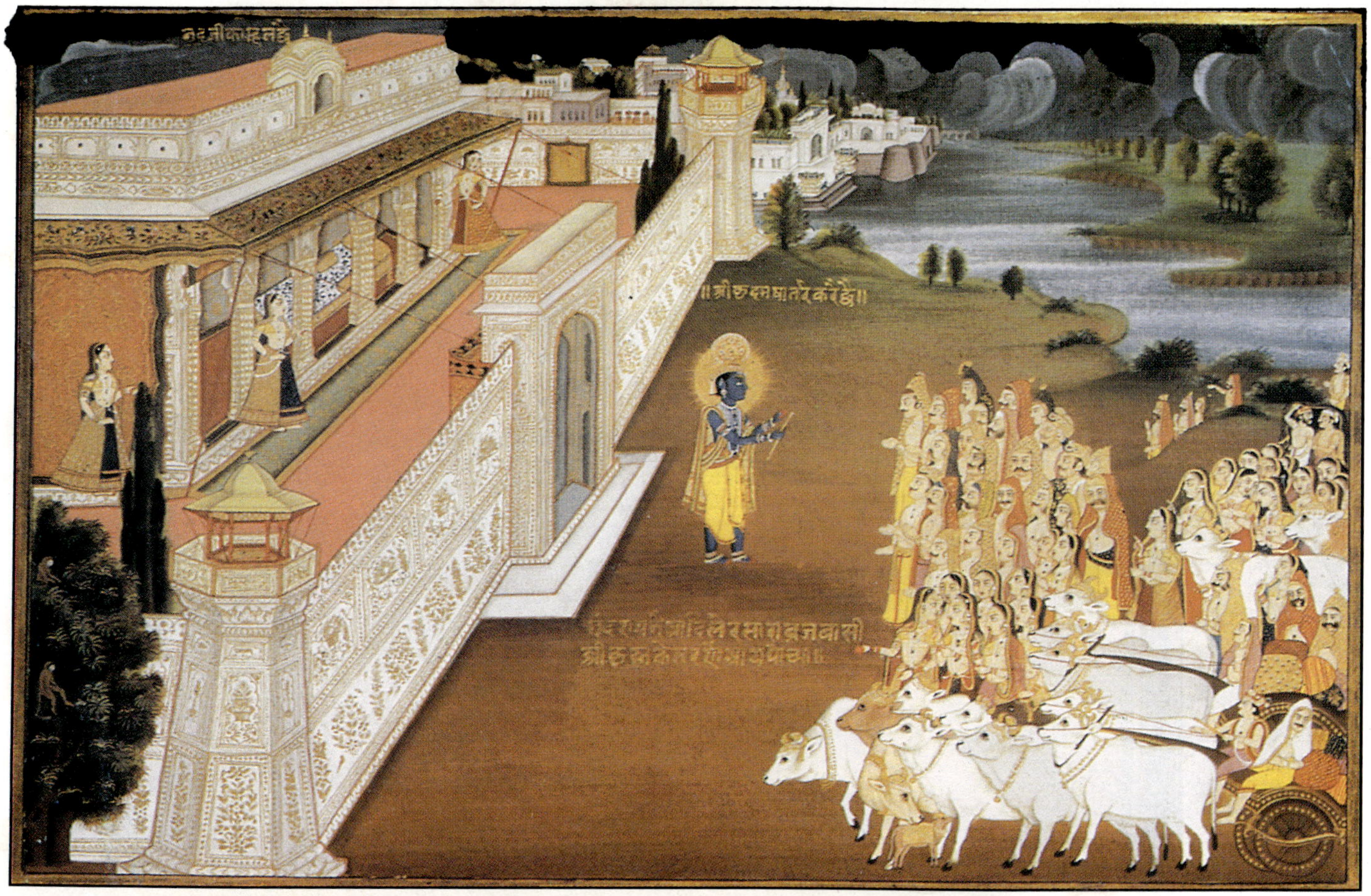

Pl. 5.1 A folio from *Bhāgavata,* dated V.S. 1792, Jaipur

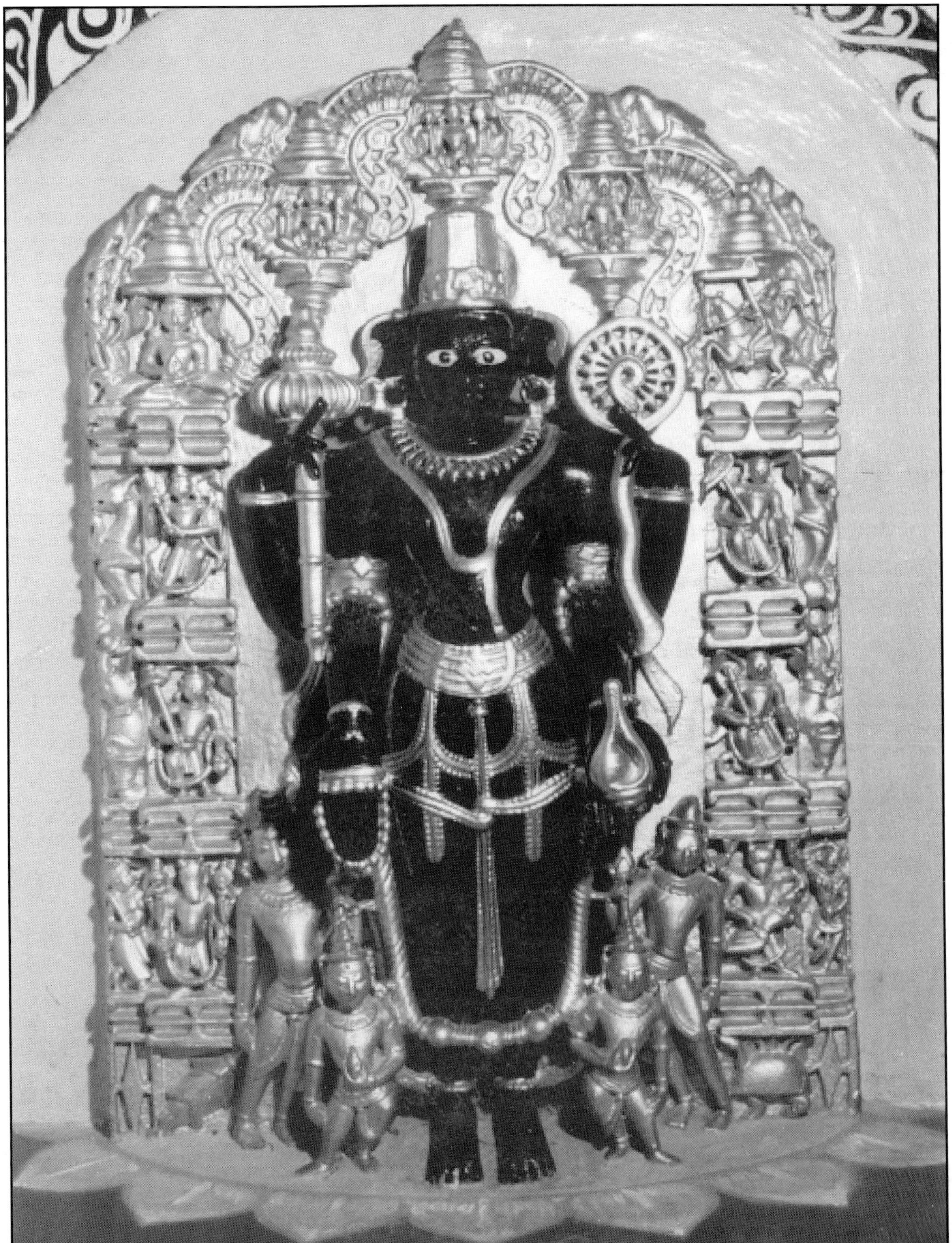

Pl. 18.1 Viṣṇu, Varanasi, *c.* 11th century AD

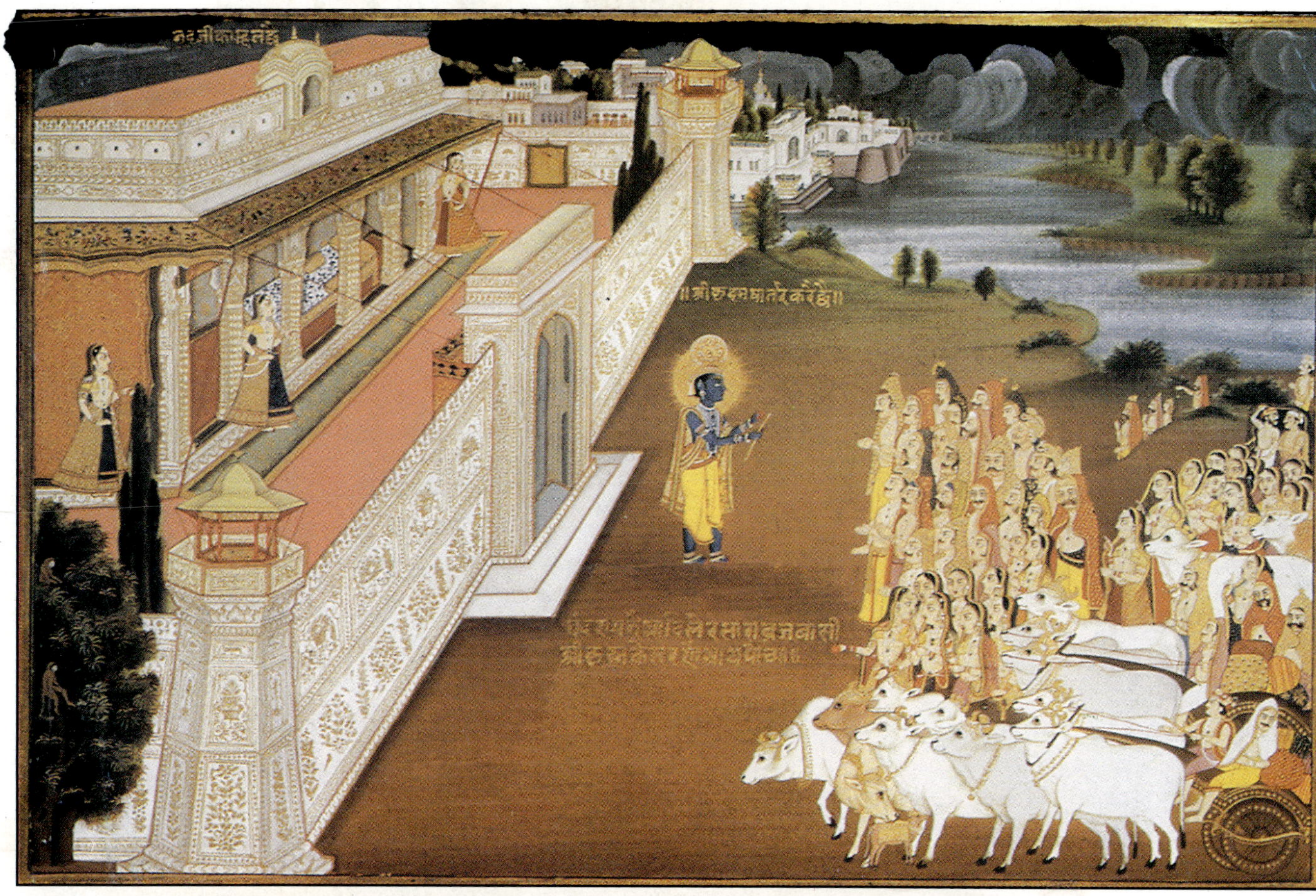

Pl. 5.1 A folio from *Bhāgavata,* dated V.S. 1792, Jaipur

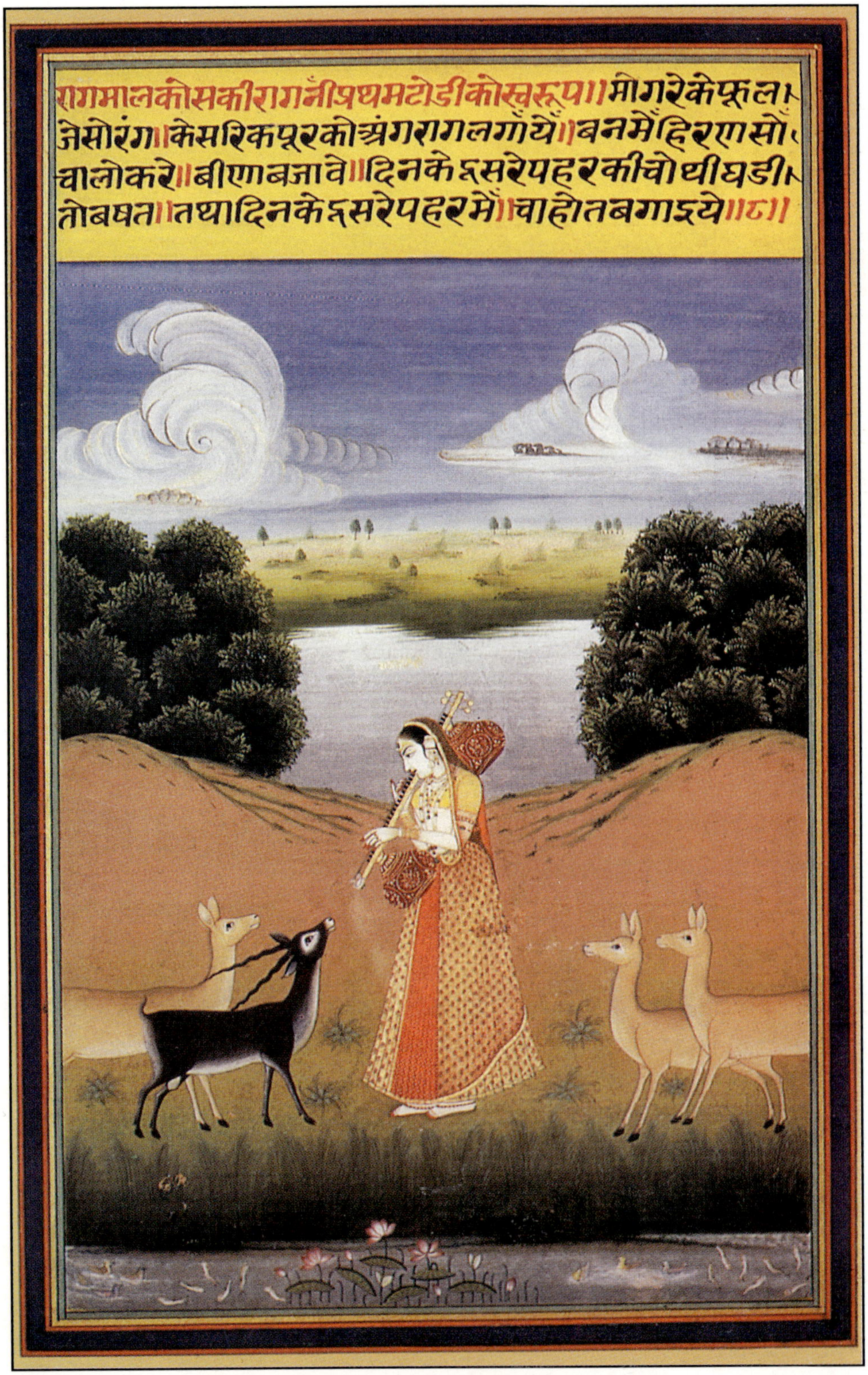

Pl. 5.2 *Rāginī Toḍī*, late 18th century, Jaipur

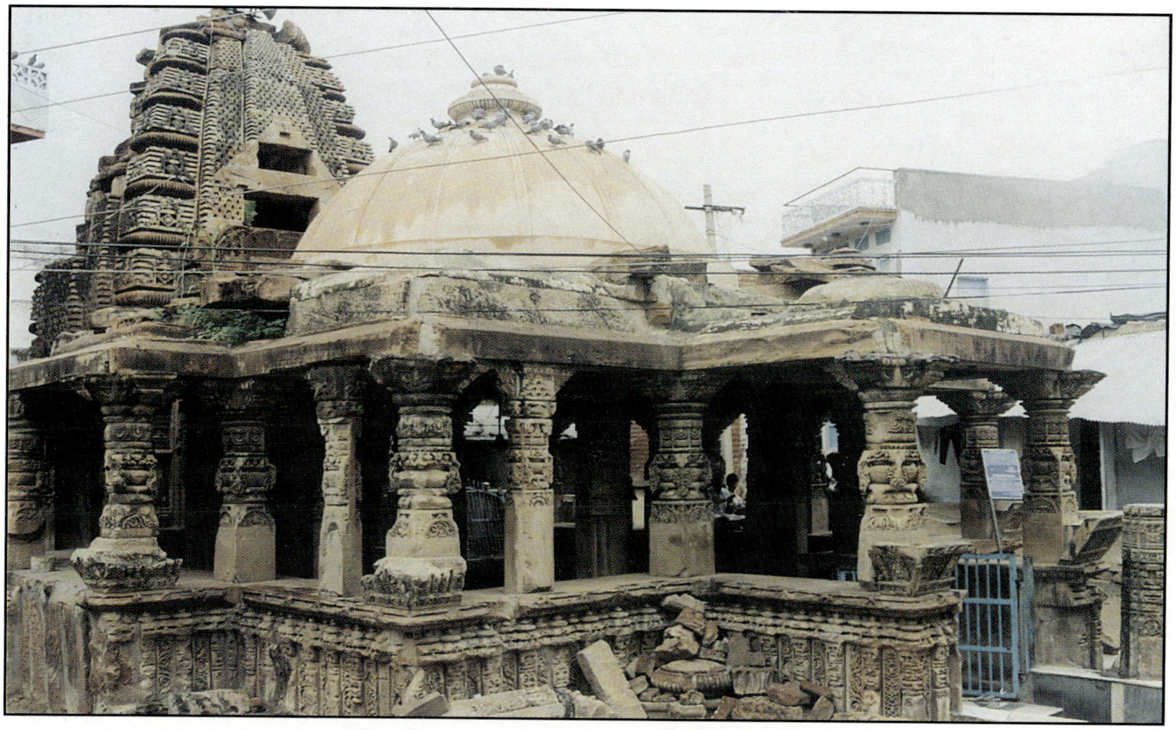

Pl. 6.1 Nīlakaṇṭeśvara Temple, Kekind (Rajasthan), *c.* 10th century AD

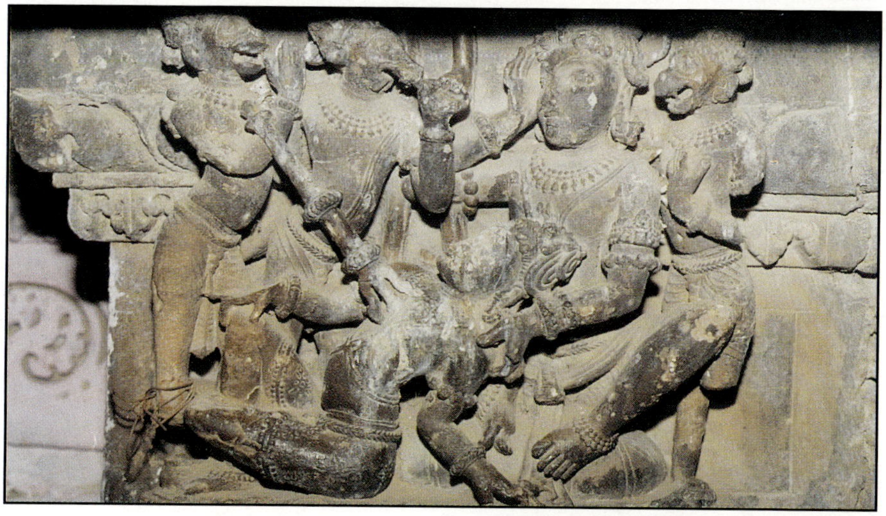

Pl. 6.2 Unconscious Lakṣmaṇa, pillar bracket, Kekind

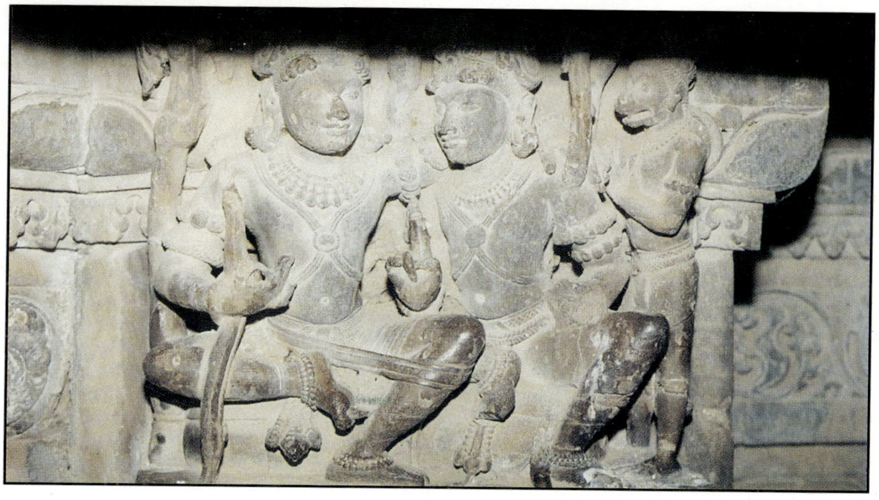

Pl. 6.3 Rāma-Lakśmaṇa-Hanumāna, pillar bracket, *maṇḍapa*, Kekind

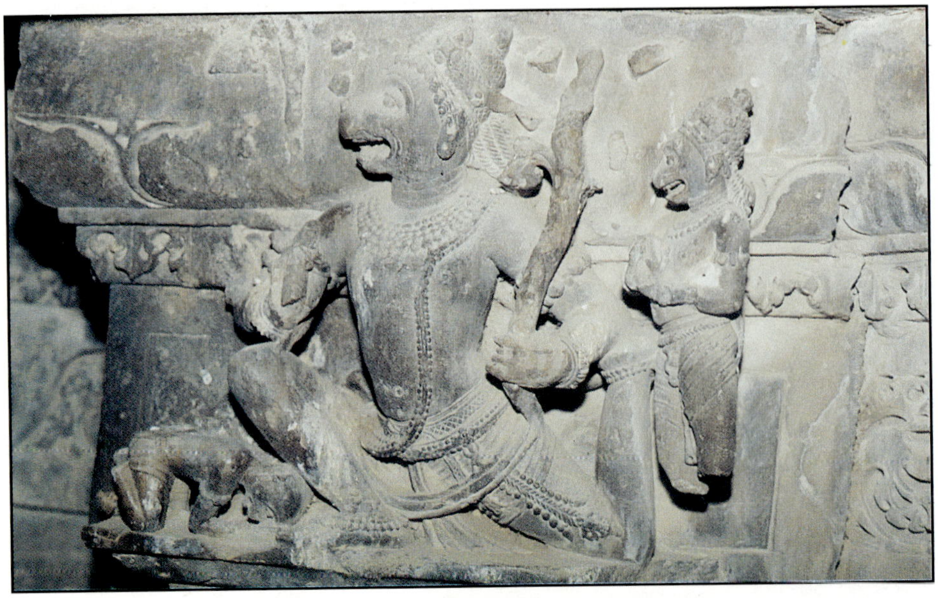

Pl. 6.4 Hanumāna and monkeys, pillar bracket, Kekind

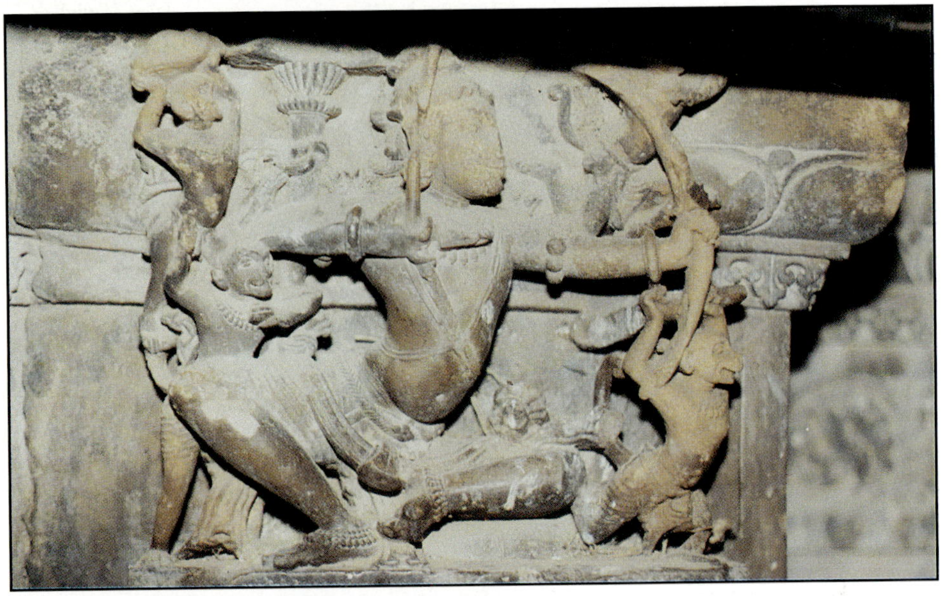

Pl. 6.5 Rāma with monkeys, pillar bracket, Kekind

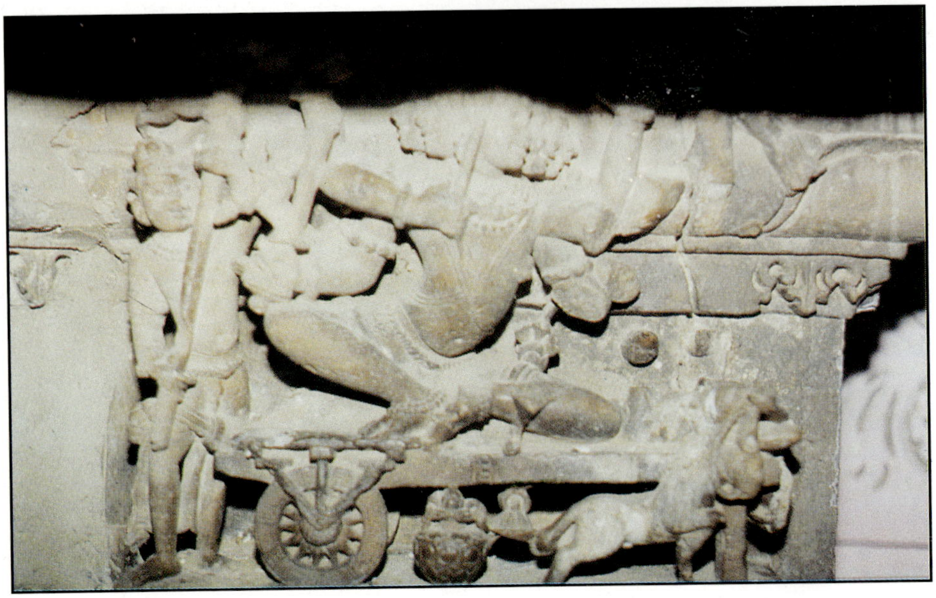

Pl. 6.6 Rāvaṇa on chariot, pillar bracket, *maṇḍapa*, Kekind

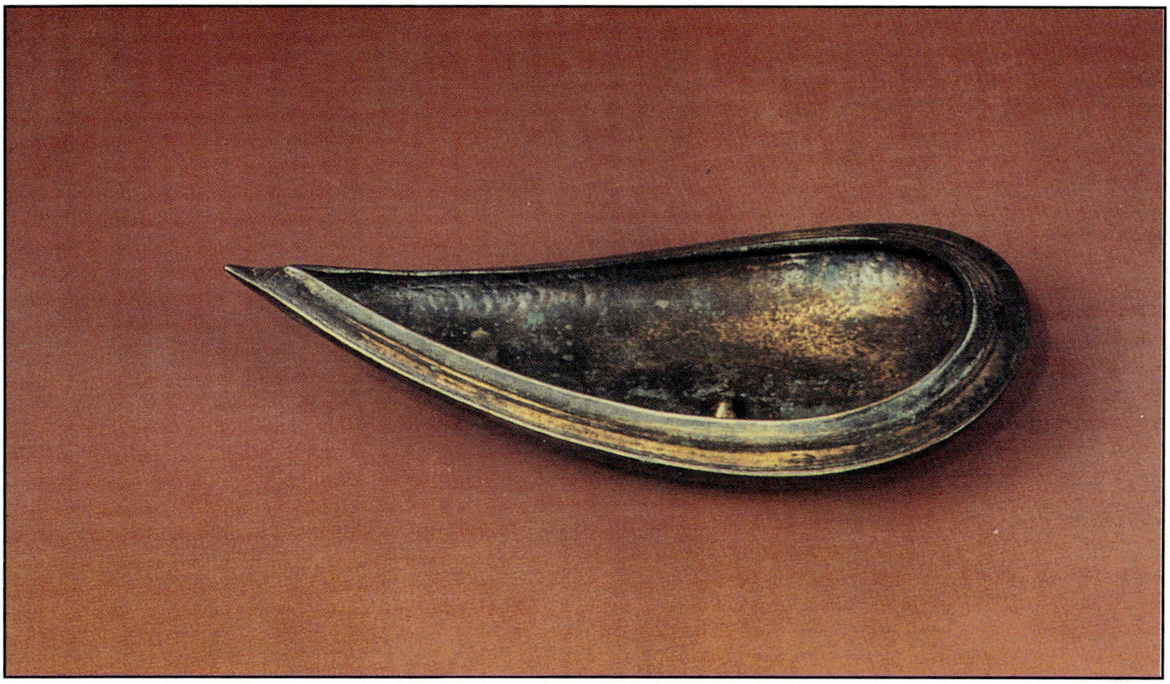

Pl. 7.1 Ritual water container, 20th century

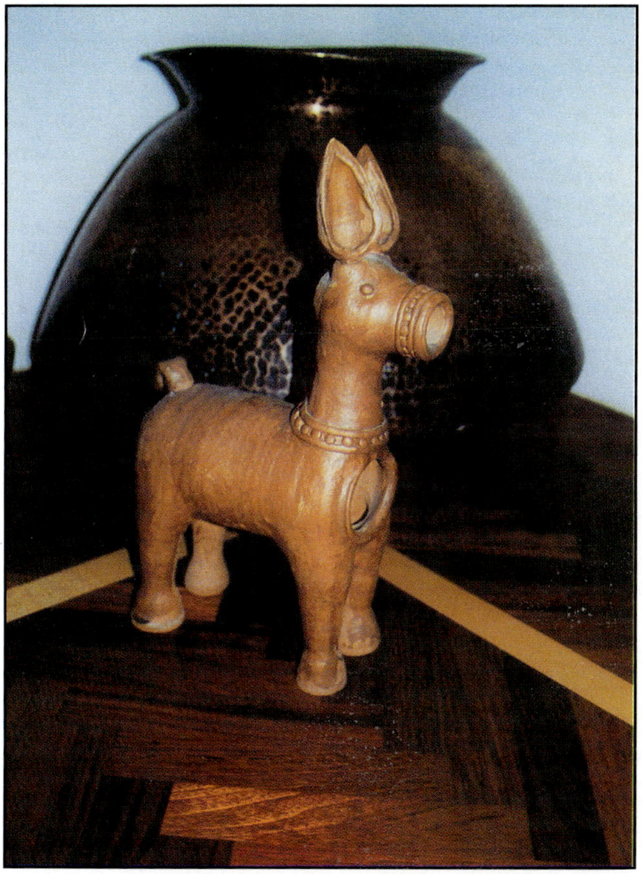

Pl. 7.2 Votive clay horse, 20th century

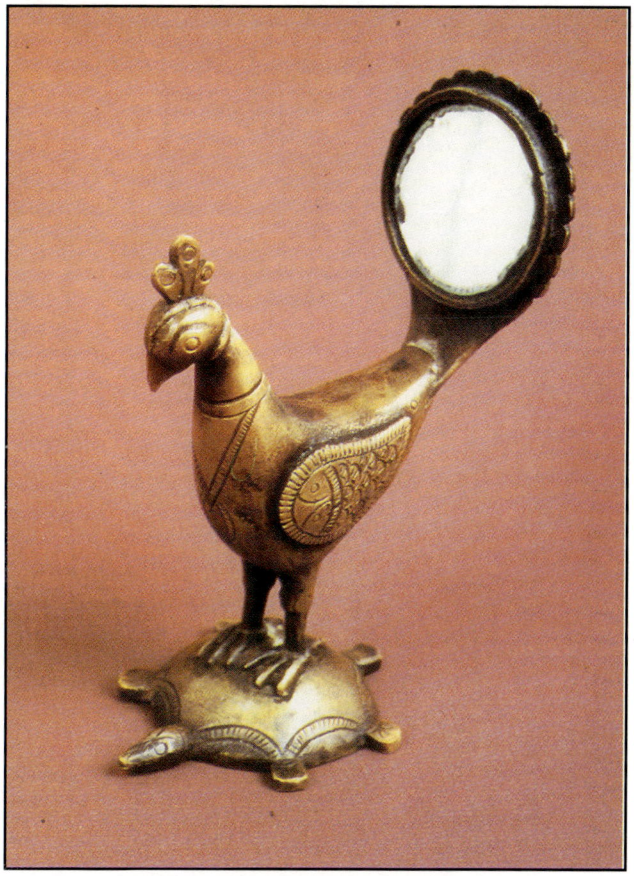

Pl. 7.3 Unguent container with mirror (brass), 20th century

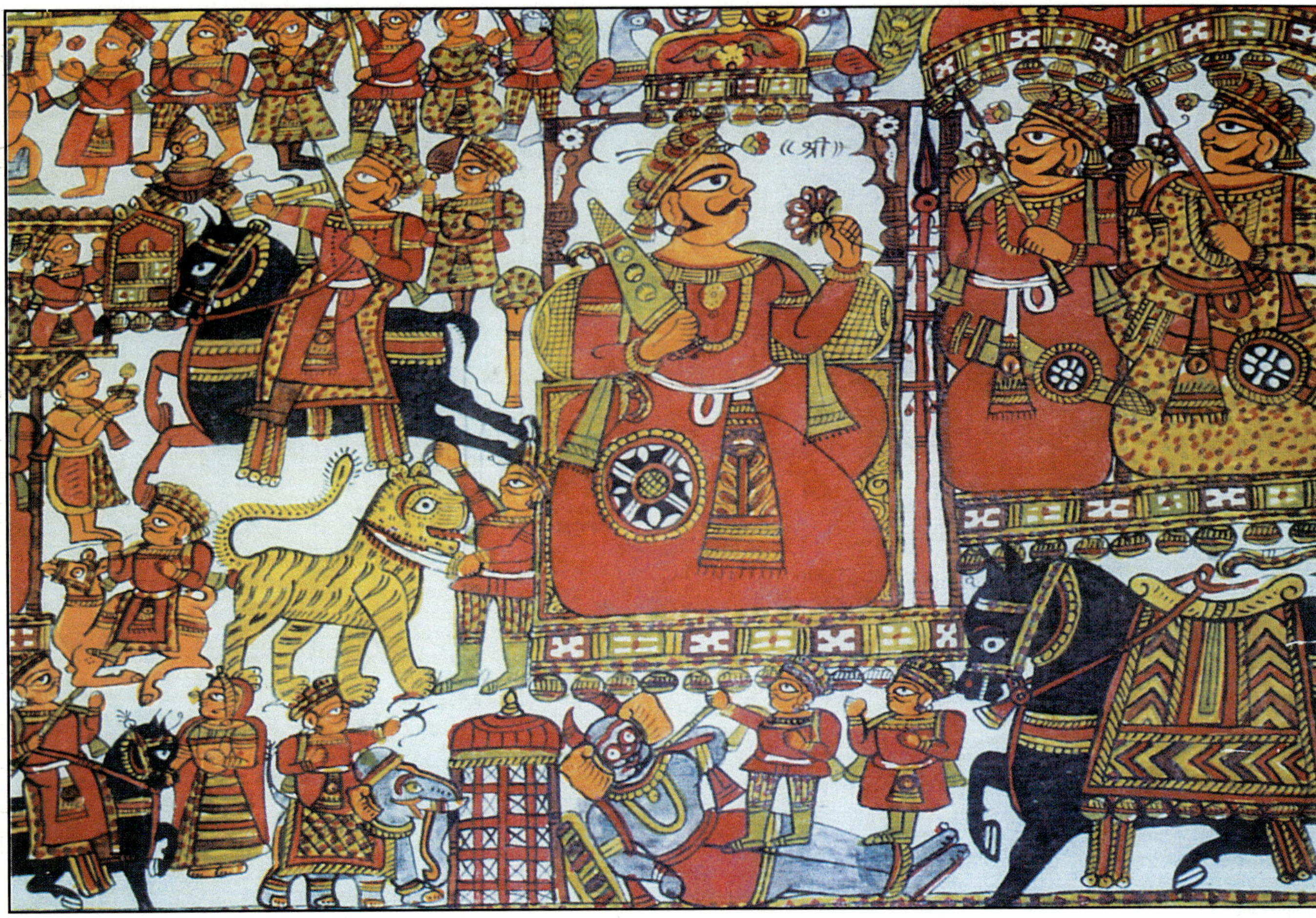

Pl. 7.4 *Phaḍa* painting, Rajasthan, 20th century

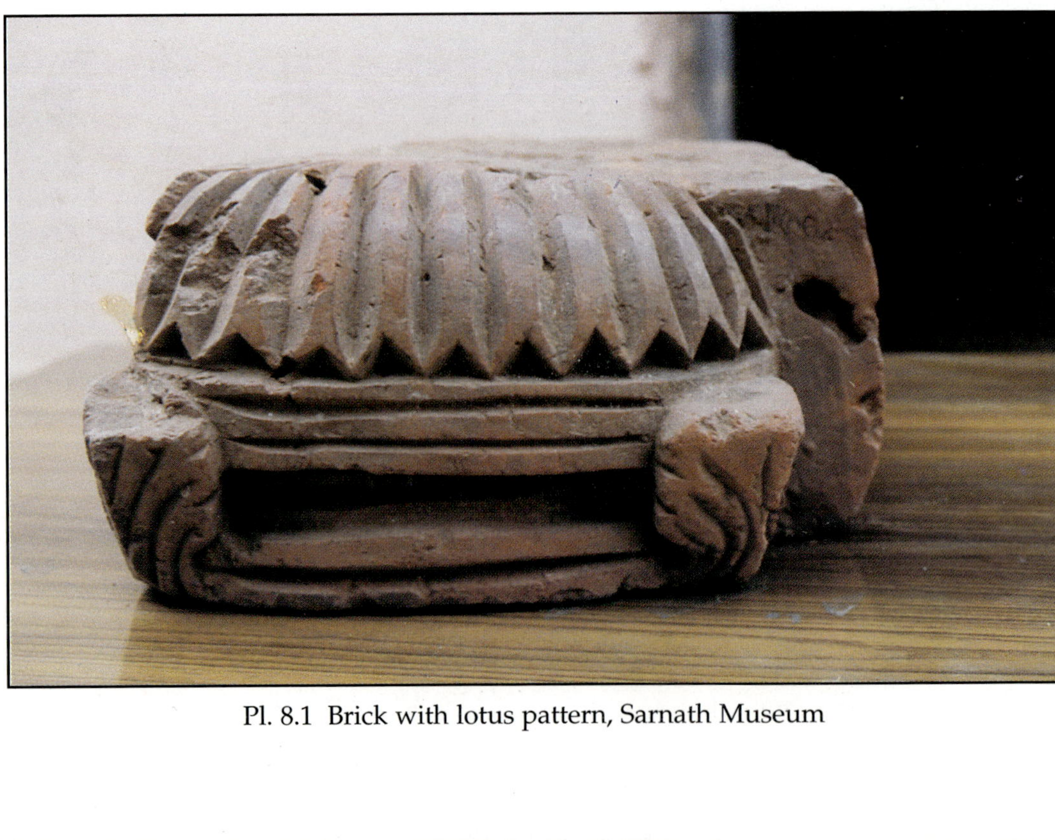

Pl. 8.1 Brick with lotus pattern, Sarnath Museum

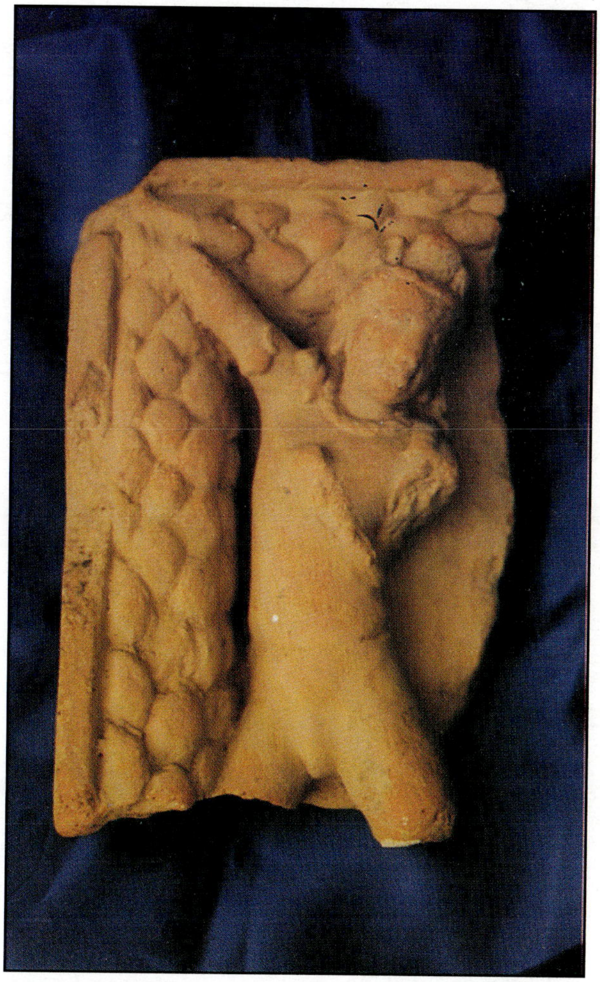

Pl. 8.2 Brick with human figure, Sarnath Museum

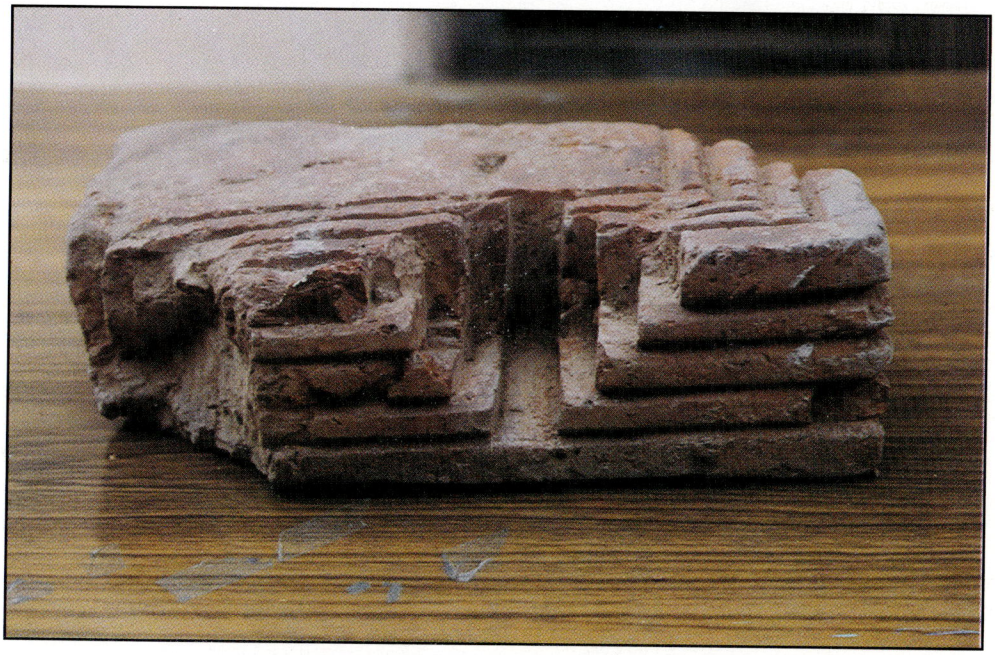

Pl. 8.3 Brick with step pattern, Sarnath Museum

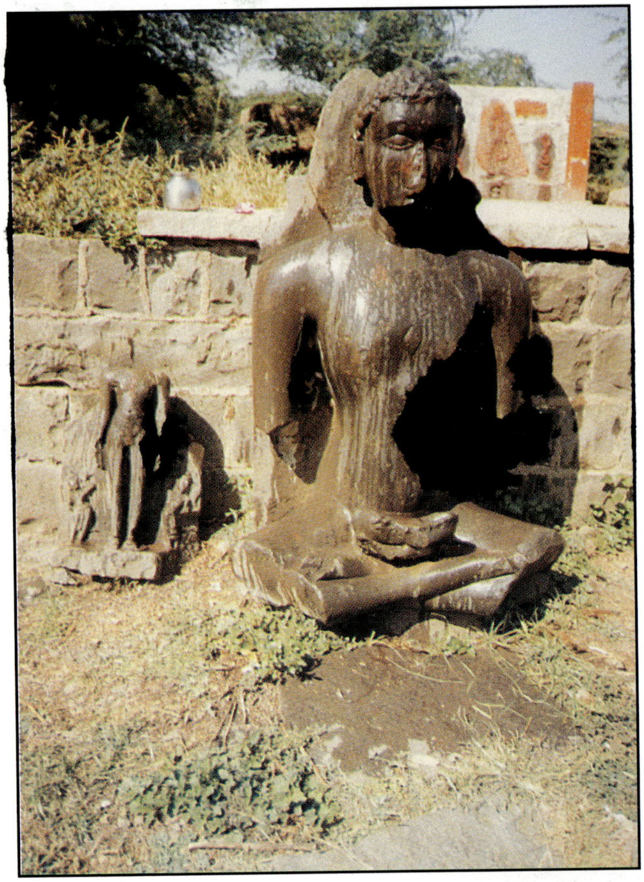

Pl. 9.1 Jina with *śrīvatsa* mark, Bhālki (Karnataka)

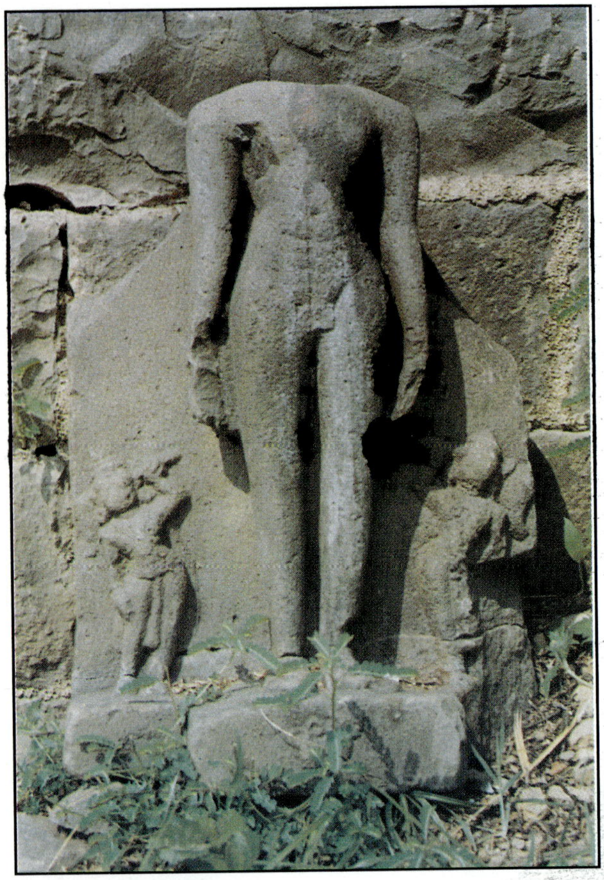

Pl. 9.2 *Tīrthaṅkara*, Bhālki (Karnataka)

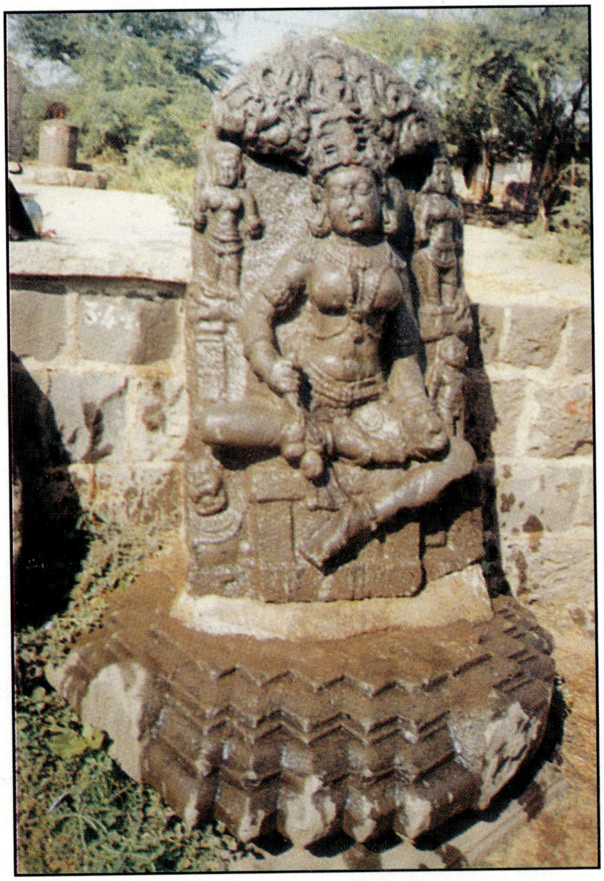

Pl. 9.3 Ambikā, Bhālki (Karnataka)

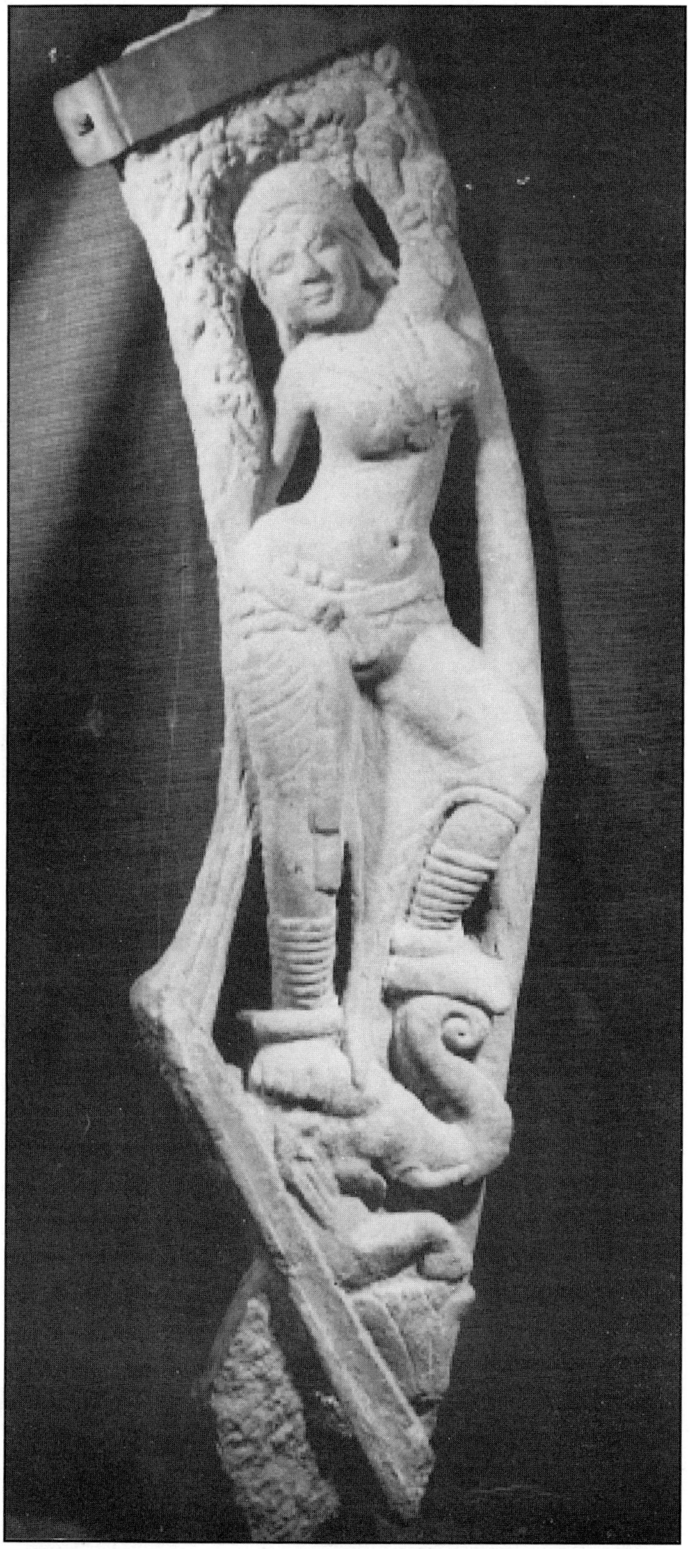

Pl. 10.1 Female figure in *śālabhañjikā* motif, Kaṅkāli Ṭīlā, Mathura

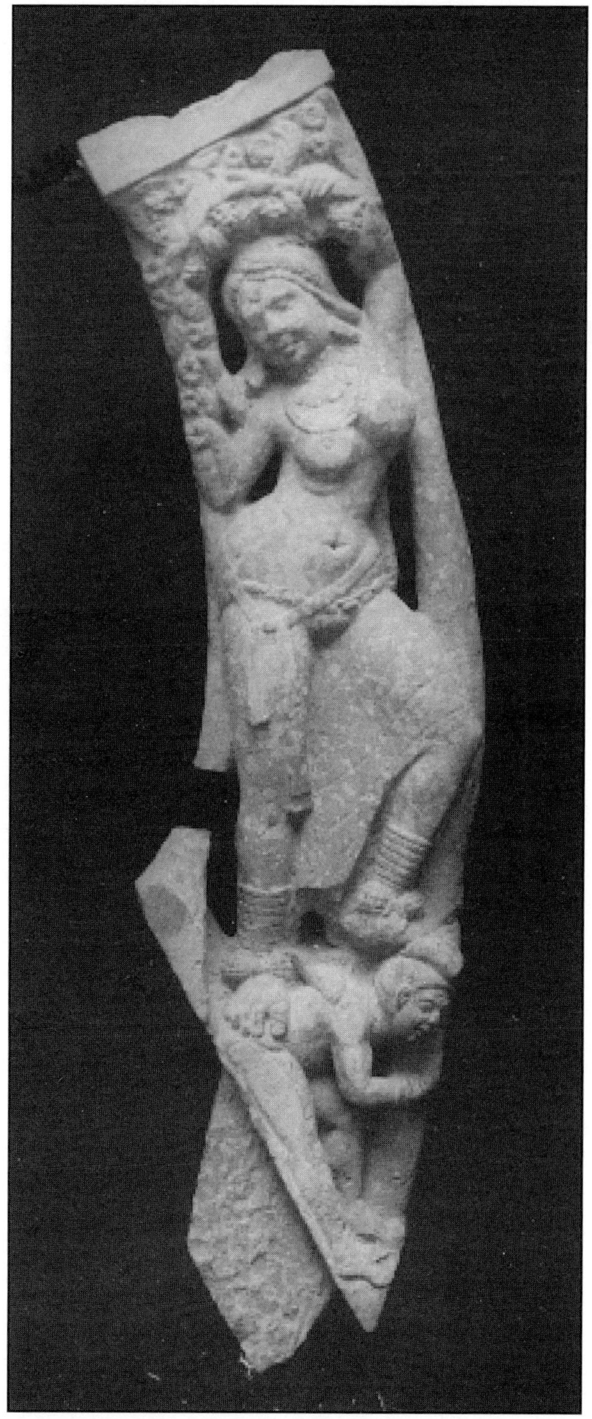

Pl. 10.2 Bracket showing female beauty, Kaṅkāli Ṭīlā, Mathura

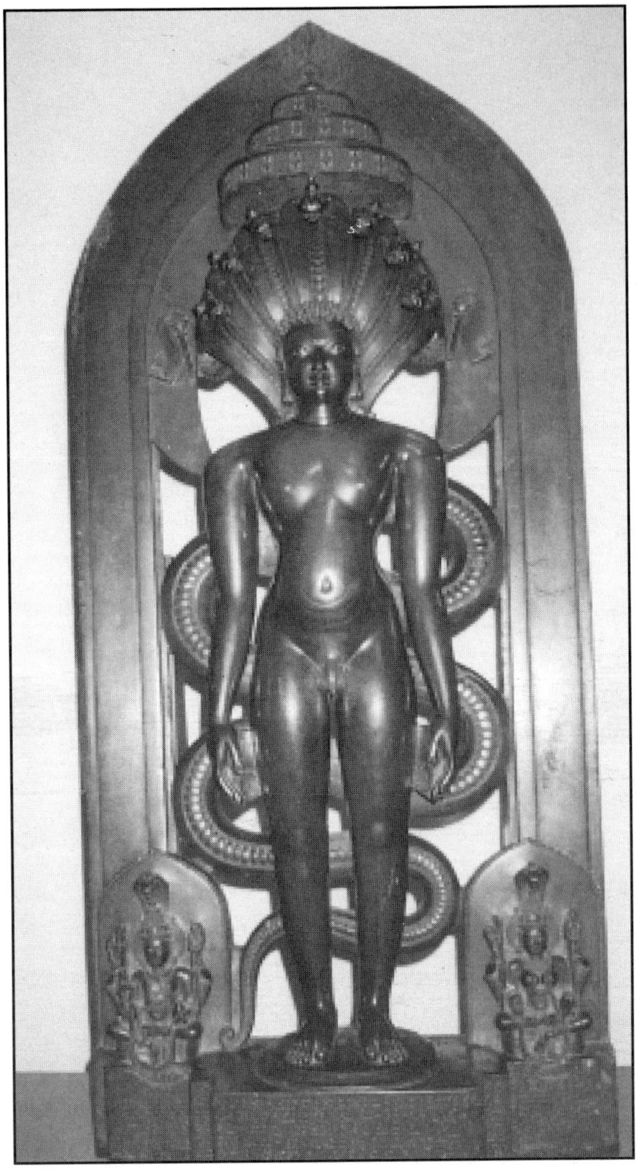

Pl. 12.1 Pārśvanātha, Gulbarga, Karnataka

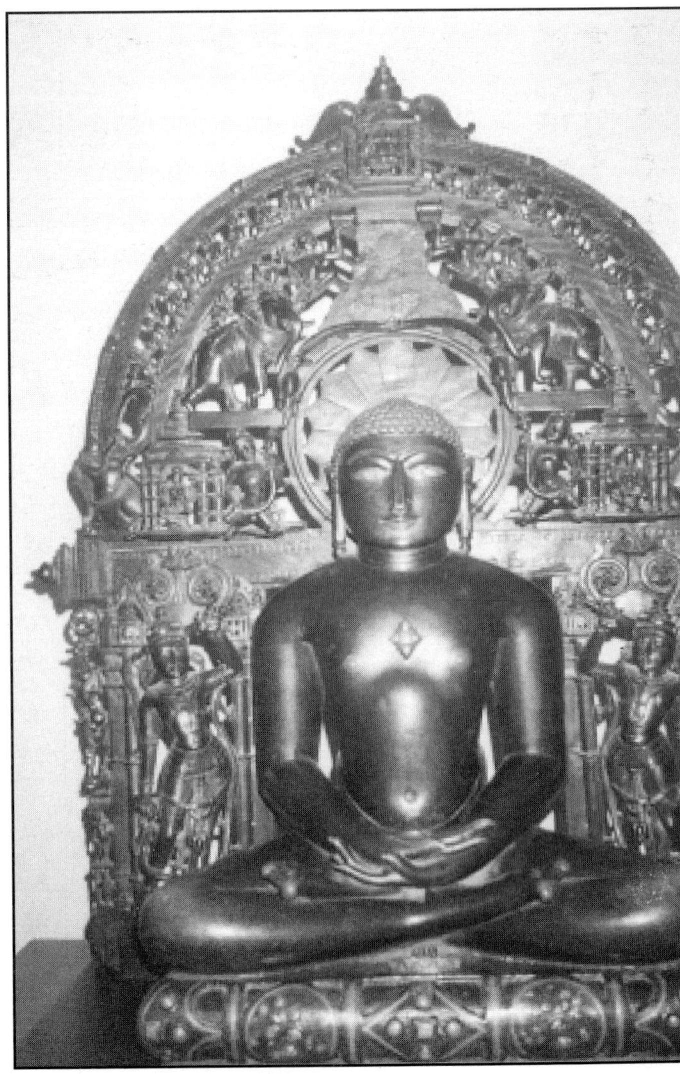

Pl. 12.2 Śāntinātha (Bronze)

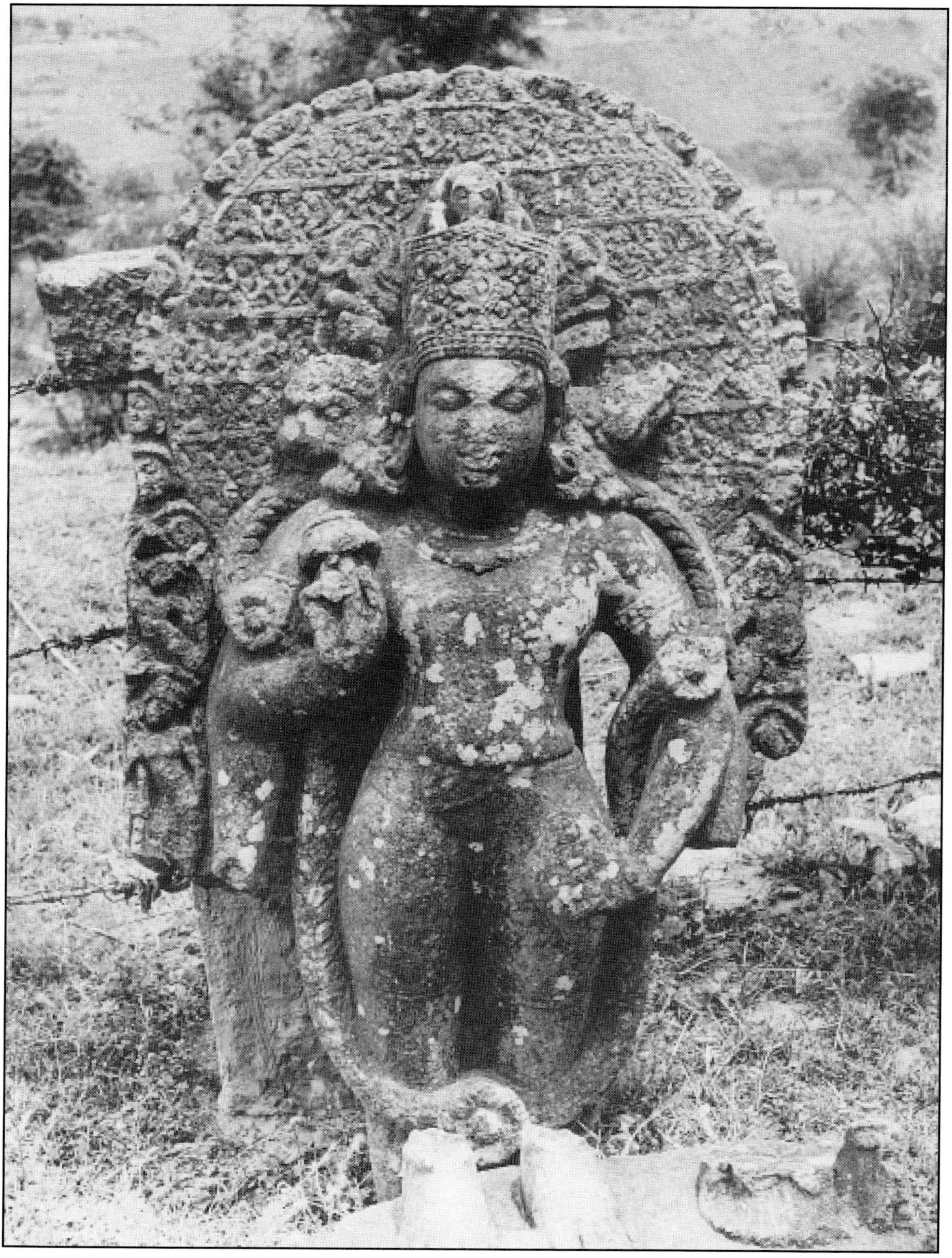

Pl. 13.1 Viśvarūpa, Bajaura, Himachal Pradesh

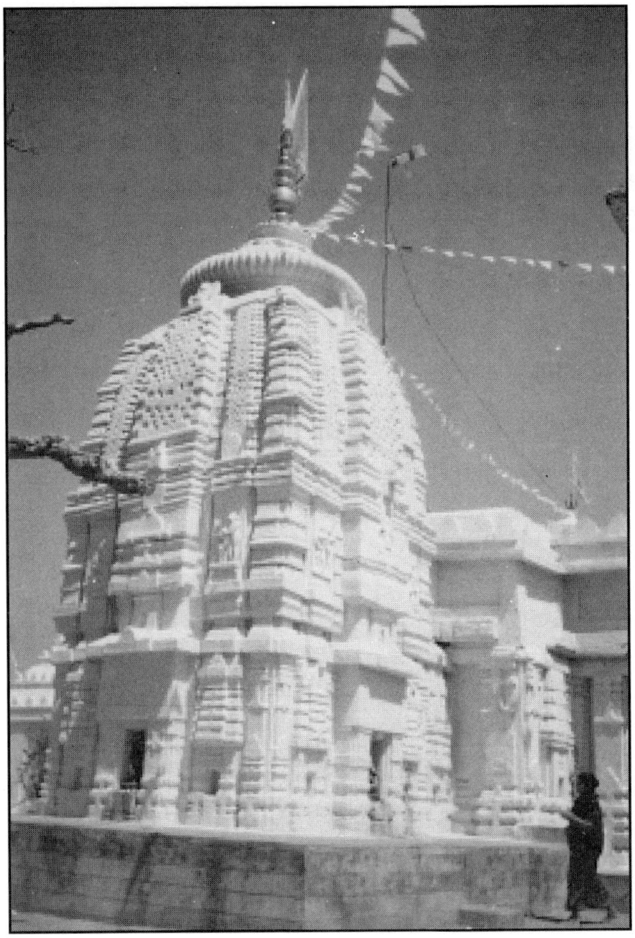

Pl. 14.1 Kapileśvara temple, Charada, Orissa

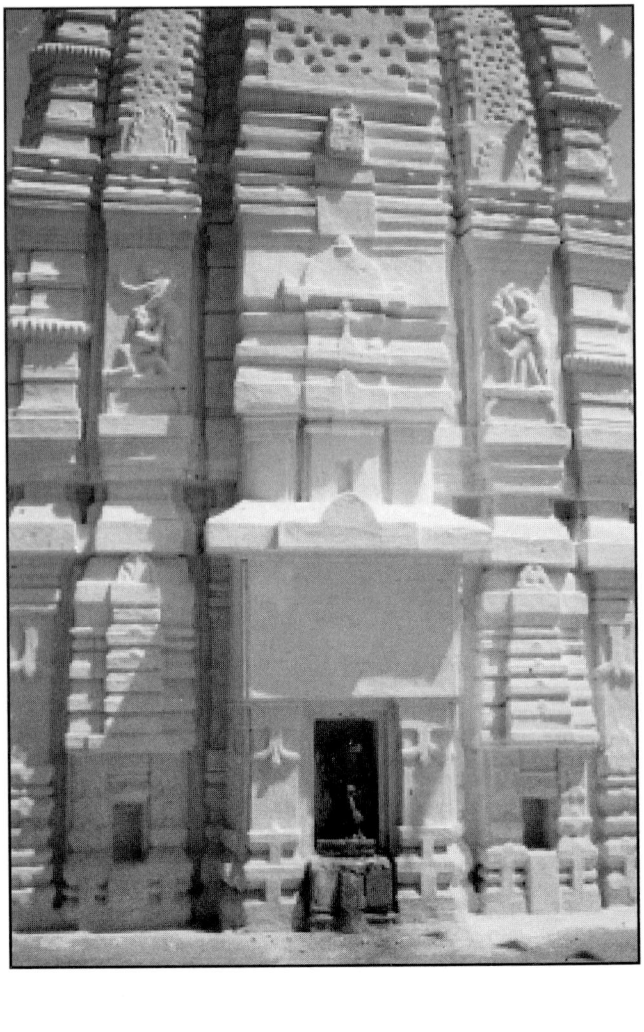

Pl. 14.2 Bāḍa, Kapileśvara temple, Charada, Orissa

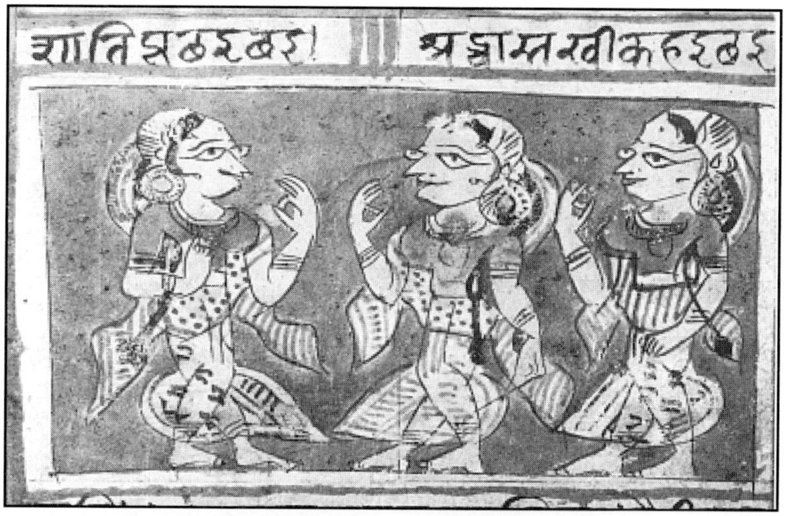

Pl. 16.1 *Prabodha-Prakāśa*, late 15th century

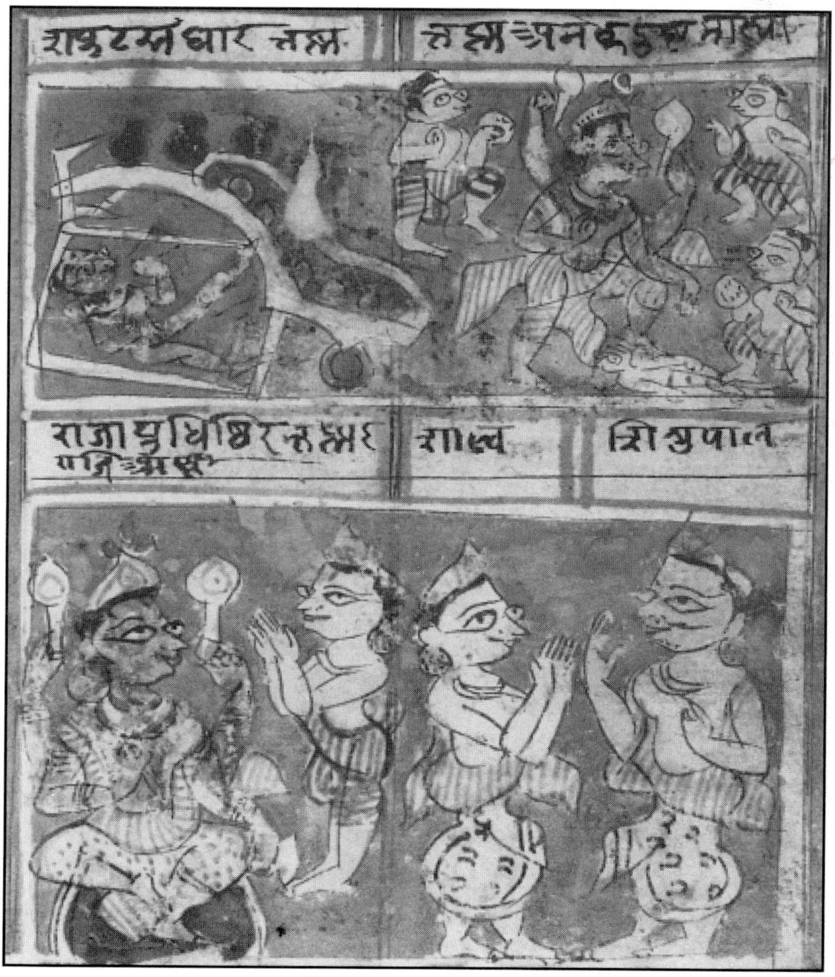

Pl. 16.2 *Harilīlā Ṣoḍaśa-Kalā*, AD 1529

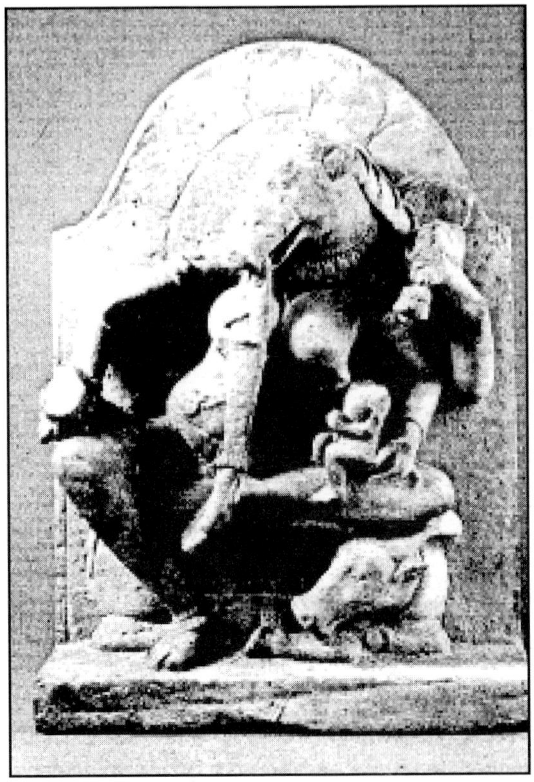

Pl. 17.1 Vārāhī

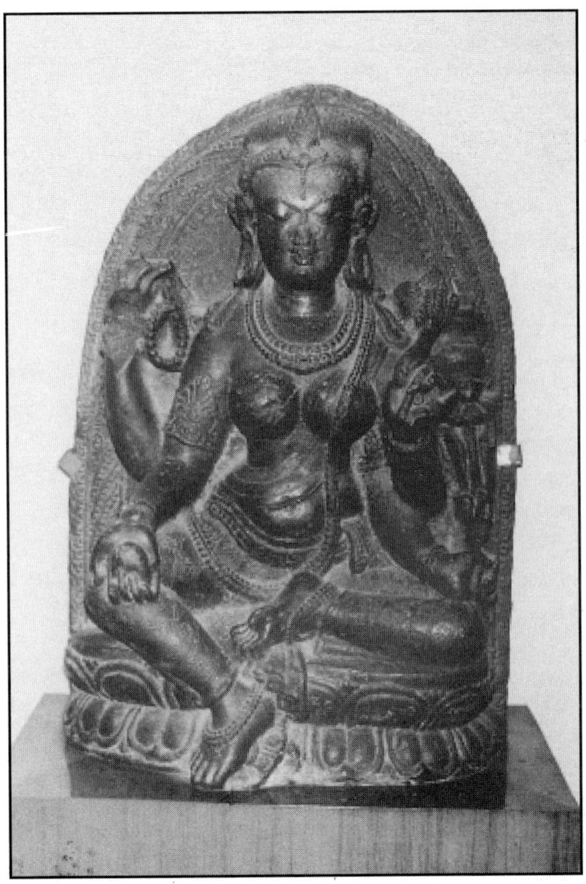

Pl. 17.2 Vasudhārā

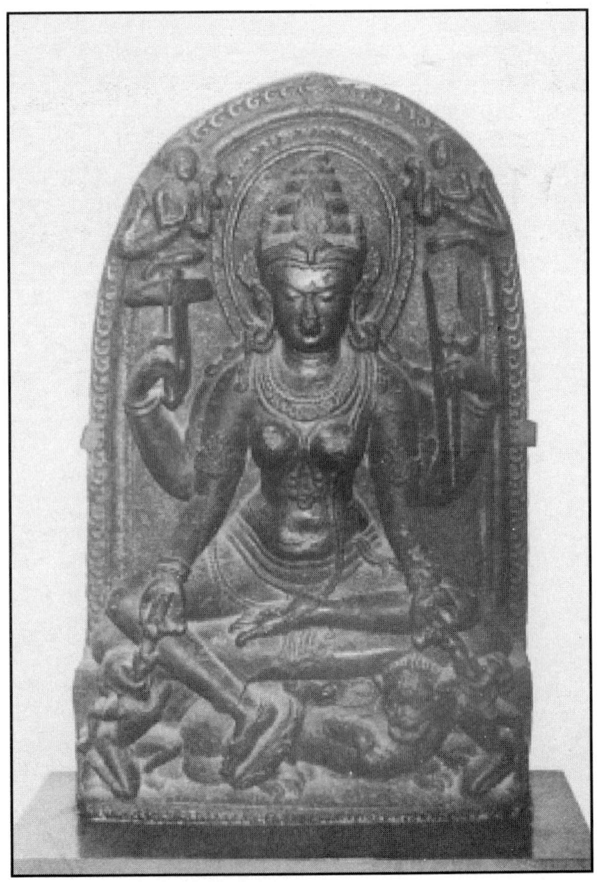

Pl. 17.3 Vāgdevī

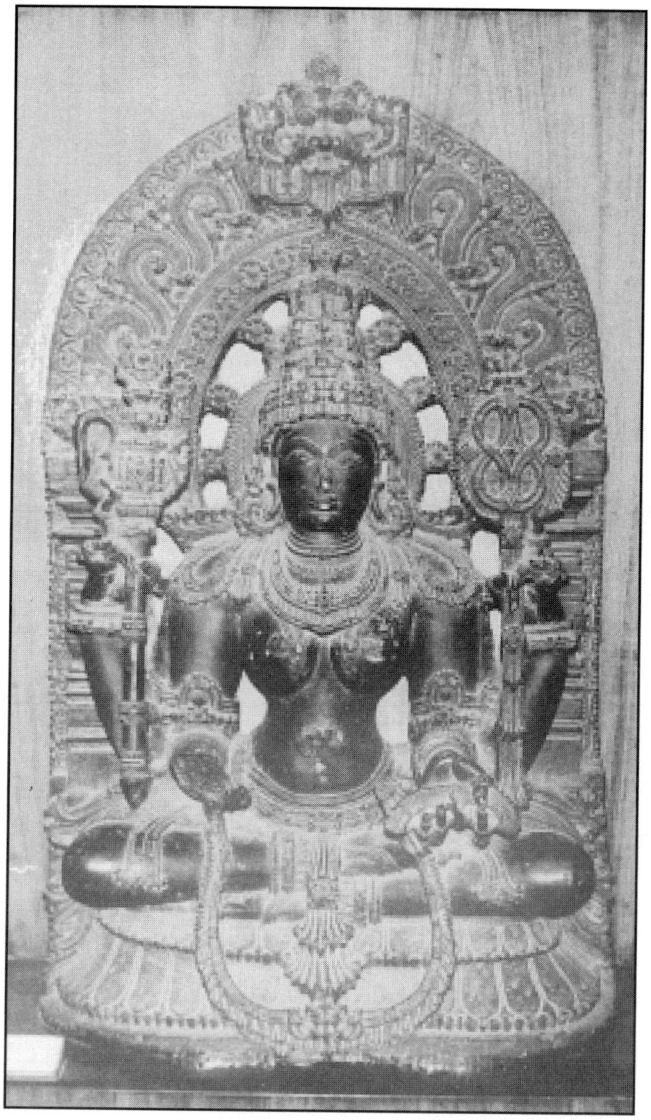

Pl. 17.4 Sarasvatī

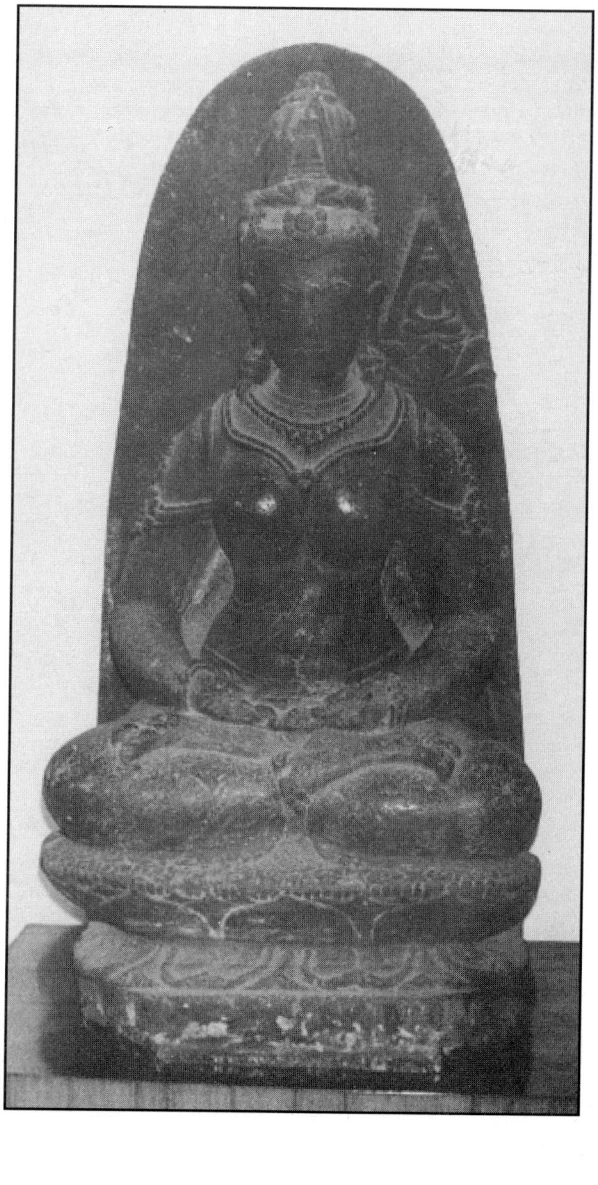

Pl. 17.5 Tārā

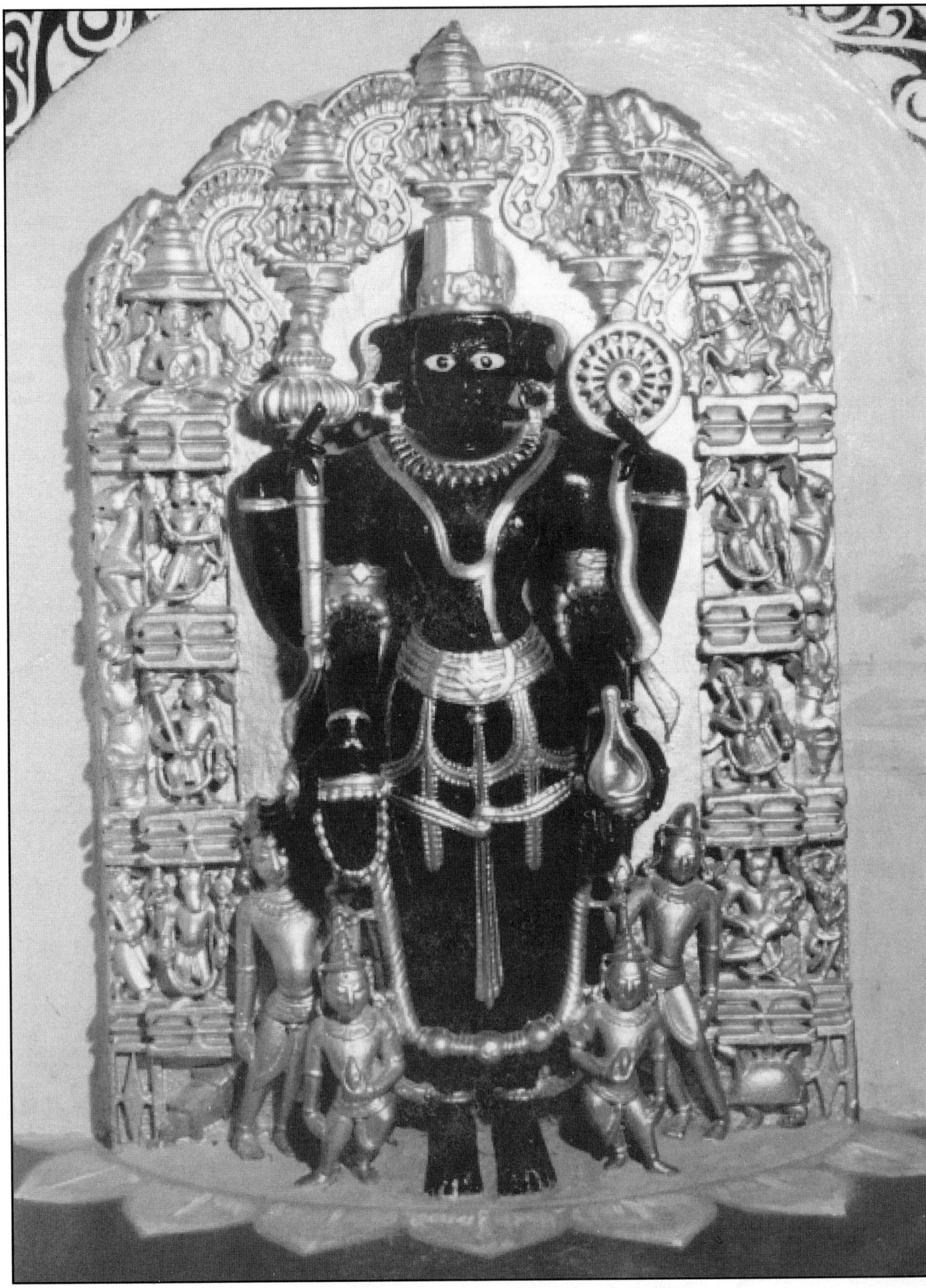

Pl. 18.1 Viṣṇu, Varanasi, *c.* 11th century AD